Lyric/Anti-lyric

Lyric/Anti-lyric

essays on
contemporary poetry

DOUGLAS BARBOUR

THE WRITER AS CRITIC: VII
Series Editor: Smaro Kamboureli

Canadian Cataloguing in Publication Data
Barbour, Douglas, 1940-
Lyric/ anti-lyric

ISBN 1-896300-50-2

1. Poetry, Modern—20th century—History and criticism. I. Title. PN1271.B37
2001   809.1'04   C00-911522-6

Editor for the press: Smaro Kamboureli
Cover photo: Tina Chang, Imaging Centre, University of Alberta
Cover design: Brenda Burgess
Interior design: Ruth Linka

The author wishes to thank the following writers and publishers for permission to quote from their publications: Robin Blaser, E.D. Blodgett, Carcanet Press Limited for Allen Curnow, Robert Creeley and The University of California Press, Susan Howe and Wesleyan University Press, the Estate of Roy Kiyooka, Ann Mandel for Eli Mandel, Steve McCaffrey, John Newlove, Michael Ondaatje, C.K. Stead, John Tranter, Sharon Thesen, and Phyllis Webb. Every effort has been made to obtain permission for quoted materials. If there is an omission or error the author and publisher would be grateful to be so informed.

The excerpts by Susan Howe from *The Nonconformist's Memorial* (copyright 1993 by Susan Howe) are reprinted with permission from New Directions Publishing Corporation.

  Canadian   Patrimoine
Heritage   canadien

NeWest Press acknowledges the support of the Canada Council for the Arts and The Alberta Foundation for the Arts for our publishing program. We also acknowledge the financial support of the Government of Canada through the Book Publishing Industry Development Program (BPIDP) for our publishing activities.

NeWest Press
201-8540-109 Street
Edmonton, Alberta
T6G 1E6
t: (780) 432-9427
f: (780) 433-3179
www.newestpress.com

1 2 3 4 5 05 04 03 02 01

PRINTED AND BOUND IN CANADA

We join our loves and others. We join relations. As a result we are trying to write an article, a piece called literary criticism about joining because in literary criticism we take a piece of something, take fragments, and string them together with our own commentary or commentary that is in reaction to something else. The commentary is designed to be narrative so as to cover up the fragmentary nature of quotation. This is the way it is with thinking, with gendering, with joining. Forms can carry all ethical positions, like people, all the positions, all the meetings and dividings. We are transition work.

—Juliana Spahr

With regard to "Neo-Formalism": ever since I studied linguistics when I was a kid, it's bothered me that the word "Formalist" has been used to talk about exactly the opposite people from those whom I think of as Formalists, to talk about people who would never question ideas of form, but are only interested in what they call content, and are really happy to use whatever Edward Arlington Robinson used in their versification. What is called Formalism displays no interest in Formalism at all. That's what is meant by Formalism in talking about European painters of the early twentieth century. If they had not been Formalists they would have been doing Poussin.

—George Bowering

Contents

Preface
Confessions of a "Formalist"

As a practicing poet, I have been writing about the work of poets I admire for close to thirty years now; the essays gathered here represent some of my thoughts over the past fifteen or so. I call myself a "formalist" because my first response to any art tends to be to aspects of what I choose to call form, in poetry the actual words, the rhythm, the placement of them on the page, the sound of them in the ear. I worry less about what many people call "meaning": as bpNichol pointed out many years ago, you can never leave meaning behind; it is always there, and it does affect us. Nichol's practice has always been important to me as a poet, but its implications play across my critical writing as well. I tend to write essays as a series of notes, little travels over the body of single works, trying to see and hear what I can, and to articulate that response as responsibly as possible.

What can I say, then, about my love of and desire for formal qualities in all the arts? Certainly, that such a partiality marks one in many ways as a kind of modernist with postmodernist proclivities. Even in popular forms of music, film, science fiction and fantasy, and comics, my enjoyment always partially depends upon various formal qualities of the works, in so far as I understand them in terms of context and convention. This is especially true of my relations with visual art. From the beginning, for whatever reasons, I have felt "at home" with modern art, and with abstract art, especially with the art of the late nineteenth century and the twentieth century that most displays itself as a "work" of art, in terms of the actual working that went into its making. This is why my favorite post-Impressionist is Cézanne, why I enjoy Cubism (especially Braque), Matisse, and later, the abstract expressionists. In my response to prints and photos, too, I look for the abstracting qualities of composition, not just the particular representations. I think the same can be said for writing, that the response is as much and simultaneously to the movement of language as to the "narrative," or "characterization," that we so often discuss.

Generally, then, I try to articulate my response in terms of formal qualities when I write. And despite a certain academic fetishism in these essays, I do hope that they remain generally clear, and open to the reading of non-experts. I have tried to resist directly engaging every critical study I have read and learned from, or recording all the links I see or echoes I hear between many of the poets I discuss. My intention, in each essay, has been to sustain an argument that locates the poetry in its relevant contexts while articulating particular elements that capture my attention as poet *and* critic.

These essays range from writing seen as centrally important during the past half-century to works seen as experimental, pushing at the boundaries of what is usually represented by the term "poetry." I do enjoy the challenges of such work, but, as I have argued in various venues, one of the things that differentiates the Canadian literary scene from those of, say, the United States or Britain, is that there is a kind of genial eclecticism at work here. While most writers have particular aesthetic biases and tend to congregate under those, they, or we, also know and even admire writers working in different modes than our own. Although I tend to champion the innovative in my critical writing, this does not mean that I find only stringently confrontational work worthwhile. I confess to a "lyric" love of beauty too. A melody, however stretched (my enjoyment of Berg, Schoenberg, post-Bop jazz, etc) in music, something of colour and form in painting, purity in sculpture—or a combination of melopoeia, first and foremost, with phanopoeia and logopoeia (Pound 1960, 25) in poetry. Although I keep finding new writers to engage, I continue to read and learn from the poets whose work I explore here. Pound's injunctions about rhythm remain true for me, even in recent work with arbitrary forms, what Marjorie Perloff has called "radical artifice" in the volume of that title, that force the line away from breath and speech as such. These are aspects of a life-long seeking that can, finally, be best named as one's poetics. At which point, I also have to admit there is no absolute consistency in my desire, or pleasure, and that for readers of the essays in this volume, such inconsistency needs to be taken, as it were, for granted.

꧁

A Preface comes before and after, especially with a gathering of essays such as this. I have written these essays (and a number of others, as well as many reviews) over a period of nearly two decades, while also writing critical monographs on John Newlove, Daphne Marlatt, bpNichol, and Michael Ondaatje. Naturally, all these critical endeavours share some basic attitudes and theoretical grounds. At the same time, I have continued to read new critics and theorists, as well as some old favorites, and their thinking cannot but have somewhat influenced mine. I would like, here, to mention a few of the most important, as I often refer to them in the essays that follow. First I would point to other poet-critics, whose writing I find so stimulating, including such figures as George Bowering, Robert Kroetsch, Daphne Marlatt, Stephen Scobie, Fred Wah, and Phyllis Webb in this country, and writers such as Charles Bernstein, Robert Creeley, Guy Davenport, Robert Duncan, Thom Gunn, Susan Howe, Denise Levertov, Charles Olson, and others in the US. These people bring a passion to their criticism which turns it into a kind of prose poetry of the intellect, and I have learned much from them all.

Among practicing critics, those who seem to have both the knowledge and the awareness of some of the most interesting writing happening today include writers like Jed Rasula and Marjorie Perloff, whose thinking about the two traditions of poetry in English in the twentieth century has clearly influenced mine. Perloff's explorations of these two traditions and of the works of individual poets strike me as ideal examples of criticism as it should be, and her thinking often provides one of the contexts in which the essays that follow attempt to construct ways of reading particular works. Perloff first differentiated the Symbolist strain of modernist writing from what she called "the poetry of indeterminacy" in *The Poetics of Indeterminacy: Rimbaud to Cage* in 1981. As she argued then, "whereas Baudelaire and Mallarmé point the way to the 'High Modernism' of Yeats and Eliot and Auden, Stevens and Frost and Crane, and their Symbolist heirs like Lowell and Berryman, it is Rimbaud who strikes the first note of that 'undecidability' we find in Gertrude Stein, in Pound and Williams, . . . an undecidability that has become marked in the poetry of recent decades" (4). A few years later, in *The Dance of the Intellect: Studies in the Poetry of the Pound Tradition*, she pursued this line of thinking further, asking the pointed question, "Pound/Stevens: whose era?" (1985, 1-32), and clearly identifying how these two masters remained at odds concerning the ways poems could be composed, structured, made to work. It should come as no surprise that she finds that Pound offered more possibilities for innovation to later poets than did Stevens, nor that I find her argument compelling. Certainly it hovers behind many of the essays here.

Most of my early critical writing was directed to Canadian literature, but in recent years I have moved out to the literatures of other countries. Visits to Australia and New Zealand granted me the privilege of meeting and reading many poets in both countries. As a result, I have begun to write about them, sometimes in comparison with Canadian poetry, sometimes on their own. As well, I have learned much from theorists in the field of postcolonial studies. Although not a theorist, I find much theory stimulating, and certainly postcolonial theory has brought many aspects of writing in such countries into focus. As a student of modernist and postmodernist writing, I find the ways in which these three nations both do and do not parallel each other's development fascinating. One of the early studies to describe the literatures of Australia, Canada, and New Zealand as postcolonial was *The Empire Strikes Back*, an introductory text to be sure. With its description of such countries as "settler colonies" (25-27), it made a case for seeing them as different from other postcolonial countries, but still definitely part of the colonial inheritance. Other critics have tried to remove them from that inheritance, but I would agree with those who argue for keeping them. As Diana Brydon argues, while altering the name slightly to "invader-settler" (9) in order to make it more complex and complicit for readers in those countries, both their implication in contemporary late capitalism and their historical relation to colonialism "provide compelling reasons for including the analysis of Canadian culture within postcolonial studies" (10). Writers like Brydon, and Alan Lawson, with his recent investigations of "the 'Settler' subject" (20-36), provide another kind of context for some of these essays, but one which my particular approach to poetic texts tends to assume precisely and only as context.

Nevertheless, I have found it useful to allude to this aspect of postcolonial theory in some of the essays that follow.

※

I have been considering what I call "lyric/anti-lyric" for well over two decades now. When I first wrote this essay, I wanted to lay out some of the possibilities inherent in such a concept. I did not think I was discovering anything new, but felt that perhaps I could articulate some aspects of the concept from a late twentieth-century, Canadian perspective. On the whole I have left the essay as it originally appeared, but it seems worthwhile to point out that many of the essays which follow tend to deal with poetry that I would call "lyric/anti-lyric" in one way or another or that finds a non-lyric way to get beyond the conventional confines of the lyric as it is usually defined.

※

Many of these essays appeared in magazines, or as papers at various conferences. I am grateful to the editors and organizers for giving me the opportunity to explore the work of these poets. Over the years, conversations with fellow poets and critics have allowed me to think my ideas through far more carefully than would otherwise have been the case, and Smaro Kamboureli, in her editing, has pushed me to think and write even more clearly, for which I am extremely grateful.

Earlier version of many of these essays were published as follows:

"Lyric/Anti-Lyric: Some Notes About a Concept." *Line*, 3 (Spring 1984). 45-63.

"The Last Time I Wrote 'Paris': Michael Ondaatje's first attempt at a poetic sequence in 'Troy Town." *Essays on Canadian Writing (Michael Ondaatje Issue)*, 53 (Summer 1994), guest editor. 107-124.

"*the man with seven toes*: Michael Ondaatje's Expressionist Version of an Australian Legend." *Australian-Canadian Studies*, 10: 1 (1992). 19-43.

"Day Thoughts on Anne Wilkinson's Poetry." *Amazing Space: Writing Canadian Women Writing*. Ed. Smaro Kamboureli and Shirley Neuman. Edmonton: Longspoon Press/NeWest Press, 1986. 179-190.

"Late Work at the Kitchen Table: Phyllis Webb's *Water and Light*." "*You Devise. We Devise. A Festschrift for Phyllis Webb*, ed. Pauline Butling. Burnaby, BC: *West Coast Line*, Six [25/3] [Winter 1991-92]. 103-117.

"Canadian Travellers on an Orient Express(ion): John Thompson's *Stilt Jack* and Phyllis Webb's *Water and Light*." *Essays in Canadian Literature*, eds. Jorn

Carlsen & Bengt Streijfert. Lund, Sweden: The Nordic Association for
Canadian Studies Text Series, Volume 3, 1989. 1-18.

"The Heavenly Rhetoric of Thine I: Some Versions of the Subject in Book 1."
Tracing the Paths: Reading = Writing The Martyrology. Ed. Roy Miki.
Vancouver: Talonbooks/Burnaby: *Line*, 1988. 172-188.

"'De tous ces mots en suspens sur mon souffle, aucun ne m'appartient': La Poésie
de E.D. Blodgett"/"'Not one of any word that floats / upon my breath is
mine': The Poetry of E.D. Blodgett." *Ellipse: A biannual review featuring
the work of Québécoise and Canadian writers in translation* 57 (Spring
1997). 55-68.

"Writing the 'trans' in *transcanada letters.*" *West Coast Line* 16 [29/1]
[Spring/Summer 1995]. 11-23.

"The Rhetorical Strategies of Eli Mandel: some notes." *The Politics of Art: Eli
Mandel's Poetry and Criticism.* Eds. Ed Jewinski and Andrew Stubbs.
Atlanta, Ga./Amsterdam: Editions Rodopi, 1992. 193-200.

"Some New Zealand Poets in Europe/Europe in Some New Zealand Poems."
"New Zealand Award-Winners Number," *The Poet's Voice*, 2:1 New Series
(June 1995), Katrina Bachinger, guest editor. 80-99.

"Writing Through the Margins: Sharon Thesen's and Bill Manhire's Apparently
Lyrical Poetry." *Australian and New Zealand Studies in Canada*, No. 4
(Fall 1990). 72-87.

"Susan Howe: Language/Writing/History: Notes around a resistant articulation."
Boxkite: A journal of poetry and poetics 1 (1997). 88-121.

Parts of "Some Thoughts on Poetry & Modernism in Australia" appeared in
review articles in *Australian-Canadian Studies* and *Australian and New
Zealand Studies in Canada.*

Lyric/Anti-Lyric

some notes about a concept

I

The possibilities inherent in this theme are virtually endless—indeed, perhaps there exists an anti-lyric for every kind of lyric expression. My two immediate candidates for the category of anti-lyric were certain short poems which deliberately flout high lyric conventions yet have their own, wild or atonal, music and certain long poems, especially those defined as "serial poems." A series of linked shorter works, often highly lyrical in character, serial poems could be taken as exemplary types of what Poe had in mind when he maintained "that the phrase 'a long poem' is simply a flat contradiction in terms" (33) and that "[w]hat we term a long poem is, in fact, merely a succession of brief ones" (22). But there are many other examples of lyrics written against the conventional concepts of lyric, and they, too, beg for attention. In these notes, I follow no specific order, nor do I cover anything like the "ground" of what I now suspect is an ever-expanding territory. I will deal mainly with contemporary poems in two forms: long poems which in one way or another seek to escape the confines of lyric though not necessarily by abandoning all lyric possibilities; short poems, which by definition are now considered lyric, yet which in one way or another interrogate the form and concept of lyric even as they apparently display them.

Perhaps one good entrance to this literary and critical maze can be made via a comment by E. D. Blodgett. In a "dialogue" with Rob Dunham, the subject of lyric arises:

> DUNHAM: Speaking of Orpheus, I note that most reviewers tend too easily to identify your work as lyric poems and you as a lyric poet. Do you regard yourself as the writer of lyric poems?
>
> BLODGETT: No. I regard myself as someone who speaks one word and then another. I can't think of anything less

lyrical than that. The very conception of the poem, to me, is how to move from word to word. This is present in "phoenix" when I talk of "the awful *the* of beginnings." It's difficult to know how to begin, and how to end. The problem is to use a lyrical form and not to be lyrical. You were quite right in talking about "breath" and "wind" as being creative signs in these poems, but in order to see those words as signs one has to cease thinking of Orpheus as a lyric poet. He is a guide with signs.

DUNHAM: But he is *the* lyrist.

BLODGETT: He is the lyrist, but what is his song? His song is a song about silence. That's the ambiguity of the non-lyric.

DUNHAM: The term, "lyric," has been reduced by making it merely the personal voice. I wish there were some way that we could recover the sense of lyrist as you have just described what Orpheus is.

BLODGETT: When one adopts the use of Orpheus in a poem, one has already abandoned one's self as a particular individual. (31)

Elsewhere in this conversation, Blodgett speaks more fully of his deliberate and increasingly successful attempt, during his first three books, "to strip himself of his empirical self," that is, to rid himself of the lyric ego. That he has not been alone in this endeavour is one of the themes of much of what follows.

Obviously, one way to get beyond the confines of "the lyric ego" is to move on to larger forms; and if the lyric is often associated with younger poets perhaps it's because young writers know only their own egocentric desires well enough to write well about them. That, at any rate, is the superficial view. Historically, though, it has been argued that, as the poet matures, he (and I note that most often it has been a "he") puts away the easy romanticism of youth and seeks larger subjects, epic or dramatic modes. Thus the shift to large non-lyric forms is one way poets of every generation transcend the lyric limitations of their youths. Aside from the fact that some great lyric poems have been written by older poets, I am not sure that the shift to larger forms must necessarily involve a denial of lyric possibilities and impulses.

One kind of lyric which seems to have surfaced seldom if ever after the great age of Greek lyric writing is the choral lyric. Modern examples would surely appear *not* to be lyrics, which is to say they deliberately seek to speak for a public "we" rather than a private "I," and to that extent can be seen as lyric/anti-lyric. In *The Idea of Lyric*, W. R. Johnson argues that Walt Whitman invented a choral epic for modern American poetry in the early versions of *Leaves of Grass*, one which sought to serve a similar function for his polis as the ancient choral poems did for theirs, but without their supports of music and dance. Of course, in a sense Johnson must define the choral aspect out of choral poetry in order to fit Whitman in. And insofar as the poems are not performed as a celebration of the American polis, they have failed to achieve what the Greek choral lyric achieved for its community.[1] Nevertheless, Johnson is not alone in perceiving Whitman's poems this way; Guy Davenport, railing in righteous anger at those who would teach poetry as "self-expression," says:

> One can think of statements that seem to explain so wry a misunderstanding of the poet as an issuer of personal pronunciamentos. Behavioral psychology, squirted into the ears of students from Head Start through the Ph.D., can account for no action not grounded in self-advancement; it follows that the poet as a voice for other people is suspect. He *must* be expressing himself, don't you see? Poor Whitman. He wrote a corpus of poems for an entire nation, to give them a tongue to unstop their inarticulateness. He wrote in their dialect, incorporating the nerve of their rhetoric and the rhythms of the Bible from which their literacy came. He wrote two elegies for Lincoln, one for grownups ("When Lilacs Last in the Dooryard Bloom'd") and one for school children ("O Captain! My Captain!"). He tried to understand the voiceless American and

to speak for him, and as much as any poet has ever succeeded, he did. Yet he has been idiotically deposed from the fulcrum he so carefully selected. He wrote not a single personal poem and yet every word is taught to students as the self-expression of an elate disk-jockey who made his scene with a poetry book, Way Back Yonder (but still pertinent, as he used symbols and sometimes undercut with irony). (132)

Whitman's particular choral gesture seems to be unique, but Johnson sees "the choral spirit and the choral gesture" (192) in the work of many of the greatest modern poets: to name just a few, Yeats, Neruda, Akhmatova, Auden sometimes, Eliot in *Four Quartets*, Ginsberg in *Howl* and *Kaddish* and other poems, and of course Pound in many of the *Cantos*. Without denying that the choral impulse is present, among many others, in some of these poets, I would argue that Whitman marks both the beginning and the end, in English anyway, of a valid choral poetry. The later poets, and even the later Whitman, could no longer believe that they spoke for all their people. A choral poetry requires a cohesive polis (of the imagination, at least), and none such exists in the West today. Nor, I would hazard, does it in the East, though some of the major Russian poets of this century wrote as if one did. Indeed, even in the sixties and seventies many poets in the USSR had the kind of followings we associate only with Rock stars; they played a clearly bardic role in their literary constituencies. Johnson argues that there is a group of choral *Cantos*, "composed of 2, 13, 45, 47, 49, 81, and 106" (194). I think, however, that Pound's massive poem can be seen as, in part, what happens when a poet seeks to give a tongue to a nation only to find it doesn't exist, and that it probably wouldn't accept his voice for its own even if it did. But then, partly because he couldn't make it choral, and partly because of his hugely didactic purpose, the *Cantos* became an awkward and resistant ongoing philosophical/historical epic attempting to contain everything, a *via impossibilia* of modern poetry. Even so, especially in some of the later moments when it begins to interrogate its own various failures, it employs or deploys lyric against itself. For example, one could argue that the *Pisan Cantos* provide a form of lyric/anti-lyric in their return to traditional lyric themes and music in the context of the longer work containing them. And then there are the final "lyric" cries of failure toward the end, as in "Notes for CANTO CXVII et seq."

M'amour, m'amour
　　　　what do I love and
　　　　　　where are you?
That I lost my center
　　　　fighting the world.
The dreams clash
　　　　and are shattered—
and that I tried to make a paradiso

　　　　　　　　terrestre.　(802)

II

Perhaps there has always been lyric-against-lyric. Many twentieth century translations of famous lyric poets of the deep past strike me as profoundly modern in voice and feeling. Translations may well reflect and be for their own age (just look at the versions of Catullus by Jonson and Campion), but, the anti-lyric intention of some of these texts is apparent.

We know Sappho's fragments were when whole of a formidable formal complexity. Having, like many other people today, "small Latin and less Greek," I cannot relish the technical subtleties of her verse. Yet, when translated by someone like Mary Barnard, Sappho's poems sound extremely contemporary and very much the passionate speech of one person to another.

50
But you, monkey face

Atthis, I loved you
Long ago while you
still seemed to me a
small ungracious child

54
Afraid of losing you

I ran fluttering
like a little girl
after her mother

If, as the critics suggest, Sappho moved far closer to the common ver-
nacular in her monodies than was conventionally the case in the traditional Greek lyric of her day, or than she probably did in her choral poems,
then we can perhaps call her one of the first lyric/anti-lyric poets. Since all
we have are fragments, perhaps we can never appreciate how complexly
formal her poems might be if complete. What does come through, in all
the translations I have read, what transcends translation in language, time,
and space, is their emotional directness, a directness I associate with such
contemporary poets as, to name just a few, John Newlove, Robert Creeley,
Denise Levertov, Phyllis Webb, and, more recently, Anne Carson, especially in her highly lyric prose meditation on the early poet, *Eros the
Bittersweet*.

A reading of Catullus, at least in contemporary translations, reveals
even more about early anti-lyric lyricism. Catullus was the gifted inheritor
of what had become, in Latin, a purely literary form (as W. R. Johnson
argues), and his success suggests that the lyric-against-itself is probably the
product of a highly sophisticated, if possibly somewhat decadent, civilization, in which there is a strong historical heritage of "high" literature. That
is, it's possible the anti-lyric lyric appears only after "lyric" establishes
itself as a tradition and generally in the culture of large cities. At any rate,
the voice of Catullus, as heard in the translations of C. H. Sisson or
Frederic Raphael and Kenneth McLeish, would not seem out of place in
many contemporary anthologies:

58 a
Caelius, my Lesbia and yours, Lesbia the great,
The great Lesbia, the very one Catullus loved
More than himself and all he ever had,

Now all roads lead to her, the city's bottleneck,
Deepthroat for suckers from Rome's noblest stem.
(Trans. by Raphael and McLeish 63)

LVIII
Caelius, our Lesbia, Lesbia, that Lesbia
More loved by Catullus than any besides

—More than he loves himself and his pleasures—
Is now, in the alley-ways and even at cross-roads
Fucked by the noble sons of the Romans.
(Trans. by Sisson 38-39)

Yet in the original Latin, if I am to trust the critics and historians, the lyric
finesse of the language and the complex control of the form surely create
an appalling abysm between the beauty of the sound and rhythm and the
barely suppressed violence of jealous anger. These English translations
lack that lyric punch; the poem might be more powerful were it couched
in rhyming couplets or quatrains, some traditional form where the angry
obscenity of the language would carry more of the original's outrageous
shock value. I'm looking for a translation by the Earl of Rochester, I sup-
pose, and only because I'm told the Latin of Catullus was of a formidably
formal elegance. Somehow the satiric aspect of Catullus's poem, one of the
factors which makes of it an anti-lyric lyric, seems to demand the conventional forms of an equally cynical period in English literary history.
And yet my point, that the obscene as lyrical/anti-lyrical *cri de coeur* is not
new, even if it is extremely popular today, is best demonstrated by these
translations as they stand.

III

Antony Easthope argues that the English tradition, from Sidney's time to
Eliot's, forms a single discourse, one of the signs of which is the attempt
in poetry to deny the *enunciation* (the speech-event) as much as possible

in order to raise to an almost perfect presence the *enounced* (the narrated event, which could be the act of speaking of a specified speaker), an activity designed "to offer an absolute position to the reader as transcendental ego" (1983, 47). Whether or not one agrees with Easthope, his points invite stimulating argument. He suggests that the poetic discourse of the fixed and transcendental ego began in the Renaissance, and offers the medieval ballad as an example of the floating or unfixed I/eye. Toward the end of his study, he examines Pound's poetry to show how, in the grand attempt "to break the pentameter, that was the first heave" (Pound 1970, 518), Pound also broke from the transcendental ego as fixed centre of the poem's universe. And, with this break, we see that Pound's "heave" was determinedly anti-lyric, even in what we might still call lyrics, as is the case with his famous haiku-like poem of 1913:

In a Station of the Metro

The apparition of these faces in the crowd;
Petals on a wet, black bough. (1990, 111)

Easthope contrasts this poem with Eliot's "Morning at the Window," where, though "[s]ignifiers are given the license to 'float' in their own autonomy," it is "only so they can be correlative to an incoherent state of mind. In Pound the effect is always more radical" (138). By undermining "the referential effect," Eliot's poem demonstrates "that language can no longer be treated as a transparent medium through which the represented speaker knows a supposedly external reality." But the single speaker remains, and although certain (Easthope would say "conventional") aspects of "the referential effect" cannot be achieved, "the poem still *represents* a speaker, an 'I' aware of itself and its feelings, even if these cannot be confidently assigned between external sensation and internal thought" (138; emphasis added). How, in Pound's poem, in contrast, is the effect more radical? All three phrases lack verbs. Although juxtaposed, they are not the unified expression of a state of mind. Rather "the reader is led to consider how these faces in the crowd are like—and unlike—petals on a bough, not to identify with a speaker represented as seeing things that way." Pound is already, then, "well on his way to the theory of the ideogram. Though idiosyncratic, this outlines a programme for a complete break with the inherited poetic discourse" (138). And, one might add, a break with the conventions of lyric, even if the acute perceptual imagism of the poem still seems lyric to us.

I am not suggesting here that Pound, or any other modern or contemporary poet, has broken entirely with either traditional discourse or with lyric as a poetic possibility. The power of lyric in its myriad forms is too great; it tends to revive and renew itself in every generation. Pound continued to create lyrics after he wrote "In a Station of the Metro," but he also embarked on projects which transcended lyric—the *Cantos*—or subverted it—*Hugh Selwyn Mauberley*, which is a set of anti-lyrics, I believe. Reading in these poems what Easthope calls a "shifting 'I'" (4) is another way of comprehending them without making what Donald Davie calls the common misreading of them "as if H. S. Mauberley . . . is no more than a transparent disguise for Pound himself" (318).

Yet the lyric impulse remains strong, and sometimes the *idea* of lyric, as a voice still to be contended with or recognized for its own sake, appears in the *Cantos*, that massive collection of voices and eyes. "Canto 75," for example, opens with seven lines of mixed rhetoric, in which, as Easthope remarks of "Canto 84," there is neither "a coherent enounced" nor "a consistent narrator or representative speaker" (147):

> Out of Phlegethon!
> out of Phlegethon,
>   Gerhart
>   art thou come forth out of Phlegethon?
> with Buxtehude and Klages in your satchel, with the
> Ständebuch of Sachs in yr / luggage
>   —not of one bird but of many (450)

The seventh line points one way into the musical notation that follows, but those staves and notes signal, equally clearly, the pure lyric cry, for when music is unheard (and Keats, you will recall, told us in one of his greatest lyrics that "Heard melodies are sweet, but those unheard / Are sweeter" [288]), it is nevertheless present, by implication, in the concept of lyric. When what is printed is only the sign of music in the text of a poem, surely we are meant, certainly we are able, to perceive lyric at that moment of the text. Especially when that music, as Pound says in *Guide to Kulchur*, is "out of Arnaut (possibly), out of immemorial and unknown, [and] takes a new life on Francisco da Milano's lute" (250-251). In various ways, then, our foremost pioneering modern poet held lyric up to question in his various writings, and that's one way of creating lyric/anti-lyric.

IV

As I have suggested, one way of avoiding the conventional confines of lyric is to seek larger forms. Yet, for many poets, this is not allied with a desire to create epic or dramatic poems. This is especially true if we accept William Elford Rogers's definitions of the three genres as "modes of relation between the mind of the work and the world of the work" (57). According to Rogers, in drama "the mind of the work" is given only "as the *effect* wrought by the world of the drama as it unfolds before us" (59). In epic, "the mind of the work tells instead of showing" and "we are given the things and events of the world not as self-subsistent entities, as in drama, but as thoughts in the mind of the narrator" (59). In lyric, however, the signal "relational concept" is "*community* or *reciprocity*" (67), which is to say "that it is impossible for the lyrical mind to present itself as detached from the lyrical world in the way that it is possible in drama or epic" (68). I am sure I do not usually use the term "lyric" as Rogers wishes to, yet I think his version of the differences among the three genres is suggestive and potentially useful.

If Poe was the first one to call for long poems made up only of the "good parts," the moments of lyric intensity, the poets have not always found the Poe poem easy to achieve. But recently a particular concept of extended form seems to come close to Poe's ideal. One of its practitioners, Robin Blaser, even calls it a narrative of sorts in his essay, "The Fire":

I'm interested in a particular kind of narrative—what Jack

Spicer and I agreed to call in our own work the serial poem—this is a narrative which refuses to adopt an imposed story line, and completes itself only in the sequence of poems, if, in fact, a reader insists upon a definition of completion which is separate from the activity of the poems themselves. The poems tend to act as a sequence of energies which run out when so much of a tale is told. I like to describe this in Ovidian terms, as a *carmen perpetuum*, a continuous song in which the fragmented subject matter is only apparently disconnected. . . . The sequence of energies may involve all kinds of things—anger may open a window, a sound from another world may completely reshape the present moment, the destruction of a friendship may destroy a whole realm of language or the ability to use it—each piece is in effect an extended metaphor (another word is probably needed), because in the serial poem the effort is to hold both the correspondence and the focus that an image is, and the process of those things coming together—so that the light from a white linen tablecloth reflects on the face of one's companion, becomes light, fire, and the white moth which happens to be in the room is also light in the dark around the table, and is thus both the light and the element of light that destroys it. I ask you to remember that every metaphor involves at least four elements—which are a story, and the bringing them together is an activity, a glowing energy if stopped over, if entered. (237-238)

Blaser's final remarks seem to hint at precisely the reciprocal relation between the mind and world of the work which Rogers speaks of.

In a statement on his own "The Moth Poem," which is a fine example of the serial poem,[2] Blaser argues that "[s]uch poems deconstruct meanings and compose a wildness of meaning in which the I of the poet is not the centre but a returning and disappearing note" (1979, 323). This is certainly true of "The Moth Poem," in which, though mostly in larger blocks than the often line-by-line shifts of focus in, say, Pound's *Pisan*

Cantos, the reader's sense of *a* "speaker" is continually subverted. So one of the purposes of this poetic form is to rid the poet of "the lyric ego," a persona perhaps too powerfully conventionalized through four hundred years of English poetry to have much that is new left to say.

And yet, if one of the signs of lyric is, as Johnson suggests, its alignment with music, either by being written to be performed to music or else by being full of allusions to music, then "The Moth Poem" almost self-consciously insists on its lyric connections (even if the music alluded to is closer to that of John Cage than that of Frederic Chopin):

> the wind does not move on
> to another place
>
> bends into,
> as in a mirror,
> 　　　　　the
>
> breaking
>
> the moth in the piano
> will play on
> frightened wings brush
> the wired interior
> of that machine
>
> I said, 'master' (1993, 40)

Here, in "The Literalist," the second poem of the sequence, the eyes watch what cannot be seen, and hear (barely) a kind of magic music issuing from the unlikely encounter of nature and machine; a speaker enters the poem clearly only in the final line, and then in order to deny his normally privileged position by announcing the "other" and its power, perceived in the unseen and the almost unheard. Nevertheless, I think most readers would hear a lyric poem in this section, and in the other sections of "The Moth Poem," simply because we conventionally call a short poem full of physically apprehended details of perception and sensuous rhythms by that term.

What do we have in such a serial poem, then? Lyric straining against itself, perhaps, and a poetic discourse very much of that modern "heave" against the consolidations of what "the pentameter" stood for. Lyric/anti-lyric.

V

In his quick overview of modern lyric, Johnson argues that what has gone wrong with lyric in modernist literature is the loss of "a speaker, or singer, talking to, singing to, another person or persons, often, but not always, at a highly dramatic moment in which the essence of their relationship, of their 'story,' reveals itself in the singer's lyrical discourse, in his praise or blame, in the metaphors he finds to recreate the emotions he seeks to describe" (3). As he sees it, two kinds of poem have replaced this pure form of lyric: meditative poetry, "in which the poet talks to himself or to no one in particular" (3); and a poetry "in which the poet disappears entirely and is content to present a voice or voices or a story without intervening in that presentation directly" (3). One thing is obvious here: Johnson's notion of the person in the poem is precisely that which Easthope seeks to call in question. However, whether or not we perceive the person in the poem as a fixed or constantly shifting entity, it is possible to see the meditative poem, which Johnson associates with the Romantics through to Eliot and his inheritors, as having changed the grounds by which lyric was judged.

Johnson does not deny that lyrics of the "I-You" type he prefers have continued to appear, but he seems to feel they are in a distinct minority and appears unaware of recent developments, pointing instead to the creation of a "fiction of the singer and his audience" (16) in the poems of Yeats, and to the self-conscious death of lyric in the poems of Delmore Schwartz and Sylvia Plath. Yet, we can see in much contemporary poetry a striking return to pure lyric, and to the kind of anti-lyric lyric I have provisionally associated with Catullus. Which is to say no more, perhaps, than that one way of defining lyric/anti-lyric is to note that such definition can only occur in contrast to a rather sentimental definition of lyric.

It is in this context that the often savagely honest poems of Robert

Creeley or John Newlove, for example, might be treated as lyric/anti-lyric. Yet one of Newlove's toughest poems deliberately calls attention to the lyric qualities it simultaneously denies and affirms. It continues "the old pronominal forms of solo lyric" and insists that it is song, yet its songs are, one might say, atonal, deliberately flat, denying the conventional music of traditional verse. The personal emotions "No Use Saying to Whom" expresses are anger, frustration, despair, and, of course, *the* lyric emotion, desire

> No use saying to whom these
> four songs are addressed.

> 1. Even being near her eases me;
>   away I am distraught and sick,
>   useless.

> 2. All my friends are my enemies,
>   they want her to stay with that man,
>   knowing nothing.

> 3. No use blaming them, because they
>   do not know what is happening
>   in this house.

> 4. When you are gone my face falls
>   into its natural frown; you are
>   the bitterness left in my mouth.

> No use saying to whom these
> songs are addressed; you know. (12)

In fact, the first three songs try to maintain a distance from Johnson's "old pronominal forms" by insisting on the third person of both friends and lover; but the final song and the coda, a near-repeat of the opening lines, focuses the pain which has suffused the whole.

The next poem in *Moving in Alone* seems to follow up the hints of illicit love in "No Use Saying to Whom." Illicit love has been a moving force in lyric poetry from time immemorial, and one could draw a continuous line from the Troubadours to modern Country & Western music (and the question of popular music's lyric qualities is an important one, although pop song lyrics are not usually studied as examples of poetic speech). Illicit love is given something of a new, and anti-lyric, twist in "Nothing Is to Be Said," where intensely physical sensation crashes into the poem leading to a series of recognitions on the speaker's part, the final one of which is savagely, painfully, comic, and brings into focus a figure usually kept out of such love poems:

> Everything ends once
> and cannot be recovered,
> even our poor selves
>
> Your tongue thrusts into my mouth
> violently and I am lost,
> nothing is to be said. I am plunged
> into the black gap again.
>
> It is not to be endured
> easily, unthought of, never
> to be dismissed with ease.
>
> What can I do. My hand
> shakes on the page. Knowing
> I am criminality, there is
> nothing I can do.
>
> Ah, I can't go home
> and make love to her either,
> pretending it's you. (13)

Both these poems are lyric—or are they? What distinguishes them and other poems like them from what we have conventionally taken to be lyric is their refusal of so many of the traditional rhetorical properties of verse—especially the various tropes. Aside from Newlove's obvious delight in flouting lyrical thematic conventions, the minimalism of such poems clearly asserts their anti-lyric nature. Yet, in their "measure," as William Carlos Williams uses the term, they achieve a real and often intense musicality, not attached to metre but to the flow of the large rhythmical unit of the stanza, or the verse paragraph. As in "The Language" by Robert Creeley:

> Locate *I*
> *love you* some-
> where in
>
> teeth and
> eyes, bite
> it but
>
> take care not
> to hurt, you
> want so
>
> much so
> little. Words
> say everything.
>
> *I*
> *love you*
> again,
>
> then what
> is emptiness
> for. To
>
> fill, fill.

I heard words
and words full

of holes
aching. Speech
is a mouth. (283)

As Thom Gunn points out, Creeley "has gone beyond, or behind, the
classic twentieth-century split between image and discourse: he does not
attempt sharpness of physical image, and the discursive part of the poetry is more aptly termed 'assertion'" (95). The "real course" this poem
"follows is that of the mind, wandering, but at the same time trying to
focus in on its own wandering and to map a small part of its course accurately and honestly, however idiosyncratic that course may seem to be—
idiosyncratic in its pace, in its syntax, even in its subject-matter. In attun-
ing our voices to that mind, in paying our full attention to the way it
moves and shifts, we become part of its own attentiveness and can share
in 'the exactitude of his emotion'" (95). Is such idiosyncrasy lyric? Anti-
lyric? Yes, and no. It *is* the kind of poetry I had in mind when I first
thought of this topic, and it still seems to me to fit the concept. Moreover,
Creeley is but one of many contemporary poets who have subverted the
modernist aesthetic of separate persona and who must be read, at least in
part, as speaking for themselves, however open and free-flowing those
selves may be. If "modernist lyric" is what Johnson perceived it as, a form
of poetry without an "I" which speaks directly to a "thou," contemporary lyric in poems like Creeley's insists upon the poet's speaking self. And
in their retrieval of the poet's self as poetic speaker, such poems attack the
idea of a *modernist* lyric.

VI

In "For Play and Entrance: The Contemporary Canadian Long Poem,"
Robert Kroetsch recalls a poem whose lyric intensities seldom fail to
impress the reader/listener, and whose affinities to the passionate lyrics of
the greatest woman poet of Greece are not hard to trace.

Our interest in the discrete, in the occasion.

Trace: behind many of the long poems of the 1970s in Canada is the shadow (Jungian?) of another poem, a short long poem.

1965: Phyllis Webb, *Naked Poems*.

A kind of hesitation even to write the long poem. Two possibilities: the short long poem, the book-long poem. Webb, insisting on that hesitation. On that delay. On nakedness and lyric and yet on a way out, perhaps a way out of the ending of the lyric too, with its ferocious principles of closure, a being compelled out of lyric by lyric:

the poet, the lover, compelled towards an ending (conclusion, death, orgasm: coming) that must, out of love, be (difference) deferred. (118)

Kroetsch is, of course, pursuing his particular poetic passions here. Webb is simply pursuing passion, to speak or sing it as clearly as possible. I am interested in what he says about her poem because he points to its lyric/anti-lyric aspects. *Naked Poems* is a serial poem of sorts; but, though it breaks away from lyric (love) song in its final three sections, the first two "suites" are exquisite in their (sometimes literal, always deliberate) mouth music. Yet, if the voice of these two suites is fairly stable (while in the final three it disappears or dissipates into a chorus of possible "I"s), it can be tenuous in the extreme. Not Sappho nor Catullus pleading; just a body (in time) timelessly speaking and making love:

AND
here
and here and
here
and over   and
over   your mouth (1982b, 66)

The merest abstractions, except for the final word: a conjunction; an adverb of place(ment); an adverb expressing temporal repetition, yet also figuring its other meanings of height, and "in excess" or "beyond what has been said"; a possessive pronoun (carefully unfocussed insofar as nowhere is the second person ever identified any further) expressing by this point in the poem an extreme possession (but on whose behalf?); and one noun, very physical, yet with the implications of speech (indeed, the specially privileged speech of lovemaking) definitely there. That one concrete word is itself abstracted in the music of the poem. Like the other terms it tends to float free of signification, to become pure signifier-in-action. All the words in this poem are things-in-themselves: the speech-act becomes far more important than the narrated event. Or rather, the narrated event exists only in the speech-act, this intensely physical fragment of broken song which is not simply song but dance. Indeed, I have always felt that the first two suites of *Naked Poems* were a series of exquisitely turned gestures, surely one possible definition of dance. Many of these gestures could be defined as lyrical, but their appearance here, in the midst of a series of fragmented moments of perception and insight, in the midst of a continuing serial narrative of enunciation, makes them something else as well. Still the central movement of the following section of "Suite II" surely deserves the adjective:

> *In the gold darkening*
> *light*
>
> *you dressed.*
>
> *I hid my face*
> *in my hair.*
> *The room that held you*
> *is still here.* (78)

In this tiny *pas-de-deux*, the focal gesture is one lovers would recognize at any period from at least Sappho's to our own.

In "Non Linear," Webb shifts focus and, in a typical post-*Cantos* move, floats the "I" of the putative speaker so that from fragment to fragment no particular voice speaks. The same is true of "Suite of Lies" (the title of which once again alludes to music), which is gnomic in the extreme as it moves to this ambiguous finale:

> *the way of what fell*
> *the lies*
> *like the petals*
> *falling drop*
> *delicately* (99)

In "Some Final Questions," Webb seems to offer us a duet and therefore two fixed voices, but there is music on only one side and that is part of the lyric/anti-lyric point. Moreover, who, precisely, speaks? The questioner is legion; the respondent is any poet; and since to question poetry's impulses is to deny the possibilities of poetic speech, only one voice achieves lyricism here, and it finally seems to disappear in silence—or do "*we* disappear" instead, "in the musk of [the Priestess of/Motion's] coming" (89), as the text prayed earlier? Either way, *Naked Poems* is, for me, not only the poem in whose shadow so many later Canadian long poems stand, but also the poem which taught us once again how we might write (sing) love without being trapped by what Kroetsch calls the "ferocious principles of closure" of the conventional lyric.

VII

An instance of what might be called "specific intertextuality"—what a number of contemporary writers have agreed to call "homolinguistic translation," translation by a variety of methods from one language into the same language—definitely denies the lyric impulse as we generally understand it, even when the results may appear lyric, upon first reading. This denial of lyric is especially obvious when the original text is a lyric.

Steve McCaffery has given us a series of homolinguistic translations of Mary Barnard's Sappho (itself a real translation from another language) in *Intimate Distortions: a displacement of Sappho*. His number "Fifty" has a lyric feel which some of his other ones clearly deny, yet the very fact that its voice emerges from some point intermediate to Barnard, McCaffery, and, yes, Sappho, means that that voice is no longer truly that of a lyric individual but that of a contemporary deconstructive process:

> Same's not similar
>
> & long ago
> is now
>
> in this remembering.
>
> i'm remembering
> your childhood &
> i'm facing that in you
>
> facing you
> facing your face
>
> as then i did you did so
>
> long to come to be
> come now. (1979, np)

In their much more stringent refusals of traditional lyric modes, "Twenty Three" and "Sixty Two" achieve an even greater distance from both their originals while simultaneously providing a contemporary commentary on them:

> 23
> And their feet move
>
> Rhythmically, as tender
> feet of Cretan girls
> danced once around an

altar of love, crushing
a circle in the soft
smooth flowering grass (Barnard)

in   crete
dis   crete

con   crete
indis   crete

in   crete

on   crete

dis   crete
con   crete

in   crete (McCaffery)

62
The nightingale's
The soft-spoken
announcer of
Spring's presence (Barnard)

nightingale on
P.S.

M.C. of
bud-break. (McCaffery)

In "Sixty Two," McCaffery plays wittily with contemporary connotations of English words. "Twenty Three" is much more radical in both form and playful wit. Displaying the words for visual effect upon the page, it insists on their concrete presence-as-enunciation while playing with both English idiom and Greek and Latin echoes in the words. Part of the enjoyment of these poems has to do with their lightly born iconoclasm; they make lyric itself no more than a trace of original texts, to be detected, if at all, only as literary artifact, ingeniously "artifantasized."

Somewhat similar in effect, though in intensity it is much closer to what we expect from lyric, is the following poem by another innovative Canadian writer, Christopher Dewdney. As its title implies, it too exists between voices: as the speaker is only the "Poem *using* lines *spoken* by Suzanne" (my italics), so too the "you" of the text floats free from particular signification, or else is no more than an absolute signifier, trapped forever in the dream of language which is the poem:

What you feel as your body
is only a dream. The mind also
is a slave. You are asleep.
You are asleep, what you feel
as your mind is only a dream. The
dream also, is only a slave.
You are a dream, what you feel
as your slave is only a mind.
The body also is a mind. You
are asleep
in the gentle theft of time.   (time) (23)

In "Boreal Electric," the epigraph (significantly a graffito, as if to say, only on walls will we now find a conventional lyric speech of any sincerity) recycles the lyric ego and his suffering, but the text itself, though it contains some "I"s and some "she"s which could possibly signify people or voices, is an extreme case of self-conscious enunciation swallowing all of the possible enounced:

For my lady, keeper of my wound.

GRAFFITI

She is the twilight intangible, a thin instruction
burning within the envelope generators. Alter
sublime in the cenozoic asylum. And

I am case-hardened. Natty causal an
auto-facsimile. Denoting cold fire.
There is nothing sentimental
about these rocks. I am
the envelope generator growling
in the shifting code facsimiles of night.

Zone traces. Indigo.

I would have her mouth the words
'statutory rape' slowly. Arrested
for intent to denote this line.
This lodestar being visible only
to the discerning eye.

The disconcerting eye. (29)

As these examples demonstrate, and I could find many more like them
in contemporary Canadian and American poetry, the outward forms of
lyric are infinitely capable of what McCaffery calls distortion and what I
might call formal subversion: lyric/anti-lyric in another of its guises.

VIII

Christopher Dewdney showed great perspicacity in suggesting that graffiti are one home for conventional lyric texts today. The other home is pop-
ular song, of course, which traverses quite a ground, from the sophisticated lyrics of Cole Porter and his ilk to the high romance of Smokey
Robinson and his. Yet, who would dare to suggest that "The Tracks of My
Tears" or "The Tears of a Clown" are not lyric in the grand tradition? Not
I, even if I also believe that Cole Porter was a master lyricist, perhaps the
finest twentieth century writer of popular music, mining ("I've Got You
Under My Skin") and undermining ("Always True to You in My
Fashion") the traditions of the love song as he inherited them. Insofar as
popular music has become the common home of lyric sentiment, it has also
developed its own kind of anti-lyric material. The whole history of the
blues traverses all the possibilities. The smartest rock groups, like The

Rolling Stones, have given us examples of both kinds, though mostly those associated with anti-lyric. Singer/songwriters as diverse as Leonard Cohen, Randy Newman, Richard Thompson and Elvis Costello have produced lyrics whose message Catullus would have no problem identifying. Some of the songs by women songwriters, such as Joni Mitchell, Kate and Anna McGarrigle, and more recent ones like Iris Dement and Lucinda Williams, also challenge all kinds of traditional lyric stances.

What is most interesting about contemporary rock music at its best is that it is a kind of technological folk art. Some songs, like certain of Bob Dylan's or David Bowie's, to choose two highly crafty manipulators of conventions, say "I" but present no specific "I" to speak through. Rather, such songs speak (or sing) for whichever person happens to be listening to or singing them at any one moment. It is too easy to dismiss all pop music as cynical exploitation of its audience's feelings, but the best and most interesting examples speak for a whole community as folk music once did. Insofar as the "I" therefore slides away from its writer's ego to embrace the unknown throng, it slips the reins of conventional lyric to become a kind of *vox populi*. No transcendent ego, of the kind Easthope sees in traditional English lyric discourse, remains, but rather an open, sliding voice we can all slip into if we so wish.

X

If Robert Kroetsch was right to point to Phyllis Webb's *Naked Poems* as an endeavour to evade lyric's "ferocious principles of closure," then perhaps what my exploration of the concept of anti-lyric has led to is a form which attempts to slip the "ferocious principles of closure" of the traditional literary essay. Lyric/anti-lyric now seems to me to be best understood as a signifier with a myriad of floating signifieds, some of which I hope I have indicated in these notes.

ENDNOTES

[1] It is interesting to note that John Adams has set one of Whitman's poems about the Civil War to music; but he has also chosen to present it for a solo voice rather than a chorus. See "The Wound-Dresser," Sanford Sylvan,

baritone, Nanko Tanaka, violin, Chris Gekker, trumpet, on *John Adams: Fearful Symmetries/The Wound-Dresser* (Electra/Nonesuch 9 79218-2).

[2] By itself it is a short serial poem, but it is also part of a larger, lifelong serial work, *The Holy Forest*, which was finally published in 1993; the way in which the whole continues to play against yet with lyric expectations is exemplary.

Ondaatje Stretches Out

Two Early Sequences

I

The Last Time I Wrote 'Paris':
Ondaatje's first attempt at a poetic sequence in "Troy Town"

Michael Ondaatje's first book, *The Dainty Monsters*, no longer appears quite as spectacularly new as it did in 1967. Though it does have a few pretensions the older writer will slough off, it is more complex and mature than is usual for a first collection, and contains far fewer poems for the older author to be ashamed of than do most such collections. Indeed, in the shift from purely lyrical separate poems in the first section to sequences of poems in the second, it enacts one of the methods by which poetry made the shift from modernism to postmodernism.

A good argument could be made that Ondaatje's epigraphs to his various books reveal his growing sophistication during the past three and a half decades, as they move from traditional literary sources in *The Dainty Monsters* to pop culture, nonfiction, ancient texts, and translations from more marginalized contemporary writers in the later texts. The epigraphs to *The Dainty Monsters* come from iconographic modern works: the poems of W.H. Auden and the novels of Fyodor Dostoyevsky. Useful introductions to each section, they also hint at Ondaatje's essentially modernist stance in these poems.[1]

On the other hand, Ondaatje's early association with Coach House Press places him in the company of a particular Canadian avant-garde, one interested in other approaches, especially the New American Poetry and Poetics. He would eventually come to his own, unique, terms with these other poetic approaches, and one of the ways he did so was by writing in extended forms. Nevertheless, as even a glance at some of the critical statements that attempt to categorize Ondaatje as a poet demonstrates, his poetry was sufficiently charged and different from the very beginning of his career to generate a multiplicity of critical responses.[2] Moreover, the critics' compulsion to find a variety of metaphors to describe his work is a testament to Ondaatje's imagistic invention.

Images and metaphors, as well as highly symbolic figures, comprise much of the text in *The Dainty Monsters*, but when these figures emerge from an implied narrative ground they seem to teeter on the boundary between modernism and postmodernism. The sequence of poems exploring the mythic material of the Trojan War is Ondaatje's first sustained attempt to break away from the limitations of modernist lyric closure. Indeed, I would like to argue that the very attempt at length and mixed viewpoints accomplishes this break.

Ondaatje's early poems are obsessed with animals and birds, often captured in some violent relation to humanity, as George Bowering, among others, points out: "In his twenties he explored and exploited the violence implied in the confrontation between people and animals. . . . Ondaatje is interested in the experiential philosophy developing from a paradox pronounced early in his verse: . . . [that] 'nature breeds the unnatural'" (1988b, 167). The dry voice of many of these poems—poised, alert, and keeping a careful distance from what it describes—is understated in the Auden or Stevens mode, and situates everything in a photographic frame or freezes it in amber. There is a felt need for control in Ondaatje's "habit of intensifying the world, of fashioning artifice" (164), where the intensification is itself somehow artificial precisely insofar as it actually manages to "freeze this moment" ". . . in immobilised time" (1967, 46). Although Ondaatje will eventually jettison the sense of closure in these early poems, they remain bright and powerful, and introduce many of the major themes of his first few books. And the desire to catch the intense moment, even if later accompanied by a recognition that such moments must necessarily disappear, remains the romantic ground of his narration-of-character to this day. That desire leads him, again and again, to create powerful moments of physically apprehended passion in the "lives" of his various revelatory figures out of myth and history. And the first example of such narration occurs in the Trojan poems.

❧

Ever since the Renaissance turn to Hellenism, young authors have found inspiration in classical sources. And although there was a change of direction in what Guy Davenport calls "the Renaissance of 1910, which recognized the archaic" (27), Hellenic myth remains the most important narrative storehouse that most beginning Eurocentric writers can find. At least since 1922, when *Ulysses* first appeared and T.S. Eliot argued that "[i]n using the myth, in manipulating a continuous parallel between contemporaneity and antiquity, Mr Joyce is pursuing a method which others must pursue after him" (177), writers have sought to wear the masks of various famous figures out of Homer and others. Homer is especially interesting because the works under his name are "the most ancient pages of Western literature" (Davenport 23), and so point backwards far beyond history. According to Davenport, *The Odyssey* was the central modernist pre-text, as opposed to *The Iliad*, which had held priority in the past. In choosing to write about "Troy Town," then, Ondaatje signaled his desire to continue in his own small way the modernist effort while resisting the general approach. In fact "Troy Town" reaches for its narrative impulses far beyond Greek mythology into Egypt, the Bible, history, and finally, in "Peter," into a kind of invention. And it approaches all its subjects in the light of its modernist epigraph, Dmitry Karamazov's contradictory boast (or is it apology?): "Indeed I can't help feeling that in telling you all about these inner struggles of mine, I've exaggerated a little in order to show you what a fine fellow I am. But, all right, let it be like that and to hell with all those who pry into the human heart" (53).[3] This epigraph sets up certain expectations, which perhaps the poems cannot live up to, especially since they are short and lack the psychological expansion of the novel. But it also suggests that contradiction, passionate struggle, and glimpses of character will occur.

Of the nine poems and sequences in this section, five are clearly personae poems, while the other four imply a specific if unidentified speaker. Of these nine, only three, one of which is "Peter," the final sequence of *The Dainty Monsters*, appear in Ondaatje's first selected poems, *There's a Trick with a Knife I'm Learning to Do*.[4] Perhaps Ondaatje chose to reject the rest because they depend so fully upon well-known mythic-literary pretexts without really subverting them. Still, simply by choosing Paris as a protagonist for the other sequence, he did undercut the heroic mode of the original sufficiently that the poem offers an at least partial new reading of the tale.

Nevertheless, the first three poems offer conventional heroic and ironic views of Prometheus and Lilith, and violent and energetic images like those in the poems of "Over the Garden Wall."[5] "Pyramid" is somewhat more interesting in its representation of an already "dead" speaker reviewing not his life but the making of his tomb.[6] The tone of near boredom might at first be mistaken as a noble's or ruler's disdain for the slaves who toil to "[break] the horizon" by "trailing their boulders to the moon" (55). The speaker finds it "Timeless here," even though he sees the others in ". . . their minutes, / distant . . . mime pains." Not by his own desire, exactly, he achieves the static perfection the lyric strives for: "positioned . . . by a mirror," a "sealed . . . form." But is that form, now sealed in place, the figure or its newly made ground, the pyramid? It is impossible to tell. Before that mirror, locked into eternity, the speaker says, "I watch / and in our conversations / grow profound." There is a suggestion of process in that "grow," but everything else undermines its hope. There is only the image of self, and this growing is only a deepening of what is already there. The poem leaves the possibility of change in doubt. In achieving even this amount of lyric indeterminacy, it sets the stage for the sequence of poems based on the myth of Troy.

The "Trojan" sequence is, in fact, larger than the seven-part "Paris," for it also contains "The Goodnight," and "O Troy's Down: Helen's Song," as well as "Philoctetes on the Island," which only appears next to "The Goodnight" in *Trick with a Knife*. Throughout the sequence, Ondaatje subtly handles a wide-ranging imagery of violence and passion, often with echoes of the poems in the first part of the book. Paris figures prominently throughout, an unheroic man of memory and sensation, who can at best articulate intense impressions rather than profound emotion and thought. Even when he gets to tell his version, he can't seem to explain anything; all he can do is represent events.

In speaking thus of Paris, I seem to be interpreting him more as a character in a fiction than as a figure in a poem. This sequence of poems is Ondaatje's first attempt to create a kind of documentary poem, even if the documents are classical myths. As will be the case in his later book-length poems, Ondaatje chooses to deal with a given and complete story rather than with the continuing act of invention, with its "ironies inherent in the act of composition, [its] acknowledgement that a writer who partic-ipates in motion cannot 'freeze' a scene for the universal literary museum" (Bowering 1988b, 169), but he also chooses to leave most of the (already-known) story in the interstices between lyric texts.[7] Thus he concentrates on text and narration, inviting readers to participate in the act of pro-duction, as it occurs. Because the story itself contains a wealth of by now complex characters, he is able to assume their fictional solidity even as he uses them as lyric images or voices.

"The Goodnight" takes a complex perspective upon its materials, and, like most poems of mythical allusion, assumes the reader's knowl-edge. The narrative voice suggests that readers join "[w]ith the bleak heron Paris / [to] imagine Philoctetes . . . in front of him" (58) bearing the full weight of his ten years of isolation.[8] Is Paris a fitting subject because he is capable of such imagining? Is such imagining the one way out of the trap of cowardice and ignoble death? By first placing reader and character on the same level of perception, the poem acts like a Chinese box. After sug-gesting that Paris (and readers) can identify somehow with his antagonist, it then steps further back to include Paris in the psychological vision of the scene. Paris as "bleak heron" might be a "true king" (13), but he is also a "perfumed stag" (58), an image that suggests the sensual man who chose Aphrodite and the most beautiful woman's love over Hera's offer of power and Athena's bribe of beauty, wisdom, and victory over the Greeks. If the first two stanzas imagine Philoctetes as if through Paris's eyes, the final stanza shifts perspective and, like a mirror, shows Paris through his killer's eyes, until the focus pulls back to show them both in the moment just before Paris is killed. Ondaatje creates a series of visual metaphors haunt-ed by abstract symbolism. The "sun / netted in the hills" is a vision of trapped power, like the Trojans themselves. From kingly heron to sybarit-ic stag to cowering "running spider," Paris diminishes to mere shadow before "the standing man" of violent strength who will conquer him. Ondaatje makes one chilling alteration to the myth with Philoctetes's still-"bandaged foot": in this world, violence seems always to bring pain, and wounds are never fully healed, be they external or internal. The ambigui-ty of the final couplet—"who let the shafts of eagles into the ribs / that were moving to mountains"—suggests both Paris's attempt to escape into the mountains where he once grazed his sheep, and his impending death, here envisaged as bone turning to stone. Only after this deadly proleptic vision does the text offer Paris's version of his story in the sequence that bears his name.

"Philoctetes on the Island" appears in *Trick with a Knife* (and also *The Cinnamon Peeler*) immediately after "The Goodnight," although none of the other Troy poems do. Thus, in both *Rat Jelly* and *Trick with a Knife*, the story of Philoctetes's exile is isolated from the larger myth of the Trojan War, possibly because Ondaatje has altered Philoctetes from the original story, in which he is presented as having a "deep love for inanimate or inhuman things" (Lattimore 45). Where the tragic Philoctetes of Sophocles rages only at the Greeks who abandoned him, Ondaatje's in "The Goodnight" is the "man who roared on an island for ten years" (58), "a mad hunter" whose "insane logic is clear" (Glickman 1985, 75): he will resist the temptation to commit suicide by committing murder. If, as Glickman argues, "the way man compensates for his own indignities by defiling the natural world is a central theme of *Rat Jelly*" (76), then "Philoctetes on the Island" may serve as a fitting transition from the early lyrics to the longer works. As a "wounded hunter" (77), Philoctetes is a figure much like Peter, Potter, and Billy, all "lawbreakers who survive in the wild places of the earth through cunning and instinct" (76). And, like Billy and Peter, at least, his mind works metaphorically; his violence creates patterns and to that degree is a kind of artistry. But the first such longer work is, in fact, "Paris," whose eponymous protagonist he murders.

As the "I" of "Philoctetes on the Island," Philoctetes is the subject of its aggressive artistry, to adapt a term from Tom Marshall (85): "Sun moves broken in the trees / drops like a paw / turns sea to red leopard" (1973, 34). As central consciousness of the poem, Philoctetes sees the sun as "broken," or wounded like himself, yet simultaneously sees it as a hunting animal. The third line is acutely ambiguous as it evokes the blood of a dying animal as well as the living animal's movements. Caught on the hinge of perception that ambiguity declares, this Philoctetes must "trap sharks" and "cut them with coral till / the blurred grey runs / red designs" (34). What he cannot escape is the capacity to impose design upon even the most chaotic deaths. As Marshall notes, "here is Ondaatje's world and his subtext of the wounded and wounding artist in a nutshell" (85). In his utter isolation, Philoctetes kills "to fool myself alive" and so not "shoot an arrow up / and let it hurl / down through my petalling skull" (34). But he is refusing the temptation of suicide because, however much he retreats from it, he cannot escape from his own thinking. Suicide is "the end of thinking," and he will "Shoot either eye of bird instead / and run and catch it in your hand" (34). The imperative and the second-person possessive here enact a suddenly doubled voice that sounds almost like a training manual on how to survive abandoned on an island.

Wounded and wounding though he might be, Philoctetes in his doubled speech is not simply in a rage against the natural world. He encounters it on its own terms. Although the advice on how to "slow an animal" is necessarily violent, it suggests how fully hunter and hunted are entwined in the hunt: "so two run wounded / reel in the bush, flap / bodies at each other" (35). And if the final advice—"then use a bow / and pin the tongue back down its throat" (35)—is a "grotesque image remind[ing] us of the mutilation of the Malayan mules . . . in 'White Dwarfs' [and saying that] guilty man has to silence the victims of his violence" (Glickman 76), it is not the end of the poem. Instead, rain "rakes up the smell of animals" still alive and "cleans me." Philoctetes cannot escape the pain of his wound, as even sunrise is a violation: "sun breaks up / and spreads wound fire at my feet" (35). Each day, he seems to say, the sun erupts from the sea and makes his wound worse; and "then they smell me, / the beautiful animals" (35). The poem does not in any way mitigate Philoctetes's violence, but it does offer a sense of balance in his lonely world. He and the natural world seem to battle on almost equal terms; if the end of his story were not known, then the unpunctuated conclusion of his narration might imply that the animals' power would eventually conquer him. The open suggestiveness of the final couplet makes interpretation uncertain, and I think it is this quality of the poem, more than its representation of humankind's defilement of the natural world, that marks it as a transition from the modernist stance of Ondaatje's early poems to the postmodernist stance of his later ones.

Paris speaks the first six parts of "Paris," and only in the final section does the focus shift outward—as in the final stanza of "The

Goodnight"—to an external representation of his death.[9] Each section stands alone, a moment cut out of the flowing stream of his life. If, in *The Iliad* and elsewhere, Paris is, in Hector's words, no more than "Paris, the great lover, a gallant sight!" but having "no backbone, no staying / power" (3, 13-70), running and hiding in battle, or lying safe with Helen (3, 408-461), here, as he remembers particular events or enacts his part in them, he might be something different. "Paris" does not alter the "facts" of Paris's life so much as provide a sympathetic—because "autobiographical"—perspective on them. But it complicates them too, because in memory events and people mix, times and places overlap.

Part I establishes an indistinct mood, the opening lines refusing any sure reference: "A lifeless night tonight, I talk to her, / the sky low, and with a surer hand / one could draw a heaven down" (1967, 59). At this point, it could be anywhere, any time, and "her" could refer either to Oinone (Ondaatje's spelling of Oenone) or to Helen. The uncertainty throughout depends on the reader's knowledge of the whole original story.[10] With the addition of the old man, possibly Priam, the poem seems to be set in Troy. But it refuses to secure this reading, for Paris could be imagining his watching on the mountain to which Priam exiled him. The still unidentified woman ". . . stretches out her palms / curves them to circle stars," and says to Paris, "I am collecting the sky for you, Alexandros." Is this a statement of faithful love or immediate passion? "At night it is cold on the mountain, / we move with fast passion from necessity" suggests this is a memory of Oinone, but the final line adds some doubt: "By calming me she removes my dreams." These could be dreams of the future, or they could be dreams of a mistaken past: as the former, they suggest Oinone, as the latter, they suggest Helen. This conflation probably signifies Paris's own confusion of the two as he remembers.

Part II seems definitely to recall the early days of Oinone's love and Paris's freedom from the gods' demands. It combines a number of visits into one image—of Priam aging, of "prudish Hector . . . calmed only by the young Polyxena" (60), his sister. Paris can even laugh at himself, a figure losing his dignity at the games, as he leaves "the chariot in a vast / ignoble, timeless tumble." Once again, the shifting tones draw readers into a confusion of emotions that assumes its own verisimilitude. From the rhythms of slapstick, in which the alliteration of "timeless tumble" seems to stop time, the next stanza turns to a slow unfolding of gentle love and beauty, Oinone's body perceived as "frail in the mornings / and white in the streams / gleaming among the dark rocks of Ida." These oppositions serve only to set up the final stanza, which leaves readers as unsure as Paris: "'For Alexandros who understands.' / 'Who understands what?' / 'Everything'." He can remember this, but he can not explain it. Readers can only share his ignorance, his failure in love and understanding signified by the very word held up only as a question. Does the text present Paris as a character in a modernist-symbolist monologue or simply as a symbol? It is hard to say.

Part III establishes an even more dramatic situation, as it is addressed to an apparently specific audience, with readers comprising a separate audience outside the action. But, once again, unclear references make it difficult to know from where, or to whom, Paris is speaking. Who are the "Sirs" who give him "all this glitter" (61)? Why does he tell them of his "whimsical past" only to warn them that he is "a curse to break your city / to kill your generations"? Even the time is unclear, although it seems to be during the war. Paris speaks with some assurance about his place in the story and, like the gods perhaps, finds his own history dependent on whim alone. His insouciance is simultaneously winning and appalling, for he does not seem to care. His final offer of "apples with a serpent's charm" slides biblical myth over the Greek story-line as if they were a pair of transparencies. In doing so, it invites a complex interpretation that the characterization refuses; yet the implication that Paris is only a temptation the Trojans failed to resist removes any responsibility from him.

Part IV also speaks to, or of, a specific audience, but here it appears as the beloved—although, once again, the missing name leaves reference more or less open. Most readers will assume this audience to be Helen. Represented as "storklike" and "thin as plants" (62), she both carries and brings scars to Paris. He seems to desire their passion, but he cannot be sure of it: "Our fires are made / with the inconsistency of sticks." Here the ancient metaphor of passion as fire is extended by the strangely abstract one of inconsistent sticks, which affirms the fragility of their union and, in the pat symbolism of "variable" wind, further suggests how fickle both gods and leaders can be. Such layered metaphors consistently add to the power of Ondaatje's writing at this stage of his career. This unsure paean achieves a lyric closure of sorts by concentrating utterly on the other: "And your body / has the muscle of birds / and the desire of their wings."

Part V is equally difficult to place in time in the story. Paris and the woman are in Troy, at some deliberately vague period during the ten-year siege. Here the focus is self-consciously inward: the speaker addresses himself in the second person and places his lover at a distance from the familiar intimacy of Part IV. Still seen as a bird "falling garroted in love / to the tangle of tall hair and bed," now "she watches" the distant ". . . fires tongue / ground and air . . ." and, "Then turning eyes drugged thin at you" (there is a note of exhortation and fear in that pronoun), "walks there key-holing night. / I even smell the fire, once she said" (63). In traditional dramatic monologuist style, Paris does not understand everything he says, but what marks his discourse as postmodern is the way it refuses to allow readers any greater (and ironic) knowledge, unless the knowledge of the story itself provides the superiority offered to readers of Browning's poems, for example. Instead, the poem grows more and more opaque the deeper it moves into the given story.

The last two sections turn to the fighting itself. Part VI is another address, to a single warrior perhaps, in which Paris admits his cowardice: "While my brothers die / and father roars, I shiver, / separate" (64). Or perhaps it is only his isolation he admits, for he insists again, "Separate, sir, / I see their dance in all its glory," and seeks to argue his case from that vantage point. It is here that the poem falters, for any explanation will seem banal, and certainly most of this one does. Paris makes this case for himself by saying he chooses to "become one-dimensional." Does this sound noble or simply vague? Again, readers can only turn to the myth, in which a not-so-valiant Paris kills Achilles with an arrow guided by Apollo, only to be then killed by Philoctetes. In myth and most literature, Paris is now a figure of sexual desire alone, and represents none of the finer virtues, but this poem seems to want it both ways. "Yes," readers might imagine Paris saying, "I will be a one-dimensional figure in the story as it is told and retold, but this was the deliberate choice I made once I comprehended my basic character."

It is good that the poem does not stop there, for this implied assertion is both too conclusive and somewhat bathetic. By suddenly shifting to external focalization in Part VII, the text returns to the violent imagery of its earlier parts in order to allow Paris a glamorous negative apotheosis:

> Paris heaving,
> > hunched in the river,
> hands on his stomach gripped
> his ripped body
> numbing in the coolness. (65)

Metaphors seem almost nonexistent in this carefully articulated poem, the only one spread across the field of the page; rather, the language seeks a physicality in which the rhythm and the sounds mime his painful dying. The rhymed series of "gripped," "ripped," "mist," "withering," "glinting," "twisted," "with," and "kisses" insistently keeps the feel of ripping in readers' minds. The alliteration of "heaving," "hunched," and "hands" has a similar effect. The total movement of the poem is downward, each stanza a repetition and intensification of the one before. The whole is directed to the loss of the body, presented in terms of physical sensation, and it all comes to a climax on "lets his stomach break." Where Part VI sounds pretentious because it strives but fails to achieve explanation, Part VII achieves a density of negative figuration, a concentration upon pure bodily and perceptual loss that dignifies its dying protagonist and satisfactorily completes his story.

As I have suggested, however, the full sequence of Troy poems includes the later story as well, and it is that aftermath which "O Troy's Down: Helen's Song" (66-67) evokes. Having heard Paris's version of his story, readers now hear Helen's final lament. Acknowledging the complexities of her aging husband, Menelaus, who, though "corporeal and crude," is also capable of a "snake dance," she perceives that even she is growing old: "I loosen like the end of spring" (66). But, in a parenthetical aside, she also remembers her own glory: "(Oh I could glitter like the stomach of the sun!)". To this point, the poem reads like a conventional lament for lost glory, addressed outward to a generalized audience, but suddenly in the fourth stanza the tone changes as Helen appears to address her "gentle proud daughter" about more complex emotional connections. In fact, her address is temporally doubled: here and now to her singular audience; there and then, and now, to the object of her continuing, useless passion. If her daughter can only show the "condescending emotion" of pity, she can still say, "I knew a man once / who never withered." Even sixteen years later she still dances in the mornings, "but with no mirror." And, even her daughter's understanding would only "stale / all this uncertain agony." She needs this agony, yet she also wants her "frail white daughter" (67) to know:

> if I should breathe
> these thoughts to you at night
> I would with all the senses
> left now to me call
> Paris, Paris, Paris, Paris, Paris. (67)

The emotional argument of the poem is complicated, a method of creating depth of character for a mythical figure who never chose to "become one dimensional" like Paris, but has been made so through the ages. Here the dramatic monologue takes a different direction than usual, for the ironies reflect outward on the reader's inherited knowledge of the character rather than inward on the character's own lack of self-awareness. Helen knows all too well who and what she is, and, in this poem at least, she accepts her character whole. Desiring what she calls "agony," rather than condescension—as much of youth for age as of child for wayward parent—Helen turns Enobarbus's famous speech on Cleopatra inside out to remember Paris as a man "who never withered," if only because he died so young. The text simultaneously denies and affirms Helen's continuing desire—both for Paris and for her daughter's emotional complicity. As "could," "should," and "would" accumulate on the final page of the poem, it becomes clear that Helen is not telling her daughter anything; she only remembers Paris in terms of a possible narration. She will not say what she is thinking, because that "would stale / all this uncertain agony," the very pain of which is necessary. Her final statement gathers her love and fear for her daughter, her undying passion, and her sad awareness of mortality into a single *cri de coeur*, which is the name of all she found and lost. In this moment, the poem achieves a romantic apotheosis of passionate desire, and on that name, cried out in love, the sequence comes to a close. Whatever the given story says, this version will validate the bonds of passion against the moralists and their disapproval through the ages.

❧

Despite its occasional flaws, the Trojan sequence is an admirable effort for so young a writer (Ondaatje was twenty-three when *The Dainty Monsters* appeared). Although he would seek out figures less constrained by mythological and legendary iconography in the longer works he was soon to essay, he had already recognized that such figures become most interesting when the writing explores their actions and motives in unknown (that is, invented) situations. As he would eventually do with Mrs. Fraser, Billy the Kid, and Buddy Bolden, Ondaatje chose to give his readers glimpses of Paris in the interstices of the known story. While no longer retelling ancient myths, he would nevertheless continue to figure the mythic in narratives that denied narrative. And, as a romantic writer, he would, with all three later protagonists, seek those moments of passionate physical engagement with the world in which to inscribe them. He has already, in *The Dainty Monsters*, begun to discover the power of tactile and kinetic metaphor, a power that will serve him more and more in his subsequent books.

II
The Man With Seven Toes:
Ondaatje's early expressionist version of an Australian legend

Michael Ondaatje's second book of poetry, *the man with seven toes* (1969), is a fine example of little press artistry: five inches high by eight inches wide, it defies librarians; sumptuously printed, with a single lyric to each page, and a glorious cover illustration ("a black & white reproduction of MAN AND DOG by London, Ontario, painter, Jack Chambers"), it invites its readers' collaboration. It is a typical Coach House Press book of the late sixties.

One of the major advantages of working with a small press like Coach House was the personal nature of the contract, and the resultant concern for craft in design. Coach House had a reputation for oddly beautiful books, and became known as a publisher of innovative and experimental texts by many of the leading Canadian postmodernist writers. That Ondaatje was from the first an integral part of Coach House's publishing program says much about its openness to writing that did not fit a narrow avant-garde or postmodern definition.

the man with seven toes is a transitional work in which Ondaatje began to explore the formal ramifications of indeterminacy. Had he remained an essentially lyric poet, it would stand as an important book-length sequence. Given his later move into the long poem and the novel, it has become an early work often ignored in discussions of his oeuvre. Yet it remains an important document of his transition toward the longer documentary works for which he is best known: it extended his craft while remaining a young man's poem, perhaps more caught up in the thinking of the period than his later works (even *The Collected Works of Billy the Kid*) would be.

※

In the early summer of 1966, having sent *The Dainty Monsters* off to Coach House Press, Michael Ondaatje was looking for a suitable subject for a new project. Given his interest in the visual arts, as the imagery and the references to Henri Rousseau, Chagall, and Epstein in his first book show, it's not surprising that the paintings of Sidney Nolan are the central "documents" from which he built his second book, the 34-poem sequence, *the man with seven toes*. Nolan, one of the first Australian painters of this century to achieve an international reputation and certainly a painter to whom the term expressionist can be attached, created a series of paintings about Mrs Eliza Fraser, who was shipwrecked off the Queensland coast in 1836, and Bracefell, the escaped convict who led her through bush and desert to a settlement only to be betrayed by the woman he had saved. Ondaatje came across the Mrs Fraser paintings in a 1961 art book on Nolan, which also contained the only version of the story he ever learned.[11] He began work on the sequence in the fall of 1966, having spent a hot dusty summer on a road gang: "'the nearest thing to desert I could get'" (cited in Ann Mandel 275). It was finally published in 1969.

The quotation from Colin MacInnes's essay, "The Search for an Australian Myth in Painting," with which Ondaatje concludes his book, appears to make an implicit claim to conventional documentary. I believe, however, that it actually serves a function similar to the original notes for T.S. Eliot's *The Wasteland*: partly parodic, partly subversive. In other words, although Ondaatje's work continually aligns him with other makers of documentary poetry, novels, or films, it also signals his ironic separation from them. Just as "Peter" "forgets" the Wayland Smith myth[12] in order to construct a new story on a blank textual site, so too *the man with seven toes* dispenses with almost everything MacInnes provides for it. Ondaatje subverts the documentary as a form even as he makes use of the way it allows him to "novelize" (Bakhtin xxxii) the lyric sequence. One could also say "dramatize" here, for the poem "has been performed as a dramatic reading for three speakers—a convict, a lady, and a narrator" (1968, 45).[13] Although it does not achieve the fully dialogized "heteroglossia" (Bakhtin 263) of *The Collected Works of Billy the Kid* and later prose works, it does begin to suggest the ways in which multiple voices both support and contradict one another. This aspect of novelization ensures a formal realization of indeterminacy in *the man with seven toes*. As opposed to Margaret Atwood in *The Journals of Susanna Moodie*, Ondaatje works throughout to undercut the obvious document. Where her text elaborates, revises, and supplements the documents it acknowledges as the solid background of Moodie's life and writing, *the man with seven toes* stringently re-writes its pre-text, gleefully overturning it, putting it under erasure in order to write something new in its place. It is a palimpsest, where the erasure of the earliest, now hidden, layer of the "original version" of the story ensures a site for the invented one newly inscribed there.

Ondaatje begins to slide away from MacInnes immediately, even in the quotation, which, coming at the end of his book, seems to cast a documentary aura back over what it cannot put under erasure. MacInnes's and Ondaatje's versions have too many differences to be easily laid over one another, like transparencies. For example, where MacInnes's commentary insists on interpreting both the incident and Nolan's response to it, Ondaatje eschews interpretation entirely, especially postcolonial political interpretation of the theme of betrayal (I italicize the portion Ondaatje quotes):

The Convict Paintings   Of these, the most remarkable are the "Mrs Fraser" series, painted in 1947-48.

Mrs Fraser (so runs the legend) *was a Scottish lady who was shipwrecked on what is now Fraser Island, off the Queensland coast. She lived for six months among the aborigines, rapidly losing her clothes, until she was discovered by one Bracefell, a deserting convict who himself had hidden for ten years among the primitive Australians. The lady asked the criminal to restore her to civilization, which he agreed to do if she would promise to intercede for his free pardon from the Governor. The bargain was sealed, and the couple set off inland. At the first sight of European settlement, Mrs Fraser rounded on her benefactor and threatened to deliver him up to justice if he did not immediately decamp. Bracefell returned, disillusioned, to the hospitable Bush, and Mrs Fraser's adventures aroused such admiring interest that on her return to Europe she was able to exhibit herself at 6d a showing in Hyde Park.*

This "betrayal" theme—in which the traitress is portrayed naked in grotesque postures, and the stripes of her saviour's convict dress in skeletonic bars—is evidently one that preoccupies the artist. . . . Of what can these potent pictures be the allegory? Possibly of some personal conception of an essential factor in the man-woman relationship (as if Bracefell and Mrs Fraser were an Adam and Eve in a latter-day and rather terrible Eden). Certainly, too, a reminder that primitive Australian life re-created, for Europeans, conditions that tested the real quality of their acquired and confident culture. And basically, perhaps, an allegory of the conflict between the European expatriots who explored and governed and 'squatted' on the land, and bullied and slew the prisoners and aborigines, but who never became the true Australians . . . and then the stalwart, authentic natives, whether white or aboriginal, who were born in the country, or were exiled there by force, and who freely chose it for ever as their home.

This hostility of the rich, essentially alien English "gentry" to the poor, working (and robbing, and often Irish) labourers and small farmers, is also the key to understanding the whole episode of Ned Kelly with whose name Sidney Nolan's own, as the pictorial biographer of the great outlaw's life and spirit, has become especially connected. (21-22)

Ondaatje alters MacInnes's commentary, rendering it simultaneously more mythic and more contemporary. He does keep the rigid outline of a story MacInnes characterizes as paradigmatically Australian, but only so we may realize how far he strayed from it in the sequence just read. As is perhaps proper for a legend, MacInnes's version skips over any details of either the six months Mrs Fraser spent with the aborigines or the difficult trek back to civilization; Ondaatje's text reverses this approach, offering no rational explanation for her presence in the bush, but concentrating with visceral effectiveness on the perceptual physicality of the experience. As he later wrote about *Tay John*, he desires writing "in which the original myth is given to us point blank" (1974, 24), the "source is not qualified" (25), and the "official" story is replaced by an utterly *other* version, full of the "original rawness" (24) of immediate sensual perception.

Ondaatje has always chosen his subjects opportunely, insofar as the documents about each of them have been few and fragmentary at the time he was writing through, around, and beyond them. This is true not only of Mrs Fraser, but also of Billy the Kid (where there was a plethora of material but almost all of it was hearsay) and Buddy Bolden. In all three cases, works of historical scholarship appeared after his books, possibly granting them an even greater fictional autonomy.[14] The nature of the documents he uses ranges far wider than the term usually covers:

There's a series of paintings by Sidney Nolan on this story

and I was previously interested in Nolan's Ned Kelly series. I got fascinated by the story of which I only knew *the account in the paintings* and the quote from Colin MacInnes. That's how it grew. It had to be brief and imagistic because the formal alternative was to write a long graphic introduction explaining the situation, setting, characters, and so on. All the geographical references in the book are probably wrong and I'm sure all Australians think that the book is geographically ridiculous. (Ondaatje 1985, 20; emphasis added)[15]

Ondaatje does not like long explanations and his poetics does not accommodate them. As primary documents, Nolan's Mrs Fraser paintings became the properly fragmented ground of Ondaatje's invented text. Insofar, then, as the poems represent "setting" at all, they do so in terms of the paintings' already expressionist representations. Although some of the poems specifically allude to individual paintings, they generally render their basic violent hothouse atmosphere while ignoring the political theme of betrayal completely. As a phenomenological representation of perception, and perception mostly cut free from rational thinking, *the man with seven toes* refuses the kind of political allegorizing MacInnes brings to Nolan's paintings. This lack of political affect, this textual refusal to take account of where Mrs Fraser came from, what she represented, and how her betrayal reinforced colonialization, is open to criticism, but the poem simply does not enter that particular debate. The woman of the poem is never named; the convict is renamed; there are some telling anachronisms (another Ondaatje game in book after book); she does not turn upon her benefactor, although he does disappear from the text as soon as she leaves him; the Australia of this poem, like the land of "Peter," is as much a wilderness of the fantasizing mind as any real place. And that latter point suggests one reason why the young Canadian poet found the story so appealing, even if he had to deny almost everything that originally marked it as historically Australian.

the man with seven toes can be read as "a mythic exploration . . . of how an unnamed white woman perceives and experiences a primitive and anarchic world totally alien to her civilized assumptions and mode of being" (Solecki 1985c, 137); as "her encounter with and her 'escape' from her own sexual wilderness, her 'shadow' self ('animus,' 'id,' what-have-you)" (Lane 151); or as a "journey through the jungle to civilization" in which the woman learns "how to release the experience of violence as well as control it" (Hunter 53, 52). All three of these interpretations accept the wilderness as a metaphor for our own internal wildness, a recurring theme in Canadian literature. Although different in many ways, Canada and Australia share a colonial history as countries where European immigration created a new society based on the British model. In both "settler colonies . . . [where the] land was occupied by European colonists who dispossessed and overwhelmed the Indigenous populations" (Ashcroft, *et. al.* 25), the so-called "primitive" indigenes came to represent for the white settlers an aspect of their own cultural inheritance they wished to deny. *the man with seven toes* makes no large cultural statements, but its narrative occurs in a literary context which both Canadian and Australian readers might recognize, as D. G. Jones writes, as "devoted to the expression . . . of a sense of exile, of being estranged from the land and divided within oneself. A number of voices have made the point that the conventional culture, largely inherited from Europe, fails to reflect the sometimes crude but authentic experience of our lives and that this experience is in urgent need of expression in native terms" (1970, 5).

Like this poem, which appeared too late to be discussed in it, Jones's *Butterfly on Rock* reflects a sixties spirit of ecological and racial conciliation, and of revolutionary social and sexual idealism, in which, to borrow a phrase from Marshall McLuhan and Wilfred Watson, psychological, social, or cultural breakdown leads to breakthrough (48-51). Both the breakdown and the breakthrough can occur on many levels of experience, but one of the most effective, both imagistically and poetically, is the sexual, which ties together body and spirit, desire and denial, action and morality in a complex weaving of motive, meaning, and behavior. *the man with seven toes* is far from alone in narrating a renewing loss of civilization, a regenerative encounter with the primitive within. What marks it as colonial writing is its representation of a white, European suffering that loss in a "heart of darkness" landscape to her eventual, if also provisional, emotional and spiritual gain.

Paradigmatic figures of rational civilization confronting their own dark other are an inheritance of modernism's revaluation of nineteenth century ethnography's sense of "primitive" art as just a stage in the development of civilized art. In modernism, "this ethnographic view was accompanied by a more radical, fearful, and complex vision in which 'primitive' art was seen as expressive of the 'other side' of the European, civilized psyche, the 'dark' side of man. This is the fear which is expressed in such works as Conrad's *Heart of Darkness* and which is summed up in Yeats's comment after seeing Jarry's *Ubo Roi*: 'After us, the Savage God'" (Ashcroft, *et. al.* 158). Africa was the central symbol here, and Conrad's novella a central text presenting the dark version of a "Eurocentric viewpoint [in which] African culture could be viewed as the liberating Dionysiac force which could shatter the Apollonian certainty of nineteenth-century bourgeois society" (Ashcroft, *et al.* 159). Ondaatje, like every other university student of the time, would have read *Heart of Darkness*; at some point he also read *Ubo Roi*, as his unacknowledged quote from it in "Letters and Other Worlds" demonstrates (1979, 44). But any "primitive" culture can serve equally as "a mirror image, or more appropriately, the negative of the positive concept of the civilized, the black Other to the white norm, the demonic opposite to the angels of reason and culture" (Ashcroft, *et al.* 159). In terms of this paradigm, the white woman's position is representative: "The weakness of the colonial mentality is that it regards as a threat what it should regard as its salvation; it walls out or exploits what it should welcome and cultivate. The same weakness is inherent in the assumptions of western culture that lead man to view the universe as an enemy" (Jones 1970, 7). The early Army settlements in Australia, although they had the additional negative duty of punishing convicts, shared with their Canadian equivalents what Northrop Frye famously termed a "garrison mentality" (225, 231). The art and literature of both nations, especially as it became caught up in the throes of modernism, often explored what occurred to those who ventured, willingly or unwillingly, out beyond the garrison walls.

Such a theme was not necessarily nationalist, especially during the sixties, when many radical thinkers were writing critiques of rational and technological civilization. The zeitgeist of the period promoted a "revolutionary" sexual, psychological, sociological vision in such popular works as Norman O. Brown's *Life Against Death* and *Love's Body*, R.D. Laing's *The Politics of Experience*, Herbert Marcuse's *Eros and Civilization*. But many who read these books also read such books as William Burroughs's *The Naked Lunch*, Thomas Pynchon's *V*, and, especially in Canada, Leonard Cohen's *Beautiful Losers*, a conjunction Ondaatje himself makes in his book on Cohen (1970, 53). Indeed, it seems likely that Ondaatje read *Beautiful Losers* as soon as it came out in 1966. Although it is always difficult to argue direct influence, he seems equally willing to avoid "a safe formal style [that would] castrate [the] powerful ideas and . . . vulgar sanctity" (1970, 49) of his text. Despite being much smaller in scale and lacking the spiritual and apocalyptic dimension of Cohen's poetic novel, *the man with seven toes* shares the same drive to explode conventional historical narrative, and to wander far into the psychic wilderness of its protagonist.

At the same time, precisely because it is not a novel, even a disturbingly non-realistic one, *the man with seven toes* provides even less in the way of characterization than does Cohen's book. Moreover, Ondaatje is not yet the master of varying styles who will make of *The Collected Works of Billy the Kid* a masterful collage of voices dialogically competing with one another. *the man with seven toes* is too purely lyric to do that, despite its attempt to provide three narrative voices. The shifts from voice to voice register few if any obvious character traits: the third-person narrator sounds no different from the woman or the convict. Ondaatje sought to create "a narrative form as a kind of necklace in which each bead-poem while being related to the others on the string was, nevertheless, self-sufficient, independent, lyrical" (1985, 24), and he succeeded; but the lyrical is enhanced more than the narrative form. Character is generalized, for this is not the story of a unique personality; rather it attempts to represent an archetypal journey into physical and psychological wilderness, as so many writers understood it at that time.[16]

That journey begins in an indeterminate space and time; and, "as with Browning's Childe Roland, we are shown primarily the perceptual present of Ondaatje's characters" (Lane 150), especially in moments of physical and emotional intensity. Although the poem begins in the past tense as history or memory, as the deliberately anachronistic train "hummed like a low bird / over the rails" (1969, 9), the highly tropic language immediately forces us to engage a scene of ambiguity. Thus "air spun in the carriages," through which an unnamed woman, presented only as a non-referential third-person pronoun, "moved to doorless steps / where wind could beat her knees." The images, and especially the synecdoche of "air spun," suggest her lack of direction, which the final stanza, with its echo of "spun" in "wheeled," confirms: "The train shuddered, then wheeled away from her" (9). She is, at this point, almost entirely passive, "too tired even to call" (9), a *tabula rasa* about to be inscribed by the raw world she has given herself up to.

"She woke and there was a dog / sitting on her shoulder" (10) reverses expectation in a surreal dream-image which introduces the unlikely rupture of this new world from her old one. The vital, sexual life beyond the machinery of her civilization is simply, suddenly there: "it sauntered / feet away and licked its penis / as if some red flower in the desert" (10). Has she been asleep until now? Is the dog real or only a projection of her unacknowledged desires? The "red flower" will be echoed in her red dress, in various images of blood, even in the "red velvet" "my love" wears in the final ballad (42). Symbolically, the general sense of red as "the colour of the pulsing blood and of fire, for the surging and tearing emotions" (Cirlot 53) suits the direction the poem is moving in. Her sense that "everything around her was empty" (10) echoes the classic Eurocentric perception of colonial space, which renders invisible the aboriginal other. But as section 3 reveals, this emptiness is all too full, and if the figures in "the clearing" (11) might be read as aspects of "the feared subconscious [and] her bad, wild desires" (Lane 154), these people are also palpably present to her and our senses. In its determined indeterminacy, the poem allows no single readings. It hesitates, always, among various possibilities, granting none of them primacy.

Every shift from one lyric to another occurs with the arbitrary abruptness of a dream, offering revelations that "come in brief and enigmatic flashes which disappear and are then replaced by new ones" (Solecki 1985c, 140). The enigmas extend to the question of point of view. Thus far the focalization has been internal but from without; the narrator has narrated. But who says "entered the clearing and they turned / faces scarred with decoration" (11) or notes that "One, whose right eye had disappeared / brought food on a leaf" (11)? The perceptions appear to be Mrs Fraser's, but, lacking pronoun pointers, we cannot be sure. Such undecidability is one of the ways the poem maintains its dream-like quality, and becomes a kind of anti-lyric.

Section 4 is clearly hers, as "they stripped clothes off like a husk / and watched my white" (12). There is a sense of self-awareness here not previously expressed, yet the metaphorical touches work to contradict one another. Her clothes "like a husk" imply a potential transformation, given the general meaning of husk as "the shell or case of a chrysalis, a cocoon" (*OED*: 1353), but "their fingers / writhing in [her] head" (12) suggest serpents, with all the negative symbolic overtones they would have for a good Christian lady. Still, they throw "the red dress back at" her (12): she had clothed and will continue to clothe herself in the color of fire and passion. The nature of their laughter is left open as a sign of both friendship and derogation.

Like her, "they" are never named, perhaps only because she can't name them. They remain unfixed images of the other that are both inside and outside the colonizing power of her language, for they manage to evade her descriptive powers, as the next few lyrics demonstrate. The best she or the narrator can do is attempt to inscribe some sense of them through a series of contradictions. First "they" are "not lithe [and] move / like sticklebacks" (13), the sound of the spiny-finned fish's name emphasizing a lack of suppleness the description of their bodies as cracking, sharp, and grey supplements. But the image of a fish swimming undercuts that perception. Any sense of constricted movement is soon contradicted by the violent energy of the description of ritual dancing and rape. Each of the woman's perceptions is of the now, but the now continually changes, and neither she nor we can maintain a single view of them or of their actions. In section 5, the referent of "you" is too open for comfort, for if *she* speaks, she is already dissociating from her self, and if the narrator does, he may be referring to her or us. The final line, "Maps on the soles of their feet" (13), is a complex metaphor combining her perception of their dry, cracked skin with an acknowledgement of their walkabout sense of their own space. It indicates they are at home in their bodies in their world. But she is not—in either their world or her own.

Section 6 presents the first rape in escalating stages as she experiences a violation of her body to remove the signs on it of her "civilized" past. The first two stanzas open with the phrase, "tongued me" (14), as if to emphasize a more "primitive" way of knowing, but the phrase also refuses to identify any one person. Where she has kept them at a perceptual distance through the "modern" sense of sight, she now feels them close in on her and literally take impressions of her body through the more "primitive" sense of taste. In implying these distinctions, the poem appears to buy into a conventional modern and colonialist concept of the "primitive." First someone invades her mouth, and removes her silver fillings, signs of an advanced technology he turns into ornament. Then someone, but it's unclear if it is the same man or another, invades her ear, and bites the lobe off, in a grotesque kinetic image: "ate it, that a wedding band / in his stomach growing there" (14). While the phrase "wedding band" may refer either to her earlobe or an earring, the surreal image of growth attached to it implies "his" sexual arousal is based on this violent act. All the way through this experience, she knows it is happening to her, as the repeated first person singular pronouns demonstrate. In the third stanza, "he" invades her body, and the movement of the verse is ambiguous in the extreme:

> then him in me
> in my body,
> like a like a
> drum a drum (14)

Although this does have the rhythm of a chant (Hunter 52), which suggests a dance, and even hints at her participation, the implied separation of self and body does not. The disruption of syntactic repetition in the final line underlines both her felt sense of violation and uncertainty about how to describe what has been done to her. The insistence on raw feeling denies the possibility of analysis; certainly the woman never attempts it. Such lack of internal commentary keeps us off balance and unsure of what it all means, even as it renders a sense of psychological breakdown.

Section 7 views the aborigines' actions in a series of transformational metaphors which define their behavior without being able to interpret it: "bodies disappeared / shrank behind tall feathers of a bird / muscled tight as fists" (15). Analogies pile up on one another—"Necks weaved out / waved like sea" (15)—creating a chaos of sensation and movement registering the ecstatic metamorphoses of event. She perceives the aborigines as miming animals and birds in ritual dancing; yet the final stanza's "yelled out souls / feasted their bodies / and in the eating grew bellies fat" (15), with its uncertain argument and unfocused parataxis, does not let the woman explain their behavior to herself. She seems stunned. Whether the narrator or she articulates this series of sense impressions, all that is clear is the powerful energy of her captors, an energy continually increasing in intensity, as section 8 indicates: "cocks rising like birds flying to you   reeling on you / and smiles smiles as they ruffle you open / spill you down, jump and spill over you" (16). The rush of violent imagery renders their masculine power as animal vitality gone berserk. If this is the woman speaking, the continual violations of her body have brought her to the edge of dissociation: all this is happening to "you," not to "me" anymore. And the "you" has lost her sense of self and other: their cocks are birds but so is she when they "ruffle [her] open," which certainly means they "disturb" her but also suggests a ruffle of feathers. She seems unable to distinguish between their actions and her responses. But, even in a "point blank" myth, would the woman think in these slang terms? Might this not be the narrator, using the "you" to implicate readers in the possibility of experiencing such violation? The descriptions of killing and eating—"and the men rip flesh tearing, the muscles / nerves green and red still jumping / stringing them out, like you"—only emphasize how their rapes of her mean no more to them than any other activities. The "cocks" which fly, reel, ruffle, and spill and "the bodies [which] / open like purple cunts under ribs" suggest her sense that their violence to animals is the same as their violence to her, but the obscene slang calls attention to itself as a kind of linguistic anachronism, while its violation of linguistic decorum registers the utter degradation of selfhood she has suffered in a world where the usual sign of self-possession, her body, is treated as communal property. Here the text's obscenity works in a manner similar to but far less overwhelming than the "gorgeous" "sensationalism" (1970, 45) Ondaatje found in *Beautiful Losers*, another work full of deliberate and outrageous anachronisms.

The rest of the section, with its jittery, nervous enactment of action, suggests how fully she has entered that violent world and identifies with it. The animals the aborigines eat are, like her, "alive still in their mouths throats still beating   Bang / still! BANG in their stomachs." That final phrase echoes ever so slightly the earring in the stomach, as the images of leaping and eating echo the ritual dancing, and these echoes as well as the expansive descriptions of this section suggest its place as the climax of the first movement of the sequence. "[T]he use of echoes is crucial to . . . myth," Ondaatje says, because "myth breeds on itself no matter what the situation or landscape" (1974, 26). Now that she has experienced the full raw force of the aborigines' life, she must begin her journey back to the world she left behind. But first, section 9 offers a small, almost classically, understated addendum to the baroque grotesqueries of the last three segments, as felt by a dissociated "you": "at night the wind / shakes in your head / picks sweat off your body" (17). Yet the quiet resolution of "The sky raw and wounded" offers no real escape. The dissociation implied by "your head" and "your body" continues. Even the wind, a supposedly disinterested force of nature, invades her mind and her body, while "they" continue to demonstrate their appalling energy nearby. Is the final image an expression of her ability "to release the violence she sees in nature in a metaphor of her own making" (Hunter 52), or does the sentence fragment mime a fragmented mind's identification, in a kind of personal pathetic fallacy, with a tormented natural world? Both readings are possible.

All this violence and disruption take up less than one third of the poem. In the larger story of her return from the wilderness, it seems fitting that she be aided by a criminal, for in a sense is she not, now, something of an outlaw herself, that is thrown beyond the laws by which she once lived? Section 10 begins by slyly mixing sense impressions: "She heard wades in the yellow fern" (18). The rare usage of "wades" as a noun (*OED* 3663) emphasizes the sudden change occurring here. The following description of movement, "Elbows out for balance . . . moving through weed and mud and water," could refer either to her or the cause of the "wades," but "crossed a stretch of sunned river / scattering reflections till / his stripes were zebras," finally introduces the potential rescuer in a visually strong image.[17] As "the hub of vast ripples," he appears to have some power, but "His eyes stammering / at the sudden colour / of the woman on the bank" registers his uncertainty. That bright colour is "her red dress tucked into her thighs," the "husk" of her never wholly abandoned past life, a sign of the civilization to which she would somehow return.

Section 11 reveals a capacity for black humor expressed more fully in later works. The most specifically dramatic poem in the sequence, it begins with a contextually outrageous demand: "Don't you touch me" (19). Although the opening line is ironically comic in the light of what she has already been through, it is, after all, her first speech to someone else in the text, someone who also has white skin, with all that implies. As does the train in section 1—and her equally anachronistic question "where's the city"—"The name's Potter then" signals the degree to which this myth moves outside the boundaries of its documentary original story. In its moment of drama, it also signals the new direction the narrative will take.

Section 12 is one of the two ballads in the sequence, which sites and cites Potter as a figure out of folksong. It also sites him in the Australian bush, as a survivor who has learned to live "on wolves and birds / down in Cooper's Creek" (20). But section 13, with its description of "tattoos on his left hand / a snake with five heads / the jaws waiting / his fingernails chipped tongues" (21), implicates him in the same wilderness the aborigines inhabit in her mind. Because he exists somewhere between civilization and animality he can guide her back. But he is an ambiguous guide, both potential saviour and ever-present danger. When he uses that snake-like hand to steady her elbow, "she tense[s] her body / like a tourniquet to him," where the synecdoche both suggests her stiffness (the stick of wood) and her sense of being wounded, losing blood.

Section 14 "explains" the title of the poem, but only through a grotesque event which defies any sense of realism. As they stumble through a swamp, they are attacked by piranha-like fish, "Teeth so sharp, it was later / he found he'd lost toes, / the stumps sheer / as from ideal knives" (22). Even as *the man with seven toes* appears to enter the story world of its documentary original, it insists upon invention, fiction. Baroque, outrageous, the similes create a world of the imagined body: the fish which bite off only three of his toes are "flesh" which hangs from their "thighs" like ornaments—"bangles." This space between the perceived "primitive" and the supposedly "civilized" place they seek is a site of eerie transformation, dangerous metamorphosis, which the next few sections revel in. The voices of sections 15, 16, and 17 shift from narrator to either or both figures, and they make the scenes come alive through the power of their imaginative engagement with the seen. Colours clash, birds and water beasts charge and retreat, everything constantly moves. Echoing the original moment of the poem, "a bird, silver . . . spun like mercury away from us" (23); and like the train which "wheeled away from her" (9) in section 1, this image seems to presage a new wilderness she, and he, must traverse. Section 16, with its insistence on "night shapes" which "spit leaf juice at you / hook and stick to shoulders, / grinned teeth nuzzle, burn" (24) provides fearful echoes of the images of violation in sections 6 and 8. Throughout these passages, reference remains uncertain within the narrative, as what he and she do and what is done to them overlap in the narration.

In section 18, they leave swamp for desert, and enter a world of bleak, black comedy. The language loses some of its lushness to match the new scene, and minimalist understatement replaces expressionist exaggeration. Within the understated imagery, the characters' thoughts are comically hyperbolic: "passed a body / rotting in the sun. / Don't look, he says, / third thing for miles around. / Don't look!" (26). In its shift of direction, the sequence briefly takes full advantage of the comedic and dramatic possibilities of the characters' voices, as it juxtaposes their all too human exasperation against the absurdly limited imagery of death and violence in this minimalist landscape. Potter's "Sometimes I don't believe what's going on" (27) also reiterates, self-consciously from within his speech, the fabulous and fabular nature of the text.

Throughout, questions arise that are never clearly answered. In section 20, another of the text's deliberately unfocused metaphors—"kept to the river, frail / as nerves in the desert" (28)—may or may not be an admission of her frailties. But if so, is it because she is with another person to whom she can speak and who can speak to her? Does the possibility of speech indicate the further possibility of a kind of community? And could there be another community in which she can also speak truthfully? In section 21, she tells someone, "listen, once he crept up and bit open / the hot vein of a sleeping wolf" (29). The hortative does double duty, suddenly emerging from the text to address a specific audience and also placing the whole speech, and perhaps the whole sequence, in memory, as a kind of tale told to others (is this the one hint within the text of her later life as raconteur of her own adventure?). Within the adventure, Potter acts like the animals in order to survive as they do, yet he retains some humanity for her as his actions of "jumping up, waving, / running to me, carrying it, smiling" indicate. In providing her with food, he gets "his striped shirt bright and red" with blood. This imagistic echo of her dress, with the colour's mixed signals of vitality and violence, looks back to one rape and forward to another similar act. Other echoes of the earlier sexual violence follow, in the eggs' "salt liquid spilling / drying white on our shoulders" (30) and in the strange metaphor of birds' "eyelids / all that's delicate in their bodies / fresh as foreskins" (31).

As I have suggested, one of the deliberate difficulties in this poem is the continual shifting of speakers. Although it seems clear that some sections are spoken by a single character, many at least allow the possibility of slippage from external narrator to internal actor. In section 22, either or both characters could be speaking, while in section 23 it could be either one or the narrator, in the latter case addressing them as "you." Even the first three lines of section 24, in which Potter rapes the woman, slip a bit. Although the image of the sky as "a wrecked black boot" (32) seems most likely to have emerged from her memory, the "Noise like electricity in the leaves" may be another anachronistic touch of the narrator's. The first-person pronoun of the rest is hers, but although the imagery of "cock like an ostrich, mouth / a salamander / thrashing in my throat" insistently echoes the images of the earlier men, the word "cock" once again indicates some slippage from her cultural context, a reminder that all this action occurs in an other world of twentieth-century invention. The "salamander / thrashing in [her] throat" suggests both the fire of passion (salamanders are supposed to live in fire) and a violent silencing which the next six sections reiterate as a return to perception unmediated by any conversation between the man and the woman.

Indeed, her sense of self-degradation, imaged in "clothes rotted, flesh / burned purple" (33), skin stinking, body "brown as a bruise," starkly contrasts with his animal vitality, "shirt / striped and fabulous / like beast skin in greenery." The confusion of perspective at the beginning (is it hers or his?) matches the confusion of perception at the end, where the major sign of his humanity, his shirt, transforms him into a beast. Essentially paratactic moments of action, sections 26 to 29 suggest no narrative development, and yet by their very appearance one after another imply a possibility of sequence. Again the voices of perception shift between and within each section, are full of contradiction. First he carries her and bathes "her face with spittle" (34), an act of giving; then he reverses the action in a parody of rape that announces his power over her: "to lock her head . . . / bend tongue down her throat / drink her throat sweat, like coconut" (35). Where the past tense implies a single action, the infinitive implies a repeated one, emphasizing his continuing power over her. The ellipses of pronouns in section 28 and section 29 once again render identification almost impossible; but Potter rips his mouth open on the "tin of SIBER'S oranges" (36) while both make the quick dive in and out of the water and both are involved in the final image of "leeches on feet," which they "scalloped . . . off / made a dinner of them" (37). The synecdoche of "scalloped them off" recalls a civilized seafood dinner rather than the desperate survival stratagems they have been reduced to, and in so doing begins to prepare for the ambiguous return to follow.

But what exactly has she, or have they, learned from all this? Do such experiences teach, as the romantic philosophers seem to argue? Section 30 renders such queries superfluous: "So we came from there to there / . . . / Things happened and went out like matches" (38). The use of the past tense marks this passage as summation; only it sums up nothing. The use of such specific terms as "there" or "things" renders the whole experience as a kind of nightmare, beyond rational explanation. There are no referents; the world they moved through is emptied of specificity and of significance. Lacking any sense of where or of what, all that is left is the suffering, and even that, because "no one" witnessed it, may not be real. As an anti-summary, this section subtly reinforces a representational doubt the whole poem never quite overcomes. We are held in suspension, continuing to follow a narration whose story may not exist.

Various ironies play across section 31, which begins in a passive voice that registers reaction rather than action: "were found bathing in a river / like strange wild animals / sticking out of the water" (39). This image mixes "normal" representation with an implied civilized judgement in the simile for which there is as yet no enunciated site. The tone is coolly distant in a manner different from the previous sections, which implies a new narrative voice the text has not yet divulged; or has it? In the second stanza someone hears her speak: "She when seeing us said / god has saved me." But who is this "us"? Has the narrator always in fact been the voice of the civilization from which she escaped and to which she now returns? If so, what does that say about her journey? Unanswerable questions, but the fact that section 31 raises them once again opens the whole narrative to ever-increasing uncertainty. Similarly, although the text has deliberately used both upper and lower case somewhat randomly throughout, I believe we cannot help but make the lower case "g" significant, even if the significance is unclear. What does "god" refer to here? Potter, who in his power has both enslaved and delivered her, might, through an identification similar to what happens under the Stockholm Syndrome, make as good a candidate as any. And like any useful "god" he disappears as soon as his job is done. Both figures are present in the first stanza, but she alone appears in the second. In Lane's psychoanalytic reading, "it is as if Potter is, in a sense, washed away. In the last section of the poem she is cleansed of him. We don't know what happens to him; she doesn't care. Nor does she remember" (154). But perhaps she does remember if the surreal past tense description of section 32 is anything to go by. There is no pronoun here to identify the speaker, but if Potter has truly disappeared from the narration, then she may be recalling him into it. If it is her memory, then "mouth a collyrium that licked my burnt eyes" (40) recalls his act of kindness in section 25, where his licking acts as "an eye-salve or eye-wash" (*OED* 468). But it could be his memory instead; as usual, the text favours neither version. After all, although the poem seems to be about her, it is titled after him.

Section 31 is the first ending, an ambiguous rescue brought to an ambiguous conclusion in the eyes of an unknown "us." Section 33 is the second ending, in the guise of a completely new story: resting her sunburnt body in "the heart of the Royal Hotel" (41), she moves her hands all over "the rough skin," "sensing herself like a map, then / lowering her hands into her body." But waking to find the remains of a bird chopped by a fan, its bloody "body leaving paths on the walls / like red snails that drifted down in lumps,"

> She could imagine the feathers
> while she had slept
> falling around her
> like slow rain. (41)

The focalization is complex here: an external narrator renders her perceptions and feelings from within, but without explanation (and to paraphrase a later Ondaatje poem, what would she wish to speak of anyway?). Critical responses are divided. Lane, insisting that the woman seeks entirely to negate her own sexuality, in which the poem has immersed her, argues that red is the forbidden colour of that sexuality and that "she relaxes blissfully under the image of this living thing, this red thing, destroyed, as under a soothing rain" (153). Solecki finds section 33 much more ambiguous in its accumulation of images from throughout the poem and its insistence, in "could imagine," that she acknowledges some meaning in the bird's destruction. "Her reaction is either sentimental and romantic, or it indicates a full acceptance of the violent natural world into which she has been thrust" (1985c: 145-46). He tends toward the second of these readings, partly because the previous section positively recalled Potter, and partly because "[t]his new attitude corresponds roughly with Nolan's later paintings ["Woman and Billabong 1952," "Woman in Swamp 1957," and "Woman in Mangroves 1957"] of Mrs. Fraser and the land as finally indistinguishable from one another" (1985c, 145).

In fact, like the whole sequence, this lyric tale holds interpretation in suspension. It begins with a strong iambic pentameter line that suggests everything will be settled now, but the next two lines stagger and deny the rush to closure. For the rest of the section, the rhythm falls away from any steady beat; even "the running heart" keeps changing pace. She is "in the heart of the Royal Hotel," the "heart" of civilization, as represented by the signifier of its ruling power, so by its decrees she is safe. But her experiences are "burnt" into the body she now senses "like a map," this latter image linking her to the aborigines in an experiential knowledge that outweighs the rational territorializing of the civilization signified by "Royal Hotel." Knowing that map of her own body, it seems she can acknowledge her own sexuality. The "then" at the end of the line hesitates syntactically, registering both the moment of her discovery that her body has become a map for her and the logical outcome, that she can therefore enter what is her own possession (one implication is that she masturbates, which cannot be read as a denial of her sexuality). The death of the bird could then signify the inability of this civilization to protect her, or anyone, from either the raw violence of or its technological violence towards nature. Like the image of "the running heart" (recalling "the heart still running" [16] of section 8), the "red snails" recall her time in the wilderness. And the final stanza maintains a deliberate sense of uncertainty with "could imagine." She could but she need not necessarily imagine this way. If she does so imagine, the resulting image is one of disturbing beauty, in which the sense of disturbance is stronger than the sense of beauty, but the balance between the two offers its own kinetic resolution of the narrative.

Finally, the third ending of the poem, the ballad of section 34, begins with a documentary borrowing, of the first stanza of "the anonymous Scottish ballad, *Waly, Waly*" (45). It is set in "Glasgow town" (42), and its imagery contrasts strongly with everything that has preceded it. Although the double-edged image of "Green wild rivers in these people / running under ice that's calm" suggests "how tenuous the equilibrium of civilization really is," the ballad's summation of the book's complex tensions does not resolve them (Solecki 1985c, 146). That it is the last of three endings (unless the MacInnes quotation is read as another, final, gesture of closure) calls attention to its ironic relations to both sequence and document. By using a known ballad source for the first stanza, Ondaatje allows the possibility of a new, fourth, speaker, who may or may not be the central character of the previous narrative. "My love . . .

in red velvet / and I . . . in cramasie" (42), the latter "a crimson cloth" (*OED* 594), are met by three mangy barking dogs, "and after them came girls and boys." Only the third stanza seems to allude to the documentary original of the poem: "The people drank the silver wine / they ate the meals that came in pans" (42). This audience appears in sharp contrast to the performers of the narrative: their very eating and drinking reveal their civilized dependence on a certain level of technology. Like the queen of "Elizabeth," they "find cool entertainment" (1979, 25) in "a lady / singing with her throat and hands," performing delicately for their pleasure. This is an image of domestic and public peace, which seems to relegate the previous horrors to nothing more than a bad dream. But, even in the cold north (of Scotland, or perhaps of the author's own country), there are hidden depths and the potential for danger.

> Green wild rivers in these people
> running under ice that's calm,
> God bring you all some tender stories
> and keep you all from hurt and harm (42)

Solecki reads this stanza through the obvious symbolism of the ice as civilized rationality and control and the rivers as unconscious, chaotic desire (1985, 146), and the ballad does not deny such a reading. But the final two lines, in which the subjunctive mood of the verbs emphasizes the lack of resolution, leave the poem even more open than he is willing to allow. Can such "tender stories" as this book ever "keep you [readers] all from hurt and harm"? And if so, how? The poem offers no clear answers, although its romantic preconceptions might. That subjunctive mood promises nothing. The whole ballad, then, retreats to a typical ballad state of historical limbo, the speaker remaining anonymous. In terms of its generic qualities it serves only to place the whole narrative in a similar indeterminate field. So that narrative and ballad reflect each other's lack of representational historicity, and any proper sense of closure is undermined.

the man with seven toes, in many ways a transitional work, still depends upon the lyric as its basic building block, yet extends the reach of conventional lyric through its implied narrative and through the use of more than a single voice. It would be superseded by the far greater complexity of construction in *The Collected Works of Billy the Kid*, a book which also avoids the problems of interpretation involved when a male writer creates a female protagonist and then submits her to a series of violations which may seem only to substantiate a traditional masculist vision of women. For the late sixties, it is in many ways both an adventurous and a thematically current work, attempting to explore in an intimate and minimal imagist register some of the implications of the theories of repression and transgression which could be found in the writings of Norman O. Brown, R.D. Laing, and Herbert Marcuse—or in Leonard Cohen's work, especially *Beautiful Losers*. Ondaatje's *Leonard Cohen* illuminates the "Black Romantic"[18] aspects of his own work at this time; its fascination with Cohen's ability to create "a diseased sensuousness that one cannot eradicate because it is also beautiful" (1970, 21) suggests the writerly desire that led to *the man with seven toes*. Ondaatje's appreciation of the way Cohen was able to write "a very funny book [,] . . . also a very poetic book" (1970, 34) also suggests that studying Cohen's methods—especially in *The Favourite Game* and in *Beautiful Losers*, which Ondaatje at the time thought "a gorgeous novel, and . . . the most vivid, fascinating, and brave modern novel I have read" (1970: 45)—helped him create a style for his manuscript. But *the man with seven toes* does not transcend its various influences with the subversive élan his later works do; in that, too, it remains a young writer's work.

ENDNOTES

[1] "Over the Garden Wall," the title of the first section, comes from the epigraph, an excerpt from Auden's "The Witnesses"; it is also the title of one of the central poems. "The Witnesses" is one of Auden's casually symbolic fables from the early thirties, full of the period's paranoia. Ironically, its speakers are the watchers, not the watched. The quoted lines create an uneasy tone that hovers over the poems in Ondaatje's text, even when they appear innocent of fear or terror. The "something" that will "fall like rain" and not "be flowers" (1945, 187) could easily be read as bombs, especially in the high Cold War days of the late sixties. Equally, the lines suggest an allegiance to the symbolic tradition to which Auden belongs, and with which most of the shorter poems in the volume are aligned.

² As a quick glance at essays by Chamberlin, Glickman, Hunter, Marshall, Scobie, and Solecki will reveal, from the very beginning Ondaatje's poetry provided a map large enough to encompass a wide range of explorations.

³ The epigraph mentions only the character, not the novel. Ondaatje quotes from the Penguin Classics edition of *The Brothers Karamazov*, shifting the final exclamation mark to a period (see Dostoyevsky 132). He has remained committed to Penguin Classics editions throughout his career.

⁴ In *The Cinnamon Peeler*, Ondaatje has even dropped "Peter"; this elision, along with the continuing out-of-print status of *the man with seven toes*, suggests that the older poet has rethought the values of these early works somewhat, perhaps finding their philosophical attitudes, so grounded in the revolutionary psychotherapeutic forces of the sixties, less tenable than they once were.

⁵ As Ondaatje points out, the "book wasn't written in [its present] order, much more mixed up. Tho 'Peter' was, if I remember, the last poem written" (1972, 20).

⁶ In this he is like Billy the Kid, who, Smaro Kamboureli points out, "does not die in the poem. He is already dead" (190).

⁷ In Canada, bpNichol's *The Martyrology* is the most sustained example of a continuing poem that contains stories but is, in Robert Kroetsch's terms, a "method, then, and then, and then, of composition; against the 'and then' of story" (1988, 120).

⁸ When Hercules dies, he give Philoctetes his bow and arrows, which the gods say are required to defeat the Trojans, but Philoctetes is bitten in the foot by a serpent and the wound smells so bad the Greeks abandon him for ten years on the island of Lemnos. Eventually, they rescue him and take him to Troy where a physician heals his wound. He immediately joins the battle and kills Paris. See Hamilton (194-195) and Glickman (1985, 75).

⁹ This could make the sequence an example—like "Pyramid," and *The Collected Works of Billy the Kid: Left Handed Poems*—of a narration from the other side of death (I include Helen as such a narrator of her own poem). See Kamboureli (190).

¹⁰ Paris is exiled to Mount Ida by his father Priam, who has been warned that Paris would bring ruin to his country. There he marries the nymph, Oenone, and lives as a shepherd until the three goddesses appear before him for The Judgement of Paris, which brings him Helen after he awards the golden apple to Aphrodite (See Hamilton 179).

¹¹ The first major book on Nolan, *Sidney Nolan*, remains one of the best studies of his work. The "version of the story" appears in Colin MacInnes's essay, "The Search for an Australian Myth in Painting" (11-35), from which Ondaatje quotes at the end of his book.

¹² It is a Norse and early English myth in which Wayland, a great jeweler and metalsmith captured and hamstrung by King Nidhad, eventually rapes his daughter Beadohild and escapes on wings he has constructed (Branston 6-9).

¹³ Although the pages of *the man with seven toes* are only numbered alternately from 11 to 41, I will provide page numbers as usual, and will number the sections from 1 to 33.

[14] They are Michael Alexander's *Mrs. Fraser on the Fatal Shore* (1971), Stephen Tatum's *Inventing Billy the Kid: Visions of the Outlaw in America, 1881-1981* (1982), and Donald M Marquis's *In Search of Buddy Bolden, First Man of Jazz* (1978).

[15] Although Ondaatje eventually visited Australia, as a winner of the Canada-Australia literary prize in 1980, he has written no more about it, almost as if his deliberately fictional creation of the place had satisfied any need he might have had to deal with the Australian environment long before he experienced its uniqueness.

[16] See Patrick White's *A Fringe of Leaves* for a more dialogic historic meta-fiction based on Mrs Fraser's story. It specifically takes up the large questions of social language and meaning to which Ondaatje's poem pays no attention, exploring the problem of how to speak of those experiences which the "unitary language of culture and truth" (Bahktin 271) of a particular, and governing, group in a society denies are real.

[17] Throughout the sections with the convict, the text responds to the expressionist surrealism of Nolan's "Mrs Fraser and Bracefell series" (Clark, *et al.* 47), including "Mrs Fraser 1947," "Escaped Convict 1948," "Figures and Lilypool 1957," "Figures in Tree 1957," and "Woman in Swamp 1957."

[18] See Scobie on Cohen's "Black Romanticism" and its cultural context in the writing of the Beats and such contemporary extremists as William Burroughs, Jean Genet, and Allen Ginsberg, and their predecessors (1978, 1-14). Ondaatje wrote *Leonard Cohen* in 1968, possibly while making revisions to *the man with seven toes*.

Day Thoughts on
Anne Wilkinson's Poetry

Passion and vision tend to go together in Anne Wilkinson's poetry: "New laid lovers sometimes see // in a passion of light" (43); thus the "message" which "the bells of matin" sing to the young: "'Wake well, my child, // . . . // Today is a holy day'"(133). While night and sleep are fixed, full of "certainty," the waking mind and body, all senses alert, in the midst of day's light, will wholly (holy) engage the continually transformed world (and word). In love with flux, she knows that nothing is fixed and day is not always privileged over night, yet she usually addresses her poetry to the reader lovingly responding in daylight (and like all poets she surely does seek love as she writes). So: "day thoughts," rather than "night thoughts."

Before her death of cancer in 1961, Anne Wilkinson published *Counterpoint to Sleep*, a pamphlet (1951), and *The Hangman Ties the Holly*, a book (1955). *The Collected Poems of Anne Wilkinson and a Prose Memoir*, edited by A.J.M. Smith, was published in 1968, but soon went out of print, as did the reprint from Exile Books, with a new afterword by Joan Coldwell, in 1992; and she is read now only through a few poems in anthologies. A reading of her work reveals intricate connections between her passionate apprehension of the "two conditions" of humanity, "the quick and the dead" (36), and the equally passionate apprehensions of such earlier writers as Emily Dickinson, a connection Smith argues at the end of his "Introduction" to *The Collected Poems*. Even her final poems, he says,

> integrate the witness of all the senses into an affirming testimony of the beauty and richness of life. They consolidate her position among the small group of women poets who have written of love and death with a peculiarly feminine

intuition, an accuracy, and an elegance that do not hide but enhance the intensity of the emotion—Emily Dickinson, Christina Rossetti, Elinor Wylie, and Leonie Adams. Her work as a whole puts her, certainly, in the forefront of contemporary Canadian poets. (xxi)

This final sentence sounds ironic: many major new poets appeared in the mid-sixties, often pursuing a poetic which appeared to be at odds with Wilkinson's, and her work has almost completely disappeared behind theirs. We have all lost by this, for, although her poetry might at first appear to be in the modernist line descending from Eliot through Auden and on, the rich, almost impudent, sensuality of it stands as a rebuke to and a refusal of the ascetic "aesthetics" of that poetry with its, essentially masculine, mind (or spirit) / body split. Because her poetry roots the spirit in the body and bespeaks a vital engagement with the Heraclitean world which is always new and necessary, it deserves to be much better known than it is.

There are few essays on her work, mostly by men.[1] Why have feminist critics thus far ignored her? As Smith's remarks make clear, she definitely belongs to a line which includes some of the major women poets of the last century or so. Her life, too, with its eccentricities and normalities, seems to fit her for feminist analysis: an admittedly privileged background and childhood, including an education by private tutors and at progressive schools in the United States and France; marriage to F.R. Wilkinson, a surgeon, plus the raising of three children; divorce after twenty years; and, during the no doubt time-consuming fulfillment of her domestic duties, the creation of an important, if not large, body of poetry. On the other hand, it is possible that as a Canadian poet she did not feel quite as cut off from the mainstream of writing in her country as she might have in the United States. As Margaret Atwood has pointed out, "although Canada was and is no Utopia for women, it has historically and for mysterious reasons favoured the production of good women poets to a greater extent than have England, the United States, or Australia" (1982, xxix). As a result,

Wilkinson wrote in an atmosphere of acceptance, in so far as poetry was recognized at all in Canada during her lifetime. And, of course, her work was recognized by Smith because it seemed to emerge from the same tradition as did his, that of the twentieth century metaphysicals. Yet, I would argue that a comparative reading of their work would reveal his poems to be dry-as-dust, engaged with other art but usually lacking the necessary intermediary connection through life, while hers are full of a vital play with ideas and emotions profoundly felt in the living body. Where his poems are too often "academic" in the pejorative sense, hers fully engage the material world we know through our senses. I do not believe that Lionel Kearns, who dismissed Smith's *Poems, New and Collected* as demonstrating no more than "a low-keyed concern with love, death, and creation, spattered with smug erudition and polite unenthusiastic Christianity," and the poet as incapable "of writing, for example, poems which are direct and 'unpoetic' enough to be somehow symptomatic of human emotion" (68), would say the same of Wilkinson's poetry. Still, the critical silence regarding her work raises the question as to whether it should be read specifically as "women's writing." Annette Kolodny's remark, in 1978, that feminist critics have not always acknowledged "that the variations among individual women may be as great as those between women and men" may no longer apply, but her desire to treat "each author and each separate work by each author as itself unique and individual" (41) does. Whether or not Wilkinson's work demands a feminist reading, she wrote out of a culture in which women were still generally regarded as unessential except as wives and mothers. As artists, they were still somehow *not present*. How does she deal with this? Does she deal with this?

❦

Perhaps it does not matter whether or not Wilkinson consciously chose to write as a woman; the fact remains that she could not help but do so. In *On Deconstruction*, Jonathan Culler points out how a particular sense of "objectivity is constituted by excluding the views of those who do not count as sane and rational men: women, children, poets, prophets, madmen" (153). Writing in the forties and fifties, Wilkinson went against the 'neutral' and 'objective' grain, writing about women, children, and poets, inscribing the excluded subjective into her poems. And her texts clearly insist upon inclusivity, on perceiving the world whole through the "five times blessed" (95) sensual soul. She might admit that her "woman's eye is weak // And veiled with milk" compared with the "working eye . . . muscled // With a curious tension, // Stretched and open // As the eyes of children" (48), but the real point here is that the "woman's eye" is adult while the "working eye" [the poet's eye] is childlike. In pointing such a contrast, Wilkinson is following a great Romantic tradition, but she is also imbuing it with a feminine cast, for her sense of the exclusions and her sensibility of what they stand for are grounded in her experience as a woman, loving, giving birth, writing poetry.

And what poetry she writes. One of the great exclusions of patriarchal discourse has been the denigration of women's discourse. Drama, history, epic, philosophy: until recently, these have been the forms of discourse deemed worthy or remark. It's only since her death that feminist scholarship and criticism have validated "Women's Writing" (which was, therefore, not "real" writing at all, just letters, diaries, romantic novels, etc., what could be defined as *not literature*). Perhaps a bit ahead of her time, Anne Wilkinson chose to define many of her poems in terms of such non-"literary" categories as folk tales, nursery rhymes, lullabies, ballads, carols, letters, and even a "P.S.". Of course, we discover how ironically subversive this is when we read the poems so titled and find they rival any male writer's poetry for complexity, subtlety, allusiveness, and richness of texture. This is especially true of two of Wilkinson's major poems, "Letter to my children" and "Letter to my children: Postscript," the titles of which sign "non-essential," "women's," writing while their texts simultaneously present the central vision of Wilkinson's poetics, a poetics of essences, if ever there was one.

༄

In "Letter to my children," the mother speaks of her failures: "I guided you by rote," she says; "Bored the breakfast hour // With 'manners make the man'"; finally, and most unforgivably.

> I churched you in the rites

Of trivia
And burned the family incense
At a false god's altar. (94)

The church of trivia opposes the "church of grass" (61) which walls the lovers of "In June and gentle oven" "holy, in" their sensual, and therefore transcendental embrace. Rote rites are dead, a form of stasis, denial of the living world. And because the children to whom she offers that "useless gift, apology," are "faultless" and therefore likely perfect little Ontario prigs, she knows that both she and they would have to "start again" by peeling away the "twenty paper layers of years" which are layers of enculturation if they would ever discover "what you know // But barely know you know," the "*one* commandment" [my italics]:

'Mind the senses and the soul
Will take care of itself,
Being five times blessed.' (95)

Lines like these, and there are many of them in her work, make it difficult to accept Wilkinson as a pure inheritor of the intellectual "metaphysical" strain. Rather, although she obviously learned much of her craft from such male writers in that line of descent as Eliot and Auden, she also brings to bear a sensibility akin to Blake, and more than likely Christina Rossetti, Emily Dickinson, Charlotte Bronte, and even more recent writers like Amy Lowell and Edna St. Vincent Millay. In many ways, that "commandment" informs all her poetry, most especially "Postscript." It expresses a Romantic vision, yet I would also argue that it expresses a hard-won feminine vision of possibilities, of accepting the natural world, not trying to remake it in masculine terms but living *in* it as fully as possible.

The poem, "Rhyme," presents another version of the mother of "Letter," but this time seen satirically as misleading and hypocritical object, rather than apologetic subject:

A mother nags her daughter,

'Beware of Dick and Harry.'
O why should she nag her daughter
When she herself was merry?

A mother begs her son
'Be chivalrous with maids,
But if they be not maidens, O
Take to your heels and run.'

And boys and girls bow low, bow low,
'Thy will be done,' they say
Then hang their clothes on a budding limb,
'Be quick, my love,' they pray. (137)

This deliciously subversive lyric not only denies the power of the rote "rites // Of trivia" it insists that they derive from a religious faith become static, life-denying, because of puritan denial of the senses. The parodic use of the famous phrase from "The Lord's Prayer" underlines the completeness of that puritan denial. Robert Lecker suggests that Wilkinson always pits "the quick" against "the dead" in her work, even if such a clear opposition therefore acknowledges the power of death, and its inevitability (35). The pun in the final line here powerfully allocates quickness (i.e., the essence of life itself) to the act of love as well as suggesting the traditional *carpe diem* motif that there isn't much time so we must take what we can while we can. Like the lovers walled "holy, in" a "church of grass," these "boys and girls" are enacting a prayer, and doing so in the holy space of nature; it is the mother who denies, negates the forces of life and love. Of course, part of the delight of the poem is the way it mocks the adult forces of denial by rendering them in a conventionally dead language, which the boys and girls know only too well how to subvert through irony. The poem's wit resides at least as much in the way the text manipulates traditional form and statement to undercut them as in the narrative twist of the final couplet.

"Letter to my children: Postscript" is a much longer and more fully developed poem than its precursor. According to Smith's notes, "Early drafts of *The Hangman* contain the whole poem, but only the first three stanzas appear in the printed volume. In one manuscript the author pencilled in the heading P.S., and I have felt justified in placing the fine major portion of the poem at the head of the uncollected pieces" (211). One cannot be sure whether or not Wilkinson finally intended two poems or one,[2] but it is interesting to note that while the published "Letter" is addressed to older children, apologizing for not giving them the right teaching, "Postscript" seems addressed to those who are still young, and offers them the advice she *should have given* the "faultless" older prigs of "Letter" when they were "newbegotten."

"With winter here my age // Must play with miracles" (127) says the writer, and the rest of the poem is the miracle, played out in the writing of such play-full advice on the senses as follows. That the text insists on its heuristic presence as writing is, it seems to me, important. One of the central points of deconstruction theory is that in our culture "speech" excludes "writing" as true presence, the presence of "truth." Moreover, as Culler points out, "many of the operations identified, for example, in Derrida's study of the treatment of writing also appear in discussions of woman," who, even if "she is considered separately . . . will still be defined in terms of man, as his other" (166). How interesting, then, to find Wilkinson, the woman, insisting that the "truths" she has to offer her children can best be said, can, perhaps in our culture, *only* be said, in writing, and in an addendum, a postscript (some non-essential women's writing space), at that. Truth, these truths at any rate, cannot be found in that "real presence" which is speech, but rather in that supplementary space, unimportant and almost off the page (if you think of how postscripts tend to appear in ordinary letters), where what cannot be said (because the proprieties which "Letter" so ruthlessly exposes will not allow such speech) can be written.

The truths of "Postscript" are "wishes . . . five," rather than three, and those wishes are

> Five full and fathomed senses,
> Precision instruments

To chart the wayward course
Through rock and moss and riddles
Hard or soft as ether, airy
Airy quite contrary
Where will the next wind blow? (127)

As this series of pun-filled allusions demonstrates, the life the senses will know revels in the kinds of mixtures and transformations both Shakespeare and nursery rhymes recognize and celebrate. And that range of reference also indicates the various nature of the world the writer wants to make available to her children. Although the reference to *The Tempest* appears to deny the original "Song," it actually plays off the fact that, in the play, no death has occurred. The allusion, then, directs us to recognize the proper maturation, in a sensuously perceived world, which the play explores. The rest of the stanza keeps the idea of tempest foregrounded in a child's verse. The apparent artlessness of the poem is just that: apparent. At the same time, the very sensuousness of its sounds and rhythms insists that the wisdom it "teaches" is real. Lecker argues that the "winter" of the first line is the writer's adulthood, and "that personal survival depends upon her ability to retain a childlike sense of wonder." But he adds that "the poet's 'age' is also her epoch—a social order suffering from the symbolism of winter," and one which therefore foolishly tries to escape its self-induced alienation (from the natural world) by putting its faith in the forms of Christianity, "a false pageant made for an adult audience insensitive to creation" (41). There is much in Wilkinson's work as a whole to support such a reading. Even here the lines "Your kingdom comes with senses // Schooled to top professionals" (128), with their parodic undercutting of our major rote prayer, definitely argues against a false faith which ignores the lived world of the senses. The letter is both "a lesson about how to remain young . . . [and] a statement about how poets themselves should see" (Lecker 41). And what one sees, hears, touches, smells, and tastes are all the various worlds we inhabit but tend, as we age and neglect the purity and clarity of sensual involvement with them, to forget are there, part of the "fivefold grace" (133) of living "with sense alive" (127).

But how does one so live?

> . . . set your heart by relativity,
> With space for slow and fast,
> Set five alarms to wake and catch
> The shadowless noon
> Before it moves to after. (127)

This time the punning turns on a scientific theory to reassert the senses'
engagement with all the "world" offers to us, living, in it. And Wilkinson
insists that we must encounter all: the wonderful—presented in a series of
almost Keatsian images—and the awful—implied in the ambiguities of
certain words and phrases. The ear, for example,

> Will mark the drop in pitch of towns
> Adrift in fog
> And the lowering of evening song
> When the strut is gone
> From the tenor birds:

but it will also hear "The sharp white nails of the moon / Scratch the slate
of midnight water" (128), the synaesthesia of which inscribes the quality
of fear the image intimates.

Although the poet wants the children to "feel a way // To linen and
lover," she also insists on the sometimes dark complexities of sexual
desire:

> Before you tar with age
> Swing to hot percussion jazz
> Of insects, dance
> To carnal charivari
> Broadcast from distended throats of frogs. (128-29)

This invokes a Dionysian play, yet as its reference to the charivari demonstrates, it allows for an awareness of the meanness sexuality can also sometimes call forth. It is in such ambiguous presentations that Wilkinson most
fully reveals the complexities of her poetic vision, what Lecker rightly

describes as the "tensions" implicit in "the whole set of polar oppositions which govern her poetry and poetic" (35). Still, if the world is fraught with danger, it is also full of excitement and delight, and, in a phenomenological gesture, the poet insists that we go out to it.

> *Uncage* the tiger in your eye
> And tawny, night and day,
> *Stalk* the landscape for the contour
> Of a fern or arm,
> *Gorge* on pigment squeezed
> From barley fields
> Or *part* the strawberry leaves
> That hungry eyes *may water*
> On the fruit and feast of colour (129-30; my italics)

Active seeking, that is what the verbs in this poem and so many others insist upon. No phallogocentric gesture of mastery, this seeking is always accepting of what *is*. But the acceptance, the apparently passive stance these poems argue, is powerfully engaged. It is meditational only if meditation is seen as a positive effort of engaged psychic energies. Everywhere in "Postscript," the writer insists that we actively "read" the text of the world in all its complex presence, using all our senses as fully as possible, for only a [w]hol[l]y committed engagement with life will give us life-as-grace. Thus the conclusion:

> 'Sleep well'—I wonder why
> We harp on sleep, our certainty.
> I'd turn the message inside out
> And have you listen
> With immaculate ear
> To what the bells of matin say,
> 'Wake well, my child,
> Don't lie on your nose,
> Today is a holy day.' (133)

It is in the world of day/light, that light which infuses so many of her poems, and in a "passion" of which her "new laid lovers sometimes see" (43), that the continual transformations of the world in process take place; and it is there, where Wilkinson urges us all, most becomingly, to pay attention, that the continual transformations of the self by which we know we are truly alive also take place.

※

I tend to read "Letter to my children" and "Postscript" as a son; one who was a youngster at the time Wilkinson wrote it, and whose mother was of her generation. I read them as a boy who grew up in a social-histori-cal-cultural context best defined as Fifties Canadian Puritan, mostly blandly ignorant of the arts, and essentially dissociated from the ethics and ideas engendered in these poems. I read them wishing that my moth-er could have written something like that to me, way back then when it might have helped (and when I probably would not have understood its gifts, I admit).

※

Daughters or sons, we find in Wilkinsons's poems a generosity of vision, an acceptance of earthly, sexual, love which is somehow profoundly spir-itual (I am reminded of "soul music," Van Morrison, and then, of course, of Donne, who worked the same metaphorical language of sexual love as prayer, the connection Smith argued). What is interesting to me is how much more intensely and wholly erotic Wilkinson's approach to sexual love is than that of someone like Irving Layton. There are various reasons for this, but one of the best was first put forward by Fred Cogswell in "Eros or Narcissus? The Male Canadian Poet," (1968). There he persua-sively argued that most male Canadian poets up to that time tended to write love poems in praise of their own powers and attributes, the "other" (the woman) of the poems perceived more as a mirror than a partner in an act of reciprocation. Cogswell suggested that the "infantile" admiration of one's own sexual powers and the refusal to esteem women except "in so far as they become adjuncts to one's will," revealed an atti-tude "that can only be called sexual atavism." Female poets, said Cogswell, were far more likely to write of the act of love as a joining, an event in which two equals participated, and because they always focused on the presence of both actors in these small erotic dramas, they infused them with a warmth and an emotional complexity lacking in masculinist love lyrics (103-111).

When she presents lovers, Wilkinson definitely presents them as full partners in the acts of love. Neither the "girls" nor the "boys" of "Rhyme" are coy; they seek out the roots of life, and ignore the hypocrisy of their elders. Others, such as the merman and the woman of "Swimming lesson" or the lovers turned enemies of "A folk tale," choose their various fates together. And when they make love, her lovers "see" clearly together in the light of their passion, which is to say that, for Wilkinson, the act of love is a way of knowledge, as the biblical term for sex implies.

I believe a powerful line of eroticism perceived as visionary clarity runs from Isabella Valancy Crawford through Anne Wilkinson, through Phyllis Webb, to younger poets (of both sexes, finally) writing today. I do not argue "influence," for the connection does not rest in their writing so much as it does in my reading. Nevertheless, in this line of descent I have found some of the most compelling and vital poetry of sexual ecstasy extant.

Crawford achieves her most complete rendering of such ecstasy in "The Lily Bed," where her symbolic lovers are "cloaked in a golden pause" which lasts a whole day or but a moment, but which lasts the length of the poem, whose language leads us far and wide yet always through the paradoxical transformations of natural love:

Of loud, strong pines his tongue was made;
His lips, soft blossoms in the shade,

That kissed her silver lips—hers cool
As lilies on his inmost pool—

Till now he stood, in triumph's rest,
His image painted in her breast. (170)

Who enters whom here cannot be answered simply. Crawford has, though her ecstatic symbolism, subverted the traditional roles, and her lovers are caught in the same timeless *now* which Wilkinson celebrates in

"In June and gentle oven":

> Honeysuckle here
> Is more than bees can bear
> And time turns pale
> And stops to catch its breath
> And *lovers slip their flesh*
> And light as pollen
> Play on treble water
> Till *bodies reappear*
> And a shower of sun
> To dry *their languor.*
>
> Then two in one the lovers lie
> And *peel the skin of* summer
> With their teeth
> And *suck its marrow* from a kiss
> So charged with grace
> The tongue, all knowing
> Holds the sap of June
> Aloof from seasons, flowing. (62; my italics)

Wilkinson's lovers also participate in transformation, and in the encounter with the timeless moment of orgasm also inscribed in Crawford's "Victorian" poem (we should be reminded of how thoroughly erotic many of the poems of Crawford's contemporary "spinster" poet, Emily Dickinson, were). Both poets use a highly sensual language, but Wilkinson's is somewhat less symbolic than Crawford's; instead it insists on the physical qualities of the act it celebrates.

Phyllis Webb, in the first two "Suites" of *Naked Poems*, goes even further toward a language of enactment in which the physicality of the words on the page enacts the loving the poem is about. Conventional referentiality almost absents itself in these connected pieces, as the words simply do what they say, and the poem itself becomes a moment, a *now*, "aloof from seasons, flowing." But, as I argue in "Lyric/Anti-lyric," it is equally as transcendental as the other two poems, as the insistence that the lover's "mouth *blesses* me // all over" (1982b, 65; my italics) makes clear.

The profound connections I feel among these poems are perhaps mine alone; I know this. Still, in my personal anthology of love poems, they are among those which provide a grammar of possibilities for writing of sexual love which I have not found in the poems of many supposedly "erotic" male poets. Although these specific poems are of major importance to me, the poems of such other Canadian writers as Dorothy Livesay (especially in *An Unquiet Bed*), Gwendolyn MacEwan, Daphne Marlatt, and, more recently, Di Brandt, Sharon Thesen, Diana Hartog, Lola Lemire Tostevin, and Lisa Robertson would also fit into that anthology, along with poems by some men, most especially bpNichol, but I won't get into that here.

⚒

Actually, Wilkinson has written few traditional love lyrics; in fact, many of her poems are about a lack of love, missed opportunities. If I read her as a highly erotic poet, it is because so many of her poems argue an erotics of living through the doubled sensuality of their imagery and their rhythms; they point the way into the lived, loved, world of the senses. It's also because other poems rigorously image the emptiness of a life in which such an approach to living is absent. "The puritan" finally finds a perverse pleasure in projecting "a whip to shrivel those / Who over ten admit the sap / That rushes them" (29). Although the world resists his denial of it and "the song / Sings straight into his drum / And white the cherry floats / Though it is wrong," he remains willfully "all unaware" (30). The woman of "The Pressure of night" "lies stiff against her saviour sleep" and "lies dumb" as well, for, while "Ice and fire die tepid on her tongue / Scorched with cold, the unbeliever / Resists her saviour" (47). That she is living a lie the double use of the verb makes clear. In this poem we see another example of Wilkinson's refusal to be held to a single vision; although she celebrates "a passion of light" for her "new laid lovers" and says

A man, alone,
Perfecting his night vision

May be struck by dark
And silenced into sight (43)

she also presents night here as "blazed with eyes," which suggests a different but necessary kind of light in the darkness, as well. She refuses to be pinned down on this, for she is only too fully aware of the ambiguous relations humans have with their world. The problem is neither light nor darkness; it is the individual's craven refusal to engage that world whole. Against such singular losers, Wilkinson places her lovers, her children, and her poets, who appear in such guises as the speaker in "The red and the green," to tell us

> Here, where summer slips
> Its sovereigns through my fingers
> I put on my body and go forth
> To seek my blood. (68)

Not a quest without dangers, but worth the risk, for she hopes to find not just the symbol of her living but the others who share her way of being in the world. "The red and the green" is a highly ambiguous poem, admittedly, for "the quest turns round" and the goal, her heart, "Goes whey in the wind / Mislaid in the curd and why of memory." Is such loss good or bad? It's a question of reading the tone of the final stanzas:

> Confused, I gather rosemary
> And stitch the leaves
> To green hearts on my sleeve;
> My new green arteries

> Fly streamers from the maypole of my arms,
> From head to toe
> My blood sings green,
> From every heart a green amnesia rings. (69)

The loss of memory seems positive here, for it makes possible the fusion with the natural world the final lines celebrate. Or do they? Is such a fusion what we really seek? The speaker has become a literal Queen of the May, enacting the Druid rituals far more fully than someone with a memory (a connection with history rather than nature) could. Is "putting on" the body actually a method for getting out of the ordinary mind? This poem is visionary, but it offers no easy solutions, only images of possibility that may prove more than we can bear.

As almost all of Wilkinson's commentators have pointed out, she deals at least as much with death as she does with love. Joan Coldwell says that especially "the poems written in her last years speak of death with particular intensity . . . [bringing] to a high pitch of horror that intimate awareness of the body she had often projected in her earlier verse" (832). Although death is one of the central tropes in her work, I must confess that I feel less of that "horror" than do such critics as Coldwell and Smith. Even when Wilkinson is writing of pain and approaching death, or, as in the powerful "A sorrow of stones," of the obdurate refusal of the afterlife to provide any escape from sorrow, suffering, and alienation, the poems sing and swing with such energy they exhilarate me even as they ask me to experience something of what they speak about. "Summer storm" (156) certainly invokes the haunted mood of waiting which precedes one, and, as Smith points out, "Skull's skin is paper thin / Migraine is seeping in" brilliantly sounds the nervous apprehension the speaker feels, an apprehension which actually covers the whole poem. For the storm does not occur; the final lines inscribe only the speaker's "fear of loaded guns." Whether or not this fear is similar to that expressed by Emily Dickinson in "My Life had stood—a Loaded Gun," it suggests that what the poem is really "about" is its mood, the nervous tension its staggered rhythms and stark images manifest in every line. But that tension is exciting to read, however debilitating it might be to live.

Smith has written eloquently of how "original and terrible" is "A sorrow of stones," yet it, too, is full of ironic twists and turns, of a cold, calculating eye cast on life and death. This recalls nothing so much as the later Yeats, and it is possible that that master should be invoked before Eliot or Auden when seeking possible influences on Wilkinson's poetry. Certainly, I hear overtones of poems like "Words for music, perhaps" in both her poems on love and in the late poems apprehending the approach of death in a world where everything is "here and now," in the body of time, the body of love. Because the poems which precede these last poems have so richly engaged the living world, I read even the darkest of the late poems as continuing to do so, if only as a rearguard action. Thus both stonecutters in the section so titled, the carver of gravestones and the weather, represent the transforming power of the material world— Heraclitean flux in action. And though the final section of the poem, "When a Body Breaks" (173), in which the speaker tells of falling down a "Commonplace abyss," deals with the terror of finding nothing to grasp in death, it is full of witty, even comic, lines which subvert the horror to something else in which horror still has its place but is no longer the dominant emotion (perhaps curiosity is?).

> Twinkle twinkle how I wonder
> What I'm falling from up yonder.
> Virtue? Vice? Abstract nouns?

Thus, even though she cannot catch the attention of any gods with her prayers, and though she is forced to confess

> It is other than I had imagined. I thought
> To travel behind two plumed white horses,
> I thought to lie like cream in a long black hearse
> I had not calculated on this
> Fall without end (174)

the poem ends not in some terrible certainty but in what can be read as either terrible *un*certainty or the exhilarating if dangerous possibility of new creation. What can be said is that it refuses the temptation of intellectual closure: what the speaker "thought" to do could be interpreted as not really all that *interesting*, if nothing else, while finding oneself in a situation beyond calculation could be taken as a creative opportunity. In its presentation of a narrative figure from the other side of the boundary line death draws, this verse has much in common with a number of Emily Dickinson's central poems, yet its wit pushes in other directions than does the earlier poet's. I mean, the mood is less religious, perhaps, less spiritually apprehensive. I do not wish to denigrate the personal suffering Wilkinson may have known in her final years; I do want to register my sense of even these final poems as one of continuing affirmation of the lived, loved world in all its recalcitrant glory.

For me, Anne Wilkinson is most profoundly a poet of celebration. That is the great gift she offers her readers. The many other aspects of her work (for example, the dark wit of such poems as "Twilight of the gods" and "Fallout," both responses to the first nuclear threat of the fifties), which I have not explored here, deserve careful consideration. Her journals were discovered in the eighties; eventually published as *The Tightrope Walker* in 1992, they proved an extraordinary addition to Wilkinson's oeuvre. It remains a disgrace that the only way most contemporary readers can learn about her work is through a few poems in anthologies, and those unrepresentative of her full range. In order that her work be recognized for the achievement it is, we need a paperback Selected Poems that will stay in print, at least, if not another reprint of *The Collected Poems*, for the transformative clarity of her vision still has the power to disturb our complacency.

ENDNOTES

[1] This was true in 1986 and still tends to be the case: they are Smith's "Introduction," a version of which first appeared as "A Reading of Anne Wilkinson" in *Canadian Literature*, 10; and Robert Lecker's "Better Quick than Dead: Anne Wilkinson's Poetry." See, however, Joan Coldwell, "Anne Wilkinson," *The Oxford Companion to Canadian Literature*, for one woman's response to her work. Coldwell also edited and wrote the Introduction to *The Tightrope Walker* in 1992.

[2] Dean J. Irvine informed me (May 2000) that his research in the Wilkinson archive reveals that she wrote "Letter" and "Postscript" as a single work, and that Smith is clearly responsible for separating them during his editing.

Some Rhetorical Strategies of Eli Mandel

 Here's Eli Mandel in a paradigmatic situation, responding to a question about "Post-Modern notions of writing as process" with intense and intelligent energy: "So the answer is: yes, I think that I'm so fascinated by process that I spend a lot of time trying to work it out in the poem, always, and to learn the ways of drama in poetry—the speaking voice, starting in the middle of the situation always, your structure being anything but a form put on. It is an event, an inevitable event of ordering" (Arnason, *et.al.* 71). The way his answer involves an awareness "of drama in poetry" suggests that he takes a rhetorical view of the problem—if we take the concept of rhetoric in its highest, most traditional sense—and attempts to mesh that view with the radically anti-rhetorical stance of process poetics (we will ignore, for the moment, that anti-rhetoric is *mutatis mutandis* a kind of rhetoric).

As the *OED* demonstrates, rhetoric has been receiving the kind of deprecatory comments we now take for granted since at least the early 17th century: "**1615** BRATHWAIT *Strappado* (1878) 24 Heere is no substance, but a simple peece Of gaudy Rhetoricke." Perhaps the worst offenders are the politicians, but then, as Mandel often mixed politics and poetry, his doubled use or investigation of rhetoric in poems seems a fitting subject of our thinking. This is especially so, when we consider that behind that early turning away from rhetoric, as demonstrated in the attempts of The Royal Society in the late seventeenth century "'to return back to the primitive Purity and Shortness, when Men deliver'd so many *Things*, almost in an equal Number of *Words*,'" as Thomas Sprat put it, "lies a distrust, even a fear, of words" (Dixon 66). But the poet, certainly a poet like Mandel, who tells us that if "a language doesn't sound, really sound, then you might as well not write" (Arnason *et. al.* 81), is in love with words, for themselves alone. In that sense, the poet can never escape rhetoric.

Let us consider Mandel's strategies under the three traditional headings of *ethos* (the persuasive presence of "the person" in the writing), *logos* (the language, how it works), and *pathos* (how "the person" and the language work to move the audience to a particular response). Mandel's writing renders these aspects of rhetoric increasingly problematic, especially through the volumes of poetry from *An Idiot Joy* (1969) to *Life Sentence* (1981), and it does so in a comprehensively political manner. (The essays, too, during these years, continually address both their subjects and their audience in political terms.) Take the way *Life Sentence* confronts various questions of writing, of the written versus the writer and any form of "his" intentional "presence" in his discourse—all the political baggage of "the autobiographical" in that text. Mandel insists on the political dimension of *Life Sentence*, arguing that the poems were "drawn to, compelled from questions of the kind we call political, various ways in which forms of inhumanity manifest themselves and then seek justification in the language of patriotism, revolution, law, virtue" (7). The book's complex arrangement of carefully edited "journals" with "the poems that had grown out of the world those journals sought to record," its insistence thereby that it be treated as a dialogue among its own parts, announces its desire to take its place in postmodern discourse. Although he began as a modernist poet, Mandel wrote himself slowly and with difficulty into the process poetics of postmodernism; his last three books signaling his uneasy balancing on the cusp between the modern and the postmodern, pre- and post-structuralist writing. But the continual questioning of both poetic possibilities which these texts enact is itself a profoundly political act.

Perhaps the best way to see how Mandel both enters the rhetorical stance and interrogates it, is to glance briefly at two poems written approximately a decade apart yet exploring a similar situation: "Insomniac" appeared in *Stony Plain* in 1973 while "Beware the Sick Lion" appeared in *Life Sentence* in 1981. Both invite and repel an autobiographical reading, both have clear political overtones which mix the personal and intimate with the public and political.

They say Stalin at night
sleepless in the suburbs of Moscow
drew up long lists of enemies

think of that dreadful paper

to be sentenced by the pen
of an insomniac sleep-writing

new stars wheel over Spain
bulldozers cut roads through groves
in Africa moors rule who once ruled Spain

sleepless I pace before barred windows
fake-andalusian arches and toward sea
a Parador only cuts lines against the dark
where dark Greeks and Phoenicians sailed

if it is love that fingers in the mind
wake with a touch
                              curious
I remember only what was lost
plotting my own purges and despairs (65)

The rhetorical strategy of "Insomniac" begins in naming, and in a sly use of the tone of rumour: "*They* say Stalin," followed by what *he* did. Then the single separate line, in the imperative, followed by the central thought "we" (you) are asked to think, and the sudden duplicitous recognition of how poetry is a kind of "sleep-writing" which can sentence us too. The poem captures our attention with its opening, apparently a straightforward appeal to our fears of the political tyrant. But as the poem proceeds, through a description of the night which becomes an allusion to humanity's "ordinary" attacks on nature (and note the precision of "groves," with its "sacred" overtones), it then takes a turn which introduces *ethos* in a most problematic manner. "I" becomes the insomniac of the title, but the text has already alerted us to read "Stalin" that way. Here the tourist, lost in fake signs of present and historic glory, is aligned with another, frightening falsity, and the reader is forced to step back from the apparently objective voice of the first half of the poem. An intriguing deconstruction of *pathos*, perhaps. Finally, the tentative subjunctive query introduces the subject of love as a personal event (and here a doubled play of sound, the "lingers" we must hear behind "fingers" brilliantly refuses the conventionally pathetic). It does so, however, only to discover its losses, sliding through that wonderfully Janus-like "curious" into the announcement of "*my* own purges and despairs," a final alignment of the personal and political, though left deliberately open, unattached so to speak, non-referential in so far as "I" has not been identified, nor his possible victim(s).

What this poem does, brilliantly, is to set up certain expectations and then deny them any normal realization. The rhetoric, if we can put it this way, is continually under its own erasure, as the poem shifts from the public to the personal and back without privileging either. By the end, we discover the two realms joined in the common discourse-space of the "dreadful paper" we are reading—the poem as a list of enemies. At which point we also discover that our response, like the poem itself, is deeply compromised. Nothing is what it seems in a discourse where the language refuses all possibility of orderliness, and insists that by doing so it can teach us something about our own political or personal behavior.

〰️

When he's worried or anxious Pinochet is dangerous
do not believe his anger is pleasant
do not think his torturers intend a polite evening
Somoza is deadly when frightened or bored
families have collapsed like shanty-houses in earthquake;
or under the roaring weight of a typhoon
when he amuses himself or finds distraction
entertaining dull-witted police captains
with examples of sodomy or truncheons in vaginas

the action of broken glass in a beaten rectum

So too the belaboured husband as tyrant
rages against imagined treachery in a young wife
there is nothing like it any where else in the world
except the endless torment practiced by dangerous men

a roman catholic priest jumps from a top window
a trial witness dies in a car accident, in the desert, no other
                                                    car for miles
fishermen have found two bodies, hands wired in their nets
                                                    (verdict: suicide)
a foreign ministry official who issued a false passport to the
                                                    key witness
investigating the junta committed suicide after lunch
with three junta generals
A peasant activist found by police, his head bashed in,
both arms broken. Conclusion: train accident. It is noted his
arms were
broken before his death.

the National Centre for Investigations in Chile.
The history of ex-political prisoners

No one talks of the secret police activities of Somoza in
                                                    Nicaragua.
Only the earthquake of anger, the typhoons of oppression.
Torturers in Brazil.
Actions of the Peruvian military
The long lost afternoons of the
Privy Council Security Officers in Ottawa.

Tropical flowers are indeed exotic: read Neruda.
The poisonous flames of the tropics will burn out your heart:
                                                    read César

Vallejo.
Thugs in the colonial backlands roam the nostalgic cities of
                                                      Borges.
Northern plants too can kill: the old lion is dangerous
especially when sick, especially eaten by the jealousy of his
                                                      wife's young
body
her ass her cunt
More knives cut deeper wounds
over that piece of flesh than you can count. (1981, 23-24)

In some ways "Beware the Sick Lion" seems to be only a larger and more up-to-date version of "Insomniac." In fact, it is much more dangerously complex, for the courage of "the author" in confronting that danger is one of the things that creates the very real *pathos* we feel after we have moved through its various layers of persuasive appeal and dismissal. Certainly, it begins in similar fashion, but what it asks us to think of is far more visceral and violent than the "dreadful paper" of the earlier poem. Doubling the number of tyrants it names, it joins proposition and proof in a hyperbolic amplification of the political horrors which appear to be the poem's subject.

But suddenly the subject-as-person erupts into the poem, as it asserts the deep and deeply disturbing connection between the domestic and the political tyrant. The text subverts ordinary rhetoric by violently subjecting the traditional orderly arrangement of a peroration to a kind of implosion, everything happening at once.

The proofs of political and domestic violence it documents disrupt and distort the discourse of the poem, transforming it into a savage breakdown of syntax, decorum, and finally sensibility. Such a breakdown appears to deny the very real rhetorical skill that went into its careful construction. The apparent simplicity of the jagged and seemingly unconnected lines and images moves us, surely, to the double gesture of violently wishing to refuse what the poem tells us about the potential tyrant in us all while being drawn in, political and domestic voyeurs, to a horrified confrontation with the central paradox of impotent power and the waste of shame that accompanies it. Moreover, although the larger text of which it is a part invites some kind of biographical reading, this poem maintains a carefully "objective," almost journalistic, distance from every figure in it, although its tone is anything but distant. Every possible reading is held up to question, and no answer can be sustained.

According to Mandel, "the writer is not just a lonely guy sitting in a room scribbling little strange interests of his own individual consciousness, though he is that. He's also at the centre of a culture. He's the point of articulateness in a culture and therefore he's the best hope of that culture. The problem is that we have never been able to solve whether the things he writes about are able to do the great moral things you want him to" (Arnason *et.al.* 75). He said this while discussing *Out of Place* (1977), and nowhere in his oeuvre does he confront "the problem" more forcefully than in certain of "The Double" poems in that volume, especially "questions a double asks" (52), a witty, subversive, troubling excavation of the writer's deepest fears of impotence. First, it raises the problem of who really writes (speaks or questions): "we" are hauled into the poem as that "you" who is both writer (but only as someone taking dictation who can be asked "why are you writing out these questions") and reader, a doubling of an already doubled figure. The poem slowly builds, sliding in its questioning between the public and the private, as when it wonders both if "his appearance improve[s] your sexual performance" and if "the government of Canada, Ontario, Canada [has] significantly improved because of his presence." Scattered among these more general queries, it asks three simple questions. In order, they travel from the earliest philosophical moment of self and social awareness to the present predicament outlined in Mandel's statement above. First, "do you know yourself," which reaches back through Goethe and Pope to the inscription on the ancient temple of Apollo at Delphi. Second, "will you change your life," which also refers to the god of reason's light, this time via Rilke's "Archaic Torso of Apollo." Finally, capturing the contemporary poet's predicament, the unanswerable question, "is poetry all you have to offer." Is there any answer to this? If there is, it seems that for Mandel it will include the writer's "responsibility to face up to the worst that he's capable of. The most honest writing will not be high-minded but the writing that can show us, if it's honest, the meanness of the guy" (Arnason et.al. 76). This leads us back to such poems as "Insomniac" and "Beware the Sick Lion," and, strangely, it also leads us back to the ancient high ideals of rhetoric, where the rhetor seeks truth in a synthesis "of ethics and style" (Dixon 17), a synthesis which, in these poems, turns on a style that confronts ugly truth in ugly language and form, but does insist on the value of even that truth as an offering to the commonweal.

Ghazals in the North

John Thompson's male romanticism
& Phyllis Webb's female subversion

⧚⧚

"drunk beginnings; / yattering histories"

Although students and amateurs of culture in the non-Arab Muslim world, all of what was once known as Persia, and the Sikh and Moghul territories of northern India, have long known something about its poetry and poetic traditions, these alien poetics have, until recently, had little impact on the English-speaking world. At worst, the poetry has simply been ignored; at best, it has suffered from poor translations. Thus, a long and great tradition, that of the classic Persian and Urdu ghazal, stretching in time from the ninth century through to the present, has remained almost completely unknown, especially to poets in the West (although Goethe knew and admired it). And hardly anyone outside their own cultures ever recognized the great masters of the tradition, the Persian poet Hafiz (1320-1389), and the Urdu poets Mir (1723-1810) and Ghalib (1797-1869). As Aijaz Ahmad, the editor of a translation of Ghalib, puts it:

> The Urdu poet, and his Persian counterpart even more, has suffered not only from neglect, but also from the wrong kind of attention. By the time the British settled down in their colonies and areas of influence securely enough to start dabbling with the native literary traditions, the nineteenth century was well on its way. This tradition of translation has suffered fatally from the fact that the first conspicuous translations were done by people who came in contact with Urdu and Persian because of their involvement with matters and consequence of the Empire; by people who were not poets themselves, nor, with the exception of Fitzgerald, even men of imagination. They knew very little about poetry

and worked with a poetic ideal derived from a post-Romantic, Tennysonized jargon in which, as Pound once noted, the same adjectives were used for women and sunsets. . . . [Under the Empire] Indians were themselves alienated from their own language and were brought up on huge chunks of Tennyson, Swinburne, Macaulay, Pater, and others. By the beginning of this century there were numerous Indians who considered Ghalib both the greatest poet of Urdu that ever lived and a sort of native Tennyson. The complex, the apocalyptic, and the moral were carefully sifted out in favor of a post-Romantic grief that fed upon itself, a synthetic nostalgia that had nothing whatever to do with the concrete stresses of public and private history that Ghalib suffered. If he wasn't already a Victorian Romanticist, he had to be made into one; if the tradition of Urdu poetry wasn't already minor or trivial, the design of the Empire demanded that triviality be imposed upon it. For decades major Urdu poets were being read according to standards set by minor English ones. (xix-xx)

Having looked through translations from such major Persian and Urdu poets as Sa'di, Hafiz, Mir, and Ghalib, I can understand Ahmad's frustration and bitterness, for most are appalling examples of Greeting Card verse. Even the simplest prose crib reveals how sadly bereft of any understanding of the poetic complexity of the originals these translations are. Ahmad's basic point is true of at least the first half of the twentieth century. The few translations were both so poor and published in such limited editions they were unknown to the English-speaking poets and readers who participated in the grand experiment of modernism.

Finally, about two-thirds of the way through this century, a number of interesting introductory studies of Persian and Urdu literature began to appear, but in even the best of these, Ralph Russell's and Khurshidul Islam's *Three Mughal Poets*, the translations of the actual poems are, at best, pedestrian. They are awkward and banal because the authors too often attempt to match the exquisitely complex rhyming of the Urdu originals in English, a language which has never been very hospitable to rhyme. It was only with the publication of *Ghazals of Ghalib*, in which such fine contemporary American poets as W.S. Merwin, Adrienne Rich, William Stafford, and others created versions of Ghalib's original poems from prose translations and notes by Ahmad, that the poetic potential of the form manifested itself for poets in English. The poets Ahmad chose ignored some of the conventions of the original form in order to create versions which would be exciting and powerful poems on their own terms. He chose them for this very reason:

> [T]ranslations of poetry, though based on scholarship, have to have a poetic pulse that transcends the limits of what a scholar can ever accomplish. For example, the ghazals in these versions are almost always unrhymed; if rhymed, they are usually not restricted to any formal scheme. The fact is that formal devices, such as rhymed couplets or closely scannable prosodic structures are, in contemporary English as opposed to nineteenth-century Urdu, restrictive rather than enlarging or intensifying devices. The organic unity of the ghazal, as translated into English, does not depend on formal rhymes. Inner rhymes, allusions, verbal associations, wit, and imagistic relations can quite adequately take over the functions performed by the formal end-rhymes in the original Urdu. (xix)

I would hazard that most readers would agree that the results, the poems translating thirty-seven of Ghalib's ghazals, make for arresting poetry. It's difficult to measure the immediate impact of *Ghazals of Ghalib* on the general poetry-reading public, but it certainly had its effect on some of the participants. Adrienne Rich, especially, found the form so congenial to her poetic explorations of the time, that she included sequences of ghazals in her 1969 volume, *Leaflets*, and in her 1971 volume, *The Will to Change*. Rich's "*Ghazals*: Homage to Ghalib" was written partly in response to her work on *Ghazals of Ghalib*, partly because the form offered her a means by which to deal with complex and recalcitrant material. As her note to the sequence says:

> While the structure and metrics used by Ghalib are much stricter than mine, I have adhered to his use of a minimum of five couplets to a *ghazal*, each couplet being autonomous and independent of the others. The continuity and unity flow from the associations and images playing back and forth among the couplets in any single *ghazal*. (1969, 59)

This suggests the richly implosive nature of the ghazal that tempted Rich and other poets to attempt their own versions of the form. Another remark of Rich's, in a letter Ahmad quotes in his Introduction, provides further insight into the ghazal's formal interest to such writers:

> I needed a way of dealing with very complex and scattered material, which was demanding a different kind of unity from that imposed on it by the isolated single poem: in which certain experiences needed to find both their intensest rendering and to join with other experiences not logically or chronologically connected in any obvious way. I've been trying to make the couplets as autonomous as possible and to allow the unity of the ghazal to emerge from underneath, as it were, through images, through associations, private and otherwise. . . . what I'm trying for, not always successfully, is a clear image or articulation behind which there are shadows, reverberations, reflections of reflections. (xxv - xxvi)

Rich's last sentence could stand for any number of statements on the poetics of contemporary innovative poetry, yet it is also a true response on her part to the possibilities a particular, and ancient, form from another culture offered her. Like many of her contemporaries, she was at a point in her career when she was feeling trapped by what Perloff calls the poetics of Symbolism, and for her the ghazal offered the best route towards a poetics of indeterminacy.[1] In contrast, I would argue that Phyllis Webb has always written in the Pound tradition, but especially so after *Naked Poems*. For that reason, the form of the ghazal probably proved even more immediately congenial to her than to someone like Rich; for Rich it was something entirely new, while for Webb it was a kind of confirmation.

Rich was not alone in recognizing how that form could provide a means by which to explore specific and complex problems facing the lyric poet in contemporary North America. Still, although there may have been some others, it was in the work of Rich and Jim Harrison that the ghazal first made its impact on readers and writers in North America, and through them that readers were led to study Ghalib and others in the original tradition. Rich's and Harrison's work in the ghazal form caught the attention of the Canadian Maritime poet, John Thompson, for example; and it is through his writing, especially in his last book, *Stilt Jack*,[2] that the ghazal entered Canadian writing.

❧

"Only Love has brought to us the world"

What then is the ghazal? And why should contemporary American and Canadian poets be interested in it? According to Reuben Levy, the word derives "from an Arabic original meaning 'lovers' exchanges'" (33). Russell and Islam enlarge on this:

> The ghazal is a short lyric, in which the themes of love predominate. (The word is derived from a root which means approximately "conversation between lovers.") Its form is bound by strict rules. The authorities on poetics vary as to the number of couplets it may contain: there seems to be general agreement on a prescribed minimum of five, but the maximum is variously stated as eleven, seventeen, or some other figure. As a general rule each couplet must express a complete and independent thought, though it is permissible within the ghazal to connect several of the couplets to

form a single statement. The unity of the poem is one not of content but of form.

. . .

While in the ghazal themes of love predominate, these may treat either of earthly love between human beings or of the mystic love of the worshipper for the Divine Beloved. Many lines are capable of either interpretation. But many ghazals include lines on themes which have no conceivable connection with love—a practice that the poet could perhaps justify within the terms of the definition of the ghazal by the argument that even lovers talk of other things besides love. In general, the only thing which gives unity to the poem is its form. There is generally not even a unity of mood between the independent couplets that compose it: the mood may vary in one and the same ghazal between tragedy and broad humour. (7-9)

Agreeing with these scholars, Ahmad adds an important point:

It should be obvious that this form, based on two lines of equal length as a self-sufficient unit of poetry, is the product of the abstract nature of the language itself, and in turn reinforces the same character. Only when a unit of poetry is meant to communicate a single thought or emotion, and only when the poet sets out to deal with just the essence rather than the many particulars of an experience, can one have so small a unit and dispense with the idea of continuity. Within these expectations, the ghazal functions with an easily identifiable and almost repetitious pattern of imagery—the rose, the tulip, the nightingale, the seasons, a handful of descriptions of this or that, human or extra-human states—as does Japanese poetry, in which a certain flower, a certain time of day, even the plunge of a stone, can signify something other than itself. (xvii)

This "repetitious pattern of imagery," which achieved a high degree of symbolism through the ages, is absolutely central to a major aspect of the ghazal tradition. "The subject of love is universal," says M. Mujeeb. "The unique feature of Persian poetry is the organic assimilation of sacred and profane love in a wealth of symbols where the sacred is seen through the profane as light through a prism, and the profane is seen through the sacred as God's light in the nature of man" (34).

These and other statements defining the ghazal only serve to bring me back to the question, Why the contemporary interest in the form? I think the answer can be found in the comments of the poets who have entertained its possibilities for their own explorations. What we should remember, always, is that translation usually involves a lot more than simply saying the same thing in another language, at least where poets are involved. Even in the "translations" of Ghalib, the poets involved realized that what they had to do was re-create the original, and it is that spirit of re/creation which animates every one of the writers who has chosen to explore the potential of the form of the ghazal in their own poetry.

I have already quoted Rich on what attracted her to the ghazal. In a note on his ghazals, Jim Harrison also points to the absence of logical order in the poems as a major attraction:

> The couplets are not related by reason or logic and their only continuity is made by a metaphorical jump. Ghazals are essentially lyrics and I have worked with whatever aspect of our life now that seemed to want to enter my field of vision. Crude, holy, natural, political, sexual. After several years spent with longer forms I've tried to regain some of the spontaneity of the dance, the song unencumbered by any philosophical apparatus, faithful only to its own music. (26)

Although he posits connections among the "crude, holy, natural, political, [and] sexual," Harrison's ghazals do not, nor do Rich's, attempt anything like the inter-penetration of the sacred and the profane found in the work of such writers as Hafiz, Mir, and Ghalib, as Peter Sanger has pointed out (7).

John Thompson's *Stilt Jack* does attempt such a marriage of sacred and profane. It is a stunning, occasionally even frightening, example of what Islam and Russell call "'real love'—that is, divine love—[which] embraces not only the love of God in the sense in which the modern understands it, but a man's complete dedication to his ideals in life, ideals which he will serve to the end, no matter what suffering this may bring down upon him" (207). In Thompson's case, the suffering is palpable, and the ideals he dedicates himself to, although they include a desperate search for God,[3] are those of what he himself calls "the essence of poetry" (5). Thus it is interesting to see, in his note on "Ghazals," what qualities attract him most:

> The ghazal proceeds by couplets which (and here, perhaps, is the great interest in the form for Western writers) have no necessary logical, progressive, narrative, thematic (or whatever) connection. . . .
>
> The link between couplets . . . is a matter of tone, nuance: the poem has no palpable intention upon us. It breaks, has to be listened to as a song: its order is clandestine.
>
> The ghazal has been practiced in America (divested of formal and conventional obligations) by a number of poets, such as Adrienne Rich. My own interest in the "form" lies in the freedom it allows—the escape, even, from brief lyric "unity". These are not, I think, surrealist, free-association poems. They are poems of careful construction; but of a construction permitting the greatest controlled imaginative progression. . . .
>
> The ghazal allows the imagination to move by its own nature: discovering an alien design, illogical and without sense—a chart of the disorderly, against false reason and the tacking together of poor narratives. It is the poem of contrasts, dreams, astonishing leaps. The ghazal has been called "drunken and amatory" and I think it is. (5)

"Against false reason and the tacking together of poor narratives": there

we hear the call of a contemporary poet seeking a way out of some popular poetic conventions which seem less and less fulfilling the more they are
used. Phyllis Webb is a poet who has long challenged the conventional formal boundaries of the poem,[4] and thus both Thompson's ghazals and his
preface excited her creative imagination when she "belatedly discovered"
them, though her "anti-ghazals" are even more subversive of both traditional (and phallogocentric) lyricism and of the essentially masculist stance
of the conventional ghazal of Hafiz and Ghalib. As she points out in the
"Preface" to *Sunday Water*, the more she learnt about ghazals, the more
she saw she "was actually defying some of the traditional rules, constraints, and pleasures laid down so long ago" (1982a, np). This is especially true of the rules which followed from what Ahmad calls "the
abstract nature of the language itself" (xvii). As Webb admits—and here
perhaps the earlier impact of Japanese poetry upon her *Naked Poems*
might still be in force—her versions of ghazal "tend toward the particular,
the local, the dialectical and private" (1982a, np). Yet Thompson's versions and preface obviously excited her interest in the possibilities of the
form, and she eventually created a book which, like his, has its own "clandestine order" or even orders. Indeed, both their sequences attain a highly
lyric tone when necessary yet refuse the traditional temptations of lyric
egotism and sentimentalism to become fine examples of lyric/anti-lyric:
this is their great accomplishment, made possible through their imaginative transformations of an alien and highly conventional form into a new
and exploratory one in English.

※

"Should it be passion or grief?"

John Thompson died before *Stilt Jack* was published. His accidental but
self-inflicted death and his personal suffering during the last few years of
his life[5] affected its reception. According to Peter Sanger, in *Sea Run:
Notes on John Thompson's STILT JACK*, the "figure made of the poet has
at times obscured the figure his poetry makes" (5). Sanger's book is, as
Webb points out, a "very careful and detailed study of the sources in *Stilt
Jack*" (1987, 156), and demonstrates how rich and complex are the allusions and associations of that book. Webb says it best:

[There is] a specific cluster of associations which, once understood, make the work much more coherent, accessible, and, for me, even more desperate. Thompson, it is clearly seen now, was writing his last will and testament. A big hand and a big heart shape this cluster: Yeats ("Yeats. Yeats. Yeats. Yeats. Yeats. Yeats. Yeats. / Why wouldn't the man shut up?"), Rilke, Melville, Isaak Walton, Levertov, Donne, Blake, Stevens, Shakespeare, especially "King Lear," [sic.] Hopkins, Keats, William Styron. And the Bible. And René Char. And Theodore Roethke. Quite a handful. And the ghazal-makers, their whole tradition. (1987, 156)

Despite this, we still need to remember that, although the final "'drunken and amatory'" paragraph of Thompson's preface (5) may be, as Sanger says, "a warning, and a confirmation, as to how carefully *Stilt Jack* was written, and how carefully it can be read" (7), it is surely also, as Webb says, "an invitation into the book, its heart of darkness, its shining spins and turns, its sober (and drunken) stains. And its method" (1987, 156). And it is to some of those "shining spins and turns" of song that I wish to turn.

Among the most "astonishing" aspects of Thompson's ghazals is the way they transform a terribly strict and conventional form in Urdu into an open and questing one in English. "Divested of formal and conventional obligations," as he says, the form "breaks," yet "its order," though "clandestine" (5), is real. In Thompson's case that "order" is strangely serial, which means that the thirty-eight ghazals of *Stilt Jack* demand to be read straight through if they are to achieve their greatest impact. Thus the first couplet of Ghazal I—"Now you have burned your books: you'll go / with nothing but your blind, stupefied heart" (11)—returns, transformed by all that has passed between, as the first couplet of Ghazal XXXVII: "Now you have burned your books, you'll go with nothing. / A heart" (47). And the revelation about inspiration in Ghazal IX—"It's all in books, save the best part; God knows / where that is: I found it once, wasn't looking" (19)—echoes behind the last lines of the book, which, despite the pain it has registered, point towards a kind of hope: "Can't believe it, knowing nothing. / Friends: these words for you" (48).

Although Thompson's dramatic death makes a biographical reading of the poem almost too easy, it is more exciting when we read the "I" as merely one more voice in a text so full of them none can be pinned down. Sanger observes that there are "shifts of address" for the "you" of Thompson's poems—a "you" that can be any number of others, Thompson himself, or Thompson's muse (9). This "shift" applies equally to all the pronouns. This is not to say that biographical factors do not impinge, but it is to say they represent only one reading of this complex poem. Thompson is clearly seeking a polyphony of voices, and the form, with its lack of "necessary logical, progressive, narrative, thematic (or whatever) connection[s]" (5), invites such polyphony. The unpredictable "I" can see and say many different things, and one of the joys of the book is the sardonic humour of many of his statements:

> I'm thinking of you. Nashe. Rats on my window sill.
> The dirt under my fingernails.
>
> Lord, lord.   I'm thinking of you.
> I'm gone. (13)
>
> Last night I died: a tired flie woke me.
> On White Salt Mountain I heard a phrase carving the world.
> (21)
>
> I'm in touch with the gods I've invented:
> Lord, save me from them. (23)
>
> If there were enough women I wouldn't write poetry;
> if there were enough poetry (26)
>
> One fish, one bird,
> one woman, one word,
>
> that does it for me, and the last word of Ulysses is
> yes. (27)

The first two couplets from Ghazal III demonstrate Thompson's mastery of complex poetic syntax. At first the "you" is open, possibly some version of "the beloved" of the conventional ghazal, but we can also read it as "Nashe," even though the period seems to deny that reading; equally, the "you" might be the rats. Similarly, although the "Lord, lord" of the next line can be read as a prayer to Christ, as Sanger argues (9), in which case the voice is thinking of Him as "you," it could equally be a casual blasphemy, and the "you" any of the possibilities mentioned in reference to the previous couplet. All these readings and more are possible, and necessary: this is one of those "astonishing leaps" (Thompson 5) the ghazal offers its practitioners. In other couplets, we hear a wide range of voices, all of which speak with various kinds of emotional power, some of which depends upon them being the voices of other writers as well as of other states of being. The six couplets of Ghazal XXVIII provide a good example of this:

> I learn by going;
> there is a garden.

> Things I root up from the dirt
> I'm in love with.

> First things: lost. The milky saucer,
> of last things a siren.

> Please, please be straight, strait,
> stone, arrow, north needle.

> I haven't got time for the pain,
> name your name,

> the white whale, STILT JACK, in her face,
> where I have to go. (38)

Here, in addition to the literary and mythical allusions, there is a gathering of various symbolic images from earlier in the sequence. But there is also the assumption of the specific voice of Roethke's "The Waking" (124), which shadows the other voices within the poem just as it brackets them. The "I"s who root, love, implore, and "haven't got time for the pain" include Roethke's "I"; in their carefully constructed polyphony and intertextuality, they require a complexity of response beyond the scope of the conventional lyric.

Stilt Jack is a demanding and difficult book, one which grows richer with every reading. Its influence is growing, too, as D.G. Jones, Douglas Lochhead, Michael Ondaatje,[6] and many others, especially Phyllis Webb, have testified. Chiaroscuro, richly textured, it remains one of the major texts of the seventies.

⚞

"Poems / of many scents and various hues beguile me"

Simultaneously loving and subversive, Phyllis Webb has approached the ghazal tradition more as bricoleur than disciple. She begins the transformative journey of *Water and Light* "semaphor[ing] for help (calling stone-dead John Thompson)" (9). But even if he appears to be another version of her "male muse in many guises" (1980, 9), her ever-expanding text soon moves beyond the putative guidance of any single figure, especially a male one. Rather, the form, perhaps because she feels she is writing "anti Ghazals," offers a freedom of polyphony which allows for a sustained subversion of the Romantic and phallogocentric ideals of the ghazal tradition. It begins in the very first "anti Ghazal," the final two couplets of which confront the problem as directly as possible:

> Four or five couplets trying to dance
> into Persia. Who dances in Persia now?
>
> A magic carpet, a prayer mat, red.
> A knocked off head of somebody on her broken knees.
> (1984, 9)

First written in 1981, this poem clearly "tend[s] toward the particular, the local, the dialectical and private" (1982a, np), presenting a particular woman's response to what was happening to other women "in Persia" under the savage conservatism of the Ayatollah's Shiite Muslim "revolution." Is this what happens to "the Beloved," there and now, in the ingrained betrayal of that patriarchy? Certainly this text has no room for "the rose, the tulip, the nightingale" (Ahmad xvii) as symbol only, though later ones may entertain them in their local manifestations as material presences in a singular person's life. No, such texts, found throughout *Water and Light*, cannot help subverting a tradition rooted, as Ahmad points out, in "a language of abstractions" (xv).

The "anti Ghazal" continually interrogates the traditional form and its contemporary possibilities. It takes nothing for granted. Though it looks like a lyric, the "anti Ghazal" allows Webb to subvert both the conventions of lyric and of lyric reading: sliding lyric tone against the lyric grain results in a feeling far more complex, compressed, and opaque than is conventionally the case with traditional lyric. "I" speaks often here, but as the object of poetic investigation, no different from any other object in the poem. Even in the sequence, "I, Daniel," the I/eye is various and unauthorized, a figure of the possibilities of writing as it both enters and leaves the subject of the poem, as both Scobie (1989, 127-133) and Ricou (1986, 210) point out. *Water and Light* achieves that transcendent "leap" Robert Bly says is the true mark of poetry[7] by taking full advantage of what Thompson calls the ghazal's "freedom . . . —the escape, even, from brief lyric unity" (5).

As one example of how such freedom works, take the following:

My morning poem destroyed by the good neighbour policy.
Mrs. Olsson, organic gardener, lectures me on the good life.

Damned dark hole! Rabbit
in her rabbit warren, pushing them out.

Oh this is cozy, all of us together watching
the news, catching each other's tics and flickers.

The square ring on her third finger, six seed pearls.
On her right index finger, tiny diamond-shaped jade.

The grand design. The setting sun.

All the big animals turn toward the Great Wall of China.
(1984, 13)

Although the "particular" and the "local" are clearly present here, they intertwine with the chance and arbitrary leaps of the creative imagination in action. While the first couplet might refer specifically to "Phyllis Webb" and her locale, the second one moves us elsewhere, at first perhaps close to Wonderland. But then, with another sudden shift, the third transports us into a textual space full of other possibilities. Who, or what, does the (female) rabbit push out , and is it out of the "damned dark hole" or only "her rabbit warren"? The situation is clearly undecidable, especially when the coy and wry speech of the following couplet suggests that "all of us together" are *in*. The voice of that third couplet certainly belongs in an animal story, a story possibly alluded to in the second. The fourth, however, appears to return to Mrs. Olsson. Perhaps. But the final one, while possibly reaching "design" from the rings, strays back to that Other world, which is nevertheless ours, always mysterious. Certainly, it is mysterious to the poet, who tells us, "I wrote that line sitting on a B.C. ferry without a thought of thoughts; it arose from out of the deep and stunned me then as it stuns now" (1987, 157). A "palpable intention" (Thompson 5) is clearly absent; but "a mystical power intrudes" (1982a, np).

If there is "a mystical power" in the poems, it is most deviously present in the way Webb's "anti Ghazals" subversively undermine the theme of "the mystic love of the worshipper for the Divine Beloved" (Islam 9), while fulfilling the desire of the form for "the complex, the apocalyptic, and the moral" (Ahmad xx). This can best be demonstrated by collating a new ghazal out of some of the couplets scattered throughout the book:

I fly from the wide-open mouth of the seraphim.
Something or somebody always wants to improve me.
(1984, 11)

Yahweh is a speckled bird pecking at treebark.
We are the insects most excellent to his taste. (14)

Pretty pebble, divine bird, honorable tree—
all in me. Take this, and this, and this—in memory of. (16)

Too hot. That star. This cross-eyed
vision. Days and nights, sun moon—the up-there claptrap. (18)

Oh You who keep disappearing
behind a black cloud like a woman

behind her veil, how do you feel
shut off like that from the perfect

obedience of your worshippers? (56)

These five excerpts could add up to one ghazal, so the critics tell us. What
a strange vision and version of the divine slips into these various poems.
Yet when connected to other couplets these ones take on an added com-
plication of tone which refuses easy interpretations. However they are
read, they will not lead to the adoration of the tradition. And although
"I, Daniel" is consistently concerned with God and His messages, it too
reneges on its grand original. In both cases, these texts slip away: into
local sights, other intertexts, the subversions of parody. They will not be
taken straight.

In other poems, "the pull, this way and that, ultimately into the pull /
of the pen across the page" (18) leads to a daring questioning of the old
ways of the form. "Drunken and amatory, illogical, stoned, mellifluous,"
this "journey of the ten lines" is sung "over and over to the Beloved who
reigns // on the throne of accidie" (20). Here the poem takes a critically
comic stance to the way its "originals" groan and whine "about love's
ultimate perfection," and then offers a final kicker:

Wait! Everything is waiting for a condition of grace:
the string of the Sitar, this Gat, a distant bell,

even the Beloved in her bored flesh. (20)

We respond here to the play of language, yet also to an investigation of its
dangerous power over the figure it supposedly seeks to honour. The feminist critique is, however, only part of what this poem is about. It is also
about breaking the rules—it is no accident that it has an extra line, a broken couplet signing the human incompleteness purdah, in both poetry and

life, imposed upon the poor "Beloved"—and about a music played against traditional music. Allusive and self-referential, the first line invokes John Thompson's description of the ghazal and the calling out to him in the first "anti Ghazal." Full of duplicitous puns, the poem moves through subtle repetitions to achieve its own, purely linguistic, "condition of grace."

Puns, allusions, echoes, borrowings, intense modalities of language, as well as the questioning refusal of "the domination of a male power culture" (Webb 1980, 9), increase as the poems progress. Although a self-contained poetic sequence, "I, Daniel" continues the investigative play with the symbols of Persian culture already noted as well as undercutting the absolute masculinity the Divine assumes in both Hebrew and Muslim belief. Other poems playfully invoke precisely those images of woman which have always signaled man's fear of her: "*Dentelle*, she-teeth, milk-tooth, / a mouthful of lace" (49). Every poem invites our participation and our delight in its music. Two of them provide sharply different examples of how complex their polyphony can be:

> My soul, my soul, who said that?
> as the rain stumbles over my mental horizon
>
> horizon which wavers, creates the mirage
> of a café in Milano where
>
> Mary, he says, what shall we do tonight?
>
> Tonight, tonight, love, what shall we do tonight?
> The mirage settles into rain falling
>
> into the harbour and onto the day I own
> feeding the heat of dry September
>
> September and the cats restless, hungry
> in view of winter, in view of cold
>
> cold as the curse of mere matter, *Mère*
> matter, the subject family, the repeated
>
> word ready to pounce out of the thunder
> out of the rain-forest where leap the wild, bereft deer. (46)

The Authors are in Eternity,
or so Blake said,

but I am here, feet planted
on the ground;

I am listening to the song
of the underground river.

I go down to the same river twice,
remembering, always remembering.

I am you in your jewel-domed reading room,
I am you in your kayak skimming.

I stand in one place risking almost everything.
I weep for the last notes.

The river-stones are polished
by the blue-veined hands of Ishtar.

Poor Fishstar! Yet—all is not lost. (57)

    In the first of these poems, the varied repetitions perform the task pre-
scribed for rhyme in the traditional ghazal while setting up a haunting and
querulous music far removed from its lovesong. A chorus of voices in
counterpoint constructs both intertextuality and shifts of subjectivity. The
former in the way the first line echoes renaissance love poems and
Jacobean tragedies while the last couplet remembers *The Waste Land*; the
latter in the way the possessive in the first couplet both does and does not
belong to the speaker, while the later first-person plural phrase shifts from
one fictional state to another between lines. Throughout, the language
leads deep into the heart of "the family romance." It does so via the pun
and through a reminder of what the mirage of love leads to, from "mere
matter" to the Great Mother herself, through "the *subject* family" (that is,
subjectively sensed, recognized as *the* subject of every repeated discourse,
and subjected to traditional patriarchal power) to the final recognition of
nature as "bereft" in a world where "mankind" plays out its "curse."

The second interrogates philosophy and religion, literature, and the whole Romantic quest. There is too much here to unravel completely. A feminine interrogation of Heraclitean flux associated with a grounded sense of being excluded, possibly happily, from the patriarchal tradition (those "Authors . . . in Eternity") contrasts with the speaker's specific insistence on entering Kubla Khan's library on her own terms (perhaps as a shaman), all the while maintaining that her reading "I" is many, not one, is an affirmation of that very flux in the realm of subjectivity (and note the way the feminine subject both speaks and is spoken to). The "I" and the "you" enter each other, they perfectly represent a "simultitude," the term Laurie Ricou borrows from Daphne Marlatt for "a crucial one-word distillation of feminist poetics" (1986, 215).[8] But then the standing in one place which may be the very act of remembering is a risk: the river of memory changes us. This shifty and complex poem does not deny pain, but celebrates the refusal to live in it. As the poem soars, the feeling is one of exhilaration, and that is the quality I find most astonishing about Webb's "anti Ghazals." In the midst of subverting the conventional form, they perfectly inscribe that "essence of poetry" Thompson discovered in it (5). Webb's "anti Ghazals" are language in flight, transcendent inspiration; though completely free of the ground, they always keep in touch.

〰

"Why Poetry *And why not, I asked*'"

If nothing more than *Stilt Jack* and *Water and Light* resulted from the North American interest in the ghazal, it would still be clear that the form had had a major impact on Canadian poetry. But others have been affected, too, and it might seem mean-minded to ask whether by Webb or Thompson. And more ghazal-influenced poetry continues to appear. In exploring an ancient and traditional Persian and Urdu form, both poets were able to alter a highly conventionalized and closed poetic towards a formal freedom which provided escape from a kind of closure they found endemic to English lyric poetry. Thus they took from the ghazal, not its closed verse structure, but a formal possibility tied to structural intent and transformative tonality. The "alien design" (Thompson 5) they found is wholly open yet precisely disciplined. In it, they have discovered a poetry of extraordinary power. Both their books stand as major texts, which a reader can return to again and again without exhausting their possibilities. A masterwork from a major writer, Webb's *Water and Light* is, I think, the more open, the more generous and innovative text, partly because its feminist poetics does more to expand the range of the transformed form they both translated into personal use. But both have already influenced and will continue to influence many writers.

ENDNOTES

[1] See Perloff "Unreal Cities" (1980, 3-44) and "Pound/Stevens: whose era?" (1984, 1-32).

[2] For his knowledge of Rich's and Harrison's ghazals, see "Ghazals" (5), and Peter Sanger, *Sea Run: Notes on John Thompson's STILT JACK* (7).

[3] As Sanger says, "The great difference between the work of Thompson, Mir Taqi Mir, and Ghalib, on the one hand, and of Rich and Harrison, on the other, is that the former poets work within explicit religious traditions. Eclectic as his use of other religious traditions was, in *Stilt Jack* Thompson wrote as a Christian poet" (7). But Sanger also points out in relation to Thompson's use of *The Compleat Angler*, that "Thompson ... unlike Walton, was haunted by an absence, the *deus absconditus*, whose presence was only beginning to be felt in England by the end of the seventeenth century" (28). Comments like these suggest just how desperate and fragmentary was Thompson's search.

[4] See Pauline Butling, esp. 197.

[5] Sanger provides a somewhat fragmentary account of Thompson's last years in his study (5-7); a fuller account appears in his "Introduction" to *John Thompson: Collected Poems & Translations* (1995).

[6] See: Jones's "Imperfect Ghazals/for John Thompson," (1983, 77-79); Lochhead's references to Thompson in *High Marsh Road*, and the ghazal-like poems in *Tiger in the Skull: New and Selected Poems, 1959-1985* (109-130); and Phyllis Webb's dedication to *Sunday Water*: "for Michael Ondaatje/who introduced me to Ghazals."

[7] In *Leaping Poetry*, Bly argues that the "leap can be described as a leap from the conscious to the unconscious and back again, a leap from the known part of the mind to the unknown part and back to the known' (1). Elsewhere he adds, "thought of in terms of language, then, leaping is the ability to associate fast" (4). Bly's insistence that "in all art derived from Great Mother mysteries, the leap to the unknown part of the mind lies in the very center of the work" (1) seems relevant to Webb's practice.

[8] Marlatt first used the term in her 1984 essay, "musing with mothertongue" (1998, 13).

The Heavenly Rhetoric of Thine I

Some Versions of the Subject in The Martyrology Book 1

In "Exegesis/Eggs à Jesus: *The Martyrology* as a Text in Crisis," Frank Davey points out, in great detail, just how many "difficult problems [of textuality, of reading, or writing, etc.] *The Martyrology* raises" (231). They are problems which the text resolutely and self-consciously refuses to resolve. Indeed, that refusal is one of the major signs by which *The Martyrology* announces itself as a postmodern text. It is also one of the ways it signals its place in the tradition of what Perloff has called "indeterminacy" (1981, 3-44). As Davey suggests, all the various "problems" he mentions continue to engage the readers as problems throughout *The Martyrology*. Part of the purpose of this ongoing text, then, is to keep us aware that they will never be solved.

One of those problems "is created by Nichol's use of the pronoun 'i,'" and, I would add, the other personal pronouns as well, especially "you." The "first person pronoun has been problematic in Western poetry at least since Rimbaud's famous observation, 'Je est un autre'"(Davey 234), but Nichol's ludic expansions on that problematic extend the range of otherness very far indeed. Throughout, *The Martyrology*'s play of various personal pronouns off each other and especially off the first personal pronoun creates an awareness of layers of discourse and shifting textual spaces both liberating for and demanding of the engaged reader. The multiplicity of the "i" (and of the writerly ego it so often signifies) is one of the major thematic threads of *The Martyrology*. From the very beginning, this ongoing poem has posited the "i" and all other personal pronouns as utterly sliding signifiers, which refuse to remain "in place" for even a single page at a time.

As Steve McCaffery has pointed out, "Nichol does not *theatricalize* a struggling subject pulverized and castrated within the mechanics of writing's general economy, but rather inscribes the relativization of a multiplicity of writings within the single textual space. As a result, the oscillations acquire a multiple dimension that serves to neutralize any potential drive to dominate with a single, uniform discourse" (74). McCaffery's essay provides a complex introduction to the various ways in which *The Martyrology* inscribes such "a relativization." Here I want to look at one of those ways by tracing the "precision of openness"(*Book 4*)[1] with which the text explores the shifting nature of what the referential pronoun is and does. Following the play of the pronouns through *Book 1* should enable the reader to see how fluid the conceptualization of "i" and its related pronouns has been from the beginning, and how deliberately the text has always entertained this and the other problems which Davey has explored so eloquently in his essay.

Of course, critical readings of any poem today tend to accept the idea of personae, but in most traditional texts a persona is usually held to be a more or less single and continuous figure. This is emphatically not the case in *The Martyrology* which continually seeks "other i's to see thru / 'in the true time and space called meaning'"(*Book 3*:V), yet also systematically interrogates the critical separation of author from speaker. Sometimes they are clearly different, but, as Davey points out, "the poem contains numerous elements which underline the possible connections of [the] 'i' to Nichol's own life" (235), and which also hold any non-referential reading up to question. Thus, as McCaffery suggests, *The Martyrology* is "a polyphonic staging of intersecting texts in which intersubjectivity (undeniably present) is never allowed to dominate and needs, in its relative status, no apologetic justification" (1986, 76).

In 1980, working on the end of *Book 5*, "Nichol" writes:

i am moving before you get the chance to move

writing out the book's already written
present's past tense in the present's
work outdistancing the theory
made old as me by time
essayed a poem with all the process prose is
the play in line a thrust defines
forward back

Like many sections of the later books, this is among other things a statement of theory. But the poetry always outdistances the theory. In showing just how slippery personal pronouns can be, *The Martyrology* begins to explore their problematic nature in the early sixties, right at the beginning of *Book 1*, long before Nichol attempts any critical analyses of the problem, both within the text (in *Books 3, 4, 5,* and *6*) and without it (in some of the theoretical explorations of the Toronto Research Group, for example). Thus, even while reading the early books of the poem, the reader must continually confront the various ways the text simultaneously thematizes and questions the first-person pronoun.

In both the first and second editions of *The Martyrology*, as Scobie has pointed out, the very first speaker is "Saint Ein" (1984, 110). The quotation marks and author citation place the implicit "i" in an intertextual context ("Let *me* recite what history teaches. History teaches."), who could be Stein herself, or simply a narrator in her text, reciting what has already been said before. This finding a new place for the already said is reiterated by the text it now finds itself in. Whose "i" cites what here, anyway?

In the second edition, the fragment containing the genealogies "of those saints we know," originally published separately, follows. The pronoun here is interesting: first "we know," then "we mention," and finally "we will be writing"; it appears to be a scholarly effort, which the plural pronoun signs as a group endeavour. Indeed, this "we" seems to imply a large effort by many critics to gather and collate the "history" of the "saints," whose names, however, already suggesting their birth in language, ludically and poetically undercut such a reading.

Immediately following the third reference, a new stanza, of what Davey calls "largely unforegrounded moral generalization" (234), shifts to a singular pronoun:

> one thing makes sense
> one thing only
> to live with people
> day by day
>   that struggle

> to carry you forward
>
> > it is the only way

The text will utilize "you" this way many times: it can be read as a semantic displacement of "i," but has to be read as a hortative "you" as well, addressed to the reader reading, and attempting to move the "you" to understanding action. The next stanza slides into the passive voice: "a future music moves now to be written" and "it will be seen," but the text does not say by whom. So throughout this listing the text refuses the singular first person a place. There is an "i" implied here, but it never surfaces in the text.

The singular "i," altered from the quoted figure of the epigraph yet equally perhaps a figure of quotation, appears in the first extended passage of *The Martyrology*, which is in fact a fragment of what might be a much larger work, "*The Chronicle of Knarn.*" The first line, "i've looked across the stars to find your eyes," appears to identify this "i" as an archetypically romantic poet, but the science fictional signifiers of the text[2] soon insist upon a reading in which such apparently symbolic statements must be taken literally. What the writer has done with this fiction is to fictionalize himself. On one level, for at least the first two books and perhaps through the whole long poem, we have to read every apparent reference through "i" to "the real bpNichol" as fictional, merely an allusion to this poet of Knarn who writes long "after the fantasy that is north america crumbles"(*Book* 2 "friends as footnotes"). And, even though this text is never opened again, occasional references to it, as in *Book* 3:V, will serve to remind readers that it stands almost at the beginning, one of the gateways to the larger text which is *The Martyrology* itself.

If this "i" of Knarn is speaking from a science fictional world, he is, nevertheless, a rather sentimental romantic poet calling out after a lost "you" to whom he speaks of "them," the saints whom he cares less about than he does for his lost lover.

> > i'm holding my hat in my hand
> standing awkwardly at the entrance to their shrine
> wishing i were near you

> were they like us? i don't know.
>
> how did they die & how did the legend grow?
>
> (a long time ago i thot i knew how this poem would go, how the
> figures of the saints would emerge. now it's covered over by
> my urge to write you what lines i can. the sun is dying. i've
> heard them say it will go nova before the year's end. i wanted
> to send you this letter (this poem) but now it's too late to
> say anything, too early to have anything to send.)
>
> i wish i could scream your name & you could hear me
> out there somewhere where our lives are

So much of the rest of this long poem is implicated in this passage. The "i" is slippery indeed as it resolutely keeps to the other world of the Knarnian fiction while simultaneously pointing to the two Books of *The Martyrology* which follow. And this reader, at least, cannot help reading the final couplet as both a lost lover's cry and the desperate desire of the writer to *speak* directly to his audience "out there" beyond the confines of the text. Yet, as he then says, "the language i write is no longer spoken," so that even within the fiction writing is the primary form that what he later calls "speech / eech to / each" takes. Thus, both "i" and "you" are multiple signifiers from the very beginning, and they continue to act as such every time they appear.

Inside *Book 1*, but before the first section of it, there is a short lyric epigraph:

> the breath lies
> on mornings like this
> you gotta be careful
> which way you piss

Here the personal pronoun partly signifies the generalized "i" who speaks from experience, yet also serves as the "you" of warning; the poem recalls and foretells simultaneously. The first line also announces from the very beginning the poem's deep duplicity.

Finally, after so many tentative beginnings, the first of the titled sections concerning the saints themselves begins. *Books 1* and *2* quote a number of excerpts from various fictional texts[3] concerning the saints as epigraphs to individual sections of the poem; the major fictional text quoted is titled "The Folk Tales of the Saints." These texts use either the passive voice or the scholarly "we," and, as Scobie has suggested, they are one of the ways by which *The Martyrology* grounds its epic explorations in a posited mythology (1984, 111-117), a mythology which differs from those of earlier epic poems only in the fact that it is private rather than public. One such epigraph heads "The Martyrology of Saint And." In the poem itself, the first pronoun is a "you" signifying "i": "you promise yourself / you won't start there / again." The next line is a date, followed by a statement in the passive voice, reflecting the writer's passivity before the vagaries of the writing: will it be found or forgotten?

Only on the second page does "i" finally speak, identifying itself with a particular "you," Saint And: "i've looked out your eyes years now saint and." The next few lines then show how the poem actually works: "How / i tell you / no // things / cannot / measure thee." Although "things" will fail to "measure thee" (and that archaic singular second-person pronoun clearly suggests the saints' transcendence, linguistically and spiritually), it's by looking "out your eyes" that "i" will "tell you" to those who read this text (who are also possible referents for the pronoun). And, like the telling of beads, this telling is a kind of measurement, the only kind that poetry as an art of measure can make. The poem continues to speak of Saint And and "you" while presenting him in the circus-clown context that points to his foolishness throughout the poem. But it suddenly distances And with a shift to the third person, then moves back to the second, back into the third for a page, and then introduces another "you": "lady lady have you met saint and?" This new "you" is connected to "him," but a sudden slippage establishes the speaker's "i" wholly behind And's eyes as the lady enters And's circus world:

slim lady   lady of light   lady who is not

i've lost my head (better off dead)   rides
are still two
for a quarter

As the narrative proceeds, the sad tales of And's romantic life will emerge, but here it's already obvious that this "saint of connections" (Scobie 1984, 115) is a figure the writerly "i" can too easily identify with. The next few pages present And's life in the circus, until he enters his dressing room, where "he rests his head in his hands & doesn't care." The text then offers another "largely unforegrounded moral generalization" (Davey 234):

despair

is not   an ocean

it is a sea you walk upon till your feet are sore

This is both a warning to every "you" (i.e., Saint And and all readers, too) and a generalization of "my" experience. The following page foregrounds this "you" again, who seems more likely to be Saint And than "us" except that the text returns to him in the third person for a couple of pages. Suddenly an other "voice" interrupts the narrative:

close the door

i didn't open my mouth

(saint and measures the levels of the moon

his spoon is full)

all questions become rhetorical if the pose holds

I TOLD HIM DIFFERENT

how can you
write the news if you
won't listen

This page (and both Nichol and various critics have pointed out how the page is a unit of measurement in *The Martyrology*) offers one of the best early examples of multiple voicing in the poem. The first line erupts from another level of text than the narrative "we" has been following. The "i" responding to the italicized order appears to be the writer, yet this isn't certain. The aside concerning Saint And seems to be an attempt to return to that narrative, but the following "cry" (by which possible "i"?) suggests other possibilities. Finally, the text proposes a "you" which is on one level the "i", on another any addressee of the poem, and still, possibly, Saint And, who may, on the following page, be the "i" who speaks a Zen-like koan of potential failure.

But what appears to be the same "i" then speaks to his "lady" on the following page, and of And as someone "without understanding," who "falls through the many levels of / *this room*." "This room" could be both the writing space and the written space, that is the text itself, which is, as the example of the pronouns shows, made up of many levels, indeed. The following page tells more of the circus ("old & jaded"), of And's aging, and of how "the major notes are lost in minor movements," where the passive voice again suggests the writer's refusal of "control." But a "man," previously unmentioned, enters, who "knows only the leaves / or the ghost / of saint and's mourning." The syntax nicely registers the ambiguity sought here: is Saint And the mourner or the mourned? All this may be occurring on "another world vaguely seen"; but here "*you* stand on this side & look up   way up" into an air "the colour of saint and's hair" to see the circus disappearing and the hills turning red "*if* you ever cross over." That "if" occurs in the final line of this first section of *Book 1*, and puts everything into question, thus suspending even aspects of textuality itself throughout the ongoing poem. Here, for example, the "you" is wholly open again: it could be "i," it could be some new figure in the poem, or it could be "us," invited, once again, to enter the text and participate in the multiple narrative the poem constantly apprehends.

If the play of the pronouns in "The Martyrology of Saint And" is complex, it gets even more complicated in the volume's following sections. "Scenes from the Lives of the Saints" is exactly that, and deals, in order, with Saint Reat, Saint Ranglehold, and the story of Reat's romance with Saint Agnes. The first epigraph suggests Reat is connected with the act of writing the poem we are reading: he is "a sort of latter-day muse, a saint of speech & song," yet he is also "unknown." Nevertheless, the writer addresses him directly in the first line, and though there is no "i" in the text, it is implied by the phrase "these halls" which, with its lack of antecedent, suggests the writer is there with Reat. At the end of the page, the line "a screaming only you can hear" appears to refer to Reat, but also floats free of specific referentiality.

The following page opens with an even deeper non-referential writing which denies the "i" any space at all:

> reach infinitely
> no sky towards which
> columns the saints pass between

This carries on to the next page until the poem refers to itself, at which point it also addresses Reat again, after which the writer enters once more to demand Reat's attention and complain at his recalcitrance: "you won't come back at me out of the poem." The "i" then adds: "if i say 'hunger' / will they call it a figure of speech" (where "they" might be the readers, or the saints), and goes on to complain romantically either for himself or for Reat (either could be speaking). The next page begins with "dedicate the poem to a whim," a statement of purpose or an exhortation to an other. The following line, "His mercy," introduces an unnamed figure, though "*He* was always telling *me*" what to do. The text then slides back to Reat as "you" but, after complaining about other saints, it addresses them all in the plural, while introducing a series of demonstratives lacking antecedents which turn the whole project in on itself.

The section on Ranglehold follows, at first dealing with him at a distance afforded by the third person. Here the poem begins mixing what we might call pop mythology (Dick Tracy, Emma Peel) with the invented mythology of the saints; it also calls attention to what it's doing. The "i" insists on being heard, addressing Ranglehold directly ("you've got me by the balls & won't let go"); but this text never allows such personal speech to go on for more than a few lines at a time, so it indicates how it alters that kind of direct speech, often from line to line: "followed immediately / by another   pitch variation." The next five lines contain four more such variations, one of which returns to the hortative, yet seems addressed to the "i" in its guise as "you." And that "you" becomes even more multiplicitous a few lines later: "were there a heaven / who would you place there heavenly angels?" The syntactic ambiguity here is simultaneously vague and precise: the "you" can be the angels, can be Ranglehold, can be the self-referential writer, can even be the reader; and the "who" has its own various possibilities. No wonder the "i" thinks it writes upon a "dear funny paper," for things are "funny" indeed in this linguistic universe where no pronoun stands still long enough to be attached to any single figure. And so it's no surprise to find that the final "you" of this section is the plural "you" addressing "sam & dick & emma peel," those figures of another mythology, which is partly to be read in the funny papers.

   The epigraph to the next section mentions that the romance between Reat and Agnes "is one of the most delightful interludes in the otherwise sombre story of the saints," and adds that it has "given us our only real glimpse into their questionable humanity." This "us" could be the putative scholars, but it could as easily be the writer and his readers, sharing the myths in which this long poem roots itself. While the latter "us" appears to be inscribed in the first few lines, a turn of the page reveals that the "us" referred to could, in fact, be Reat and Agnes, for there Agnes appears as "you" to a speaking "i" who should be Reat: "saint agnes / you were the best thing to happen to a guy." Still, even though "you taught me how to cry," this reading isn't necessarily the only one: the writer, caught up in the story he is reciting, could be the one learning here. And on the next page, clearly the writer addresses Agnes as "you," begging her to help Reat. An often quoted passage of *Book 1* follows:

suddenly it makes sense. is it the poem makes us dense?
or simply writing, the act of ordering
the other mind
              blinding us
to the greater vision
                what's a

poem like you doing in a
poem like this?

Each one of the pronouns in this passage does at least double duty. The "us" could be the figures in the poem, the writer and his writing, the writer as a member of a species, the writer and reader collaborating, and all involve that "other mind" which blinds the "us" "to the greater vision" of the poem, or of the poem's transcendent ground. The punning rewrite of a famous vaudeville joke reminds us once again of the duplicities of poetic language and of the structure of the palimpsestic text we are reading. The next line, first line of the last page of the section, again resists placement: "may you be laid to rest in Shanghalla / someday." As Ranglehold appears in apposition a line further on, the "you" may address him, but equally it can refer back to "the poem" and, as it is on a separate line, it might be aimed at "us," the readers, inviting us into the mythic space the poem keeps implying it inhabits. Whatever, after asking some direct questions of Saint Ranglehold and Saint And, the text's "i" again complains about his work, then prays to some pop myth figures before admitting "all these myths confuse me," and begging Shanghalla (is it person or place?) to "take them away," whether to safety or simply out of his confused mind is deliberately left open.

The title of the next part, "The Sorrows of Saint Orm," raises expectations of a narrative about its eponymous mythic character. Yet it begins with a lyric cry from an "i" to "my lady." Although this "i" could be Orm, it rapidly shifts to an "i" who speaks of holding "your body" and prays to Saint Orm to "keep her from harm." This speedy syntactic alteration continues on the following page:

saint orm you were a stranger
came to me out of the dangerous alleys &
the streets

      lived in
that dirty room on
comox avenue

                    me &

    my friends

                    playing what lives we had to
    the end

            i want to tell you a story
    in the old way

                    i can't

Orm could be the one living on Comox, but so are "me & / my friends."
The line break of the next line is also ambiguous in its implications (and
that "had to," its sense of fate, will reenter the text many times in the
future of the poem). But this "i," who now seems to be the figure of the
writer, suddenly acquires layers of possibility: he continues to address
Orm, confessing his failure, but also clearly addresses "us," the readers,
and, as the statement "& this circus   this noise in / my brain" suggests,
he could also be Saint And, calling out to his fellow saint.

    The next page shifts again, offering a kind of explanation of the
saints' origins in the mythic cosmologies of a child (whom "we" are invited to identify with the writer). A page further, a generalized question,
"how do you tell a story?" moves to a specific addressee, Orm, and
beyond that to a statement about Orm, in the second person, which suddenly includes the "i" with him as a part of a "we" which needs the
knowledge of "REVELATIONS," then back to a personal speech which tells
"us" that that "you" which is Orm "told me the difference between now
& then." The next page is a prayer to Orm to "bring my lady / back" from
a stormy sea "to / my arms," followed by a lyric epigraph of namings and
a description of the lady to Orm, but also, of course, to the reader over-
looking these personal correspondences.

    Now the text returns to the real life situation on Comox, with specif-
ic references to "barb & dave" and the pain of "being part of history." But
the pronouns continue to float free of specific references: "you told me not
to mention it & dave did." This "you" is impossible to pin down: it could
be Orm, could be Barb, could be someone else, and the poem never says
what "dave did." Yet the text insists that Orm, as "you," is "the grey we

passed thru," almost an experience "we" shared, but is also "that pilot i took on board" when "i" "didn't know what to do." The text is entirely self-conscious about the symbolic and cliché aspects of the ship image here; it suits the self-pity of the "i" at this point, which is both deeply felt and ironically distanced. One line in particular points specifically to the deceptive nature of the text's pronominal play: "lost in the absence of being where everyone assumed me not to be," the writer is "lying as i knew would fit / their worries." Not "*our* worries," though he has placed himself among them in the earlier use of "we" for himself and his friends; rather, because of the lies, because of the writing, he finds himself outside the community he once felt he was inside. In this passage, the shifts of pronominal address provide a clear vision of how they enact the problems of writing which the poem continues to explore in later volumes.

The following page again addresses Orm, and registers some of the difficulties of the writing process before offering an image of the writer as onlooker, who "watched the clouds climb / out of your head & / lost you." This losing will become an underlying theme of *Books* 2 and 3, and will recur throughout the poem, as will the rediscoveries which the poem (and the poet) cannot yet know will happen. But for the moment it is a sign that "i shall / return again to you," an open address (is "you" the saints, the friends, the readers?) before the stanza break to "my lady." On the next page, after another epigraphic image of loss in the sky where the saints are supposed to dwell, "i" writes of "my lady" in the third person, in a traditional lyric address to "you" (both Orm and the readers) describing her beauty and loving powers. But it is only a lyric moment and cannot last, for the "i" returns to what is lost: "notes in my journals" and the relationships of the past this whole section has kept circling without quite being able to enter. Now the writer will try again, praying to Orm for help: "saint orm i need the rage to lead   drive my hand // tenderness / carry it to the end." What he can tell is this:

nights that run together on the bed

you fill yourself with someone else's loneliness

i've had enough of my own

only thing i wanted to do
somehow bring them with me into something better

always thot would happen
we'd remain as friends
ended those months on comox

boxed with faded photos
somewhere in the corners of these rooms

The "you" here is generalized, a version of "i" that we may all identify with, until the next line contradicts that reading. The text then goes on to present the writer's desires, and their failure. The first line of the next page reiterates the ambiguity of reference: "opened & told them." Is "i" opening himself and telling Barb and Dave what he now knows or is he opening the boxes of photos to tell them the way people tell a Tarot pack, for example? When he says, "saint orm these are far shores you carry me to," has Orm become the muse the text earlier marked Reat as? Whatever, "i" does tell of Barb and Dave's separation, and his own restlessness, which leads to another comment on the process of making the poem: "funny the way / the thots break." Finally, he invokes the saints, possibly Orm, or just the power to write ("it is a voice   a presence close to sleep / speaks from that too familiar world") before promising his lady to return even though "these worlds burn" and "i cannot stop the flow // single vibratory wave that goes   back / into all history." But these lines return both writer and reader to Knarn, and thus reiterate the always potential fictional quality of narrator and narration. And there this first section to deal with the real life of the writer leaves us.

If "The Sorrows of Saint Orm" refused to narrate Orm's tale, "Saint Reat and the Four Winds of the World" does a much better job with its titular figure's quest. Still, rather than simply place the tale in the third person, the "i" continues to shift in and out of the story, sometimes identified with Reat, sometimes speaking to him; the focus of the pronouns remains ambiguous, continuing to keep the reader off balance and engaged.

The epigraph tells us that Reat was sent to find "the origins of all breath," and thus the section begins:

stirred the leaves are
come to this land

sounds we walked in
before the last death visited the world

The opening lines are unfocussed, anyone could be speaking, but the "we" which follows would appear to be either the saints or some figures from Knarn, unless "last" simply means the latest, in which case it could still be anyone, but is likely the writer. The next line, "(weary walking to you)," appears to clarify the situation: "you" is probably Reat; but the parenthesis could also be Reat speaking of the travail of reaching the goal of his quest. So reference is still up in the air, and is not simplified by "i do know you" which seems to float both "i" and "you" free of specific reference, though "we" will likely try to place them in terms of our read-ing of the previous sections. If "how you dwelt in that place filled with questions / the rest (written in a book) destroyed my childhood" seems to imply that "you" is indeed Reat and "i" is the writer, the final couplet throws everything up in the air once again. The line break, on "drifting focusless twist of speech i / you reach towards saint reat," becomes a site of any number of possibilities, including the reader, as co-producer of whatever story, let alone whatever meaning, the text is generating.

The next page offers autumn imagery, plus this admonition: "bite into your arm / stop the pain / again & again." If we follow the title's invi-tation, this "you" is Reat, who has begun his lonely quest. But what then does the series of namings on the following page refer to? Possibly all the terms are only alternate ways of saying the final one, "'loon'"; neverthe-less, the passage exemplifies how words only have significance in relation to other words. In apparent response to the nightmare imagery of the list, someone feels the "moments the eyes ache / not from seeing:" a turn of phrase which implies an "i" speaking. But the narrative voice, having removed to the distance of the third person, returns in italics to a personal cry, *"wind home / how shall i reach you with all speech gone,"* before coming all the way back to the impersonal first person implications of the first line in "the moving pattern of / the eye's lid." None of this holds still, even for a single reading; the personal cry, especially, would appear to be Reat's, but for the fact that the writer has, in a sense, been trying to reach "wind home" (which might also be "cloudtown") all through *Book 1*.

The pronominal indeterminacy so firmly established continues. The writer may accept or question Reat's suffering, as when he questions the traditional metaphor, "& when you fell in love you died," and spends a page analyzing it in terms of "the image i read in a poem / years ago." "i speak lip tongue / no throat" may inscribe the loss of speech, but it's not clear whose when "never learned to dance to / my voice // sing // praises // rejoice," seems another fitting overlap of Reat and the writer. He may continue what appears to be Reat's tale. The text neatly recapitulates the ikons of a heroic quest, yet it also turns them all to the service of a poem about language and silence. The actual encounter is presented as a series of questions which lead to a putative conclusion, in which "you" apparently refers to Reat, but could refer to the writer as well: "it was the end of that phase of being // you dreamt // woke without knowing what the dream meant." At which point, the adventure leaves off and the text begins to explore the earlier lives of the saints, in a passage addressed to Saint Reat: "saint reat this is all a dream / you could've seen if you'd stopped to think." With an allusion to Knarn, the writer reminds Reat of how he left Saint Agnes and of how the other saints behaved. He returns to Reat, however, and keeps addressing him in the second person while recounting the deaths of "these other saints / ump & rap," the encounter with "a saint named aggers," and the love and compassion Agnes gave him. A parenthetical passage, separated from the others, and lacking any names, containing only the pronouns "she," "you," and "they," yet it seems to hold to the story, thus allowing for the possibility that it refers to something in the writer's own experience. This possibility is reinforced when the "i" confesses, "i get lost." The poem then returns to the free flow of the whole text, loosening its hold on the singular story of Reat's quest, but never completely.

There's lots of slippage here, leading to the moment an implied "i" writes both that "this is a love poem" and that "i" "wrote it on the long road," which neatly folds Reat and the writer into one.

This doubled "i" then becomes a doubled "you," as the story seems to carry on but a memory of "your" childhood again insists that "you" could be both Reat and the writer. The "old man" who "told you his name was raits" responds to "your" questions with a pure Zen action, a sign to be read but no explanation. At this point, writer and muse are fused, yet a reference to "the rim worlds" pulls the "you" toward the figure the writer presented in "*The Chronicle of Knarn*," only to then turn the "you" back into Reat, being questioned by a writer capable of making bald statements about birth and death. The final few pages keep that "you" in play, tying up the threads of the narrative implied by the title and epigraph to this section. At which point the "i" addresses Reat directly one last time:

saint reat this is all nothing

do you understand?

there are no myths we have not created
ripped whole from our lived long days

no legends that could not be lies

you were simply a man
suffered the pain of silence in your head

let your sounds lead you out of that dead time

were made a saint
for lack of any other way of praising you

But even this is duplicitous: the "you" of the second line is Reat, all right, but it is "us" as well; and the "we" could be the community of saints telling their tale as much as it could be the community of poets telling theirs (a possibility that will take on weight in the later books of the poem). This means that the "you" of the following couplet could also be the "i" writing, the poet who has somehow managed to escape "that dead time" of "the pain of silence" into the act of creating the poem we have been reading. The final couplet does return to Reat, and supports a reading of "you" as him but isn't strong enough to insist upon it. This section of *Book 1* remains as open as the rest.

※※

As its imagery and syntax continuously demonstrate, *The Martyrology* is a text of Heraclitean flux and transformation from the very beginning. Although the text and its implied author do not address the theoretical questions such a processual writing raises until later, the writing confronts their possibilities. The play of the "i"s is but one of the many ways in which this text interrogates singular readings, and my rather laboured examination of that ludic interrogation may seem to many readers to be too drawn out and picky. I can only argue that *The Martyrology* has achieved a solid enough reputation that the kinds of critical generalizations which I and other critics have made concerning its various dimensions, all of which I believe to be valid, now require the kind of close analytical backing which this partial reading of *Book 1* has tried to provide. It seems clear to me that such a reading demonstrates how fully polyvalent *The Martyrology* has been from its inception. Similar readings of the later Books will only bear this out, whether they are made in terms of the text's handling of pronouns, or in terms of any of the other problematic activities which such a continuing and multiplex program necessarily inscribes.

ENDNOTES

[1] *The Martyrology* is unpaginated; as opposed to dated references elsewhere, all references to it will be in terms of Book number, and, where possible, to sections of Books.

[2] See the references to "stellar banks," "inter-galactic crowds," "the sun is dying," etc.

[3] These quotations appear to have been taken from a scholarly text, but that text is either a fictional work previously written by Nichol or invented on the spot. In either case, it is only a possible text, and does not, for readers, exist outside *The Martyrology*.

The Poetry of E.D. Blodgett

"Not one of any word that floats / upon my breath is mine"

"Blodgett's poems bear witness," says Paul Hjartarson in his Introduction to *Da Capo*. "They speak the incessant pain, the weight of loss, the density of absence" (xii), but "they also sound the hope, the promise that can temper despair and enable us to speak the future tense" (xiii). On the back cover of *Arché/Elegies*, D.G. Jones calls the poems therein "civil elegies," and then calls the whole book "a post-structuralist pastoral lament." In a similar vein, Robin Blaser writes that *Musical Offering*, "posed as it is in thoughtfulness of silence and absence," is a work belonging "to a tradition of larger concerns: I think of Rilke and Mallarmé" (back cover). The book is, he says, "an *ecstasis*, contrapuntal and startling—Bach-like in its care, both an offering and a *passacaglia*." These terms, and others like them in various reviews, point readers to one end of the spectrum of Blodgett's poetry, its elegiac meditation on what's lost, the absences that surround us in the world and in its words. But other readers might find something supplementing that, and not just in his latest volume. If there is darkness in his poems, there is also light. If there is loss, there is also a finding, the act of which is the writing act, an act also of love. One could read the poems of the Governor General's Award winning *Apostrophes: woman at a piano* (1996), as something new in his oeuvre, love poems to the world and to a beloved, but this tendency has always been present in his work, albeit intermingled with the elegiac strain. Like Phyllis Webb's, his poems articulate an awareness that all his "desire goes / out to the impossibly / beautiful" (Webb 1982, 101).

In the beginning, a purity of diction. And, as we see in the first poem in the first book, *Take Away the Names*, also a desire to achieve that purity. That desire has not abated however much the rhetorical complexity of his poems has increased. As Blodgett told Rob Dunham in "A Sentence Like A

Snake," "I wanted to know what the words were that I could use. So I deliberately restrained the vocabulary. But one of the marvels of the limited vocabulary is that, although the same word is repeated in a different context, it begins to change its own signifying function and therefore it begins to make the world increasingly more elusive" (28). That elusiveness, together with the elegiac mood it fosters, has been a constant in Blodgett's poetic. Thus, although early poems like "Language" might seem at first similar to those of the Imagists—

> the bird
> has left
> my tongue
>
> the tree
> is bare
> of birds
>
> my tongue
> is the tree
> stripped
>
> it speaks (1990, 52)

—the program is different. Not the sharpness of image as such but a purity of statement, of enunciation: the tongue, stripped bare.

Ricou ruefully admits that Blodgett's poetry "is unforgivingly polylingual and allusive and demands a reading capacious as the man who wrote it" (1990, 29). Perhaps. Blodgett is uniquely fitted to write a new kind of postmodern poetry, one that owes as much to medieval lyric poets as it does to such different modernist masters as Rilke and Stevens, Mallarmé and Pound and Williams. Many of his readers will be unable to match such learning and such mastery of languages, yet they can, and are meant to, discover beauty and substance in his poems. Still, the point is well taken. Although Perloff has provocatively inquired of contemporary North American English poetry whether the era belongs to Pound or Stevens, quite rightly pointing out that each poet has offered his successors very different gifts (1985, 1-32), it seems Blodgett has evaded this particular oppositional controversy by the simple expedient of constructing his poetic from a much wider range of possibilities, including continental ones stretching all the way back to the Troubadours (if not the Roman and Greek masters) and up to the savage silencings of Paul Celan and beyond. His training in Comparative Literature has allowed him these choices; making them has broadened his poetic reach. That he also has learned from the North American masters seems equally clear, but his palimpsestic borrowings make it difficult to place him in any single line of poetic inheritance. This has perhaps had the effect of isolating him and his work. Certainly, he has not received the kind of critical attention his poetry deserves, yet a number of very different poets and critics have expressed their admiration for his work over the years, including D.G. Jones and Robin Blaser, names not usually found in the same sentence. A demanding poetic, a poetry that insists its readers come to it asking, as Phyllis Webb would put it, will not achieve instant or widespread popularity.

The poems of *Take Away the Names* especially look essentially post-Imagist in form, and sound a lot like something a poet in the Pound-Williams tradition might have written. Yet, as Blodgett himself points out, there is something else going on in them too. In response to Dunham's remark that the significance of repeated words in the volume "becomes hallucinatory. And the poems, instead of conjoining, begin to evade one another, and one feels that one is in a maelstrom of words," he responds:

> The only other poets I know of who used to do this are
> medieval lyric poets, and it's become apparent to modern
> critics that even that limited vocabulary is very deceptive.
> There's a constant sliding from denotation to connotation
> with the same word, because the form of the poem con-

tinually modifies the weight of the word. This is particularly true in old Provencal love songs, when the poets got
very, very adept at what they were doing, particularly
Arnaut Daniel. He would constantly "file off" the word,
and then let it slip into another possibility. (28)

Even as later books would investigate more complex situations, the art of
Van Gogh, the *esse* of animals, and the archeologies and archival longings
of becoming and being Canadian among other possibilities, Blodgett
would never forget that early lesson of "filing off" words. One of the central pleasures of his poetry is its indeterminacies, and that is another way
by which he can be read as convincingly, if eccentrically, belonging to the
tradition that runs from Rimbaud through Pound to such postmodern
poets as John Ashbery. The poems refuse to close partly because their
words refuse to stay in place. Repeated so often they lose any sense of
conventional representation.

The rhetoric of Blodgett's poems becomes increasingly complex. Since
Take Away the Names, where the fragment appears to be the main syntactical unit,[1] the sentence of apparent commentary or interrogation has
become the core syntax of the later poetry. But it is a sentence that cannot
seem to reach its own conclusion. As Blodgett tells Dunham, "The sentence, which is what I'm really trying to play with, moves through auditory changes to arrive where it must. Its logic belongs to the auditory
change that goes on as it is elaborated. The real work in these poems was
learning how to write a sentence, and then learning how the sentence is
self-conscious—a sentence that is thinking itself as it unfolds. It's almost
like a snake—a sentence like a snake" (29). But what do these sentences
do? In "O Canada," for example, they seem to express an argument, yet
in their very unfolding of that argument they create gaps that finally
undermine the possibility that the sentence can sustain anything like an
argument at all:

    . . . In this field the simplest words

deceive most: I want to say *the*,
but how do I stand to know where all that
finitude would rise, so precise
it stands, early winter unseen before,

a winter where *a-a-a* is no trick
of light, no dullness of lemons un-
remembered, no rot of small towns
choking air, but one beast of no
name, calling, untrapped by myth,
at large in absence of apocalypse,

standing over Saskatchewan its roads
stretching north to locate, to get lost,
to start decaying at four in the afternoon,
the year now forgotten, standing within
the space of lost heart and dead end,
calling, a merest *the* in an autumn of sighs,

wind in the small towns blowing, my arms
become tangents, and snow as space falling,
infinite end of seasons striking the void
of somewhere saying *a*, Lucretian sound
of snow intact. (1990, 146-47)

But, if anything was intact when that sentence began, all is loose and
flowing, falling, by the end. There is nowhere in this sentence to stand,
one of the words it so artfully demolishes in its incessant repetitions. But
then, it's about the way sounds, let alone complete words, slip from our
grasp, even in the attempt to speak a love of country, to say its name. We
read this snaky sentence with a wry delight, following its twists and turns
with pleasure but feeling meaning slide away with every turn of a line.
And as we watch a sentence defoliate through carefully crafted rhythmic
lines, we hear a lyric querulously turned against itself, another version of
lyric/anti-lyric.

The ostensible themes of Blodgett's later work may alter but this play
with the sentence, a complex and insistent confusion that syntax under

pressure yields, remains constant no matter what form the poems take, from the run-on, formally different sections of such poems as "Fire Music" to the carefully formal stanzas of recent poems. As he puts it in "Dickinson's Dash":

> For the act of poetry is not to name, but to articulate, as it edges from word to word in the course of the verse's evocation, the world's change and metamorphosis. Why the line, why the verse, which is the entelechy of the poem? Because the line does not conclude—it reaches the silence that it wishes to discover. It appears to end in a kind of failure, only to resume in a new line. It deliberately misses definition for the turn and the return, the incarnation of the trope, turning against the silence in its surprising, Lucretian swerve. (33)

A quick glance at any of the poems in *Apostrophes* will reveal how fully he continues to explore such turns and returns, not only in the repetitions of certain key words throughout the book, but in the cadenced syntax of the long lines always swerving back upon each other.

In "O Canada," as in other poems of *Arché/Elegies*, a profound irony emerges in the paradox that this learned poet, a master of poetry's European past should choose to write (in) Canada, the "empty" country of "a few acres of snow." Or perhaps not: the poems of *Arché/Elegies* admit what the poems of such great predecessors as F.R. Scott did not: that "perhaps this happened once in Cree" (8), and many other languages too. Blodgett emigrated to Canada from the United States, and he chose to become a Canadian citizen. Not coming upon Canadian culture until his maturity, he worked hard to discover a place for himself in the traditions of Canadian poetry too. He quotes Scott in an epigraph to *Arché/Elegies*, and he has written eloquently of some other Canadian poets. He knows Québec literature better than do most English Canadians. All of which means he understands the politics of this country, and of its culture(s). In an important manner, his multilinguism becomes a form of multiculturism, and, to that degree, his poetics is a politics, as his scholarly and poetic collaborations with Québecois writers attest.[2] Yet, he is wary of political or didactic art, and does not seek to turn his poetry into propaganda.[3] Instead, as the poems of *Arché/Elegies* demonstrate, he is interested in exploring possibilities: what languages speak this place, or spoke it? if the artists (the Tom Thomson he questions in "North," for example) are explorers, are the explorers (the Henry Kelsey of "Explorer," among others) not artists? Or, the great question he asks in the "Postscript," which echoes through all the later books, as I have already intimated:

> Is there, and should it be asked, a Canadian sentence, and how long would it last? No end in sight, it is the sentence of endless arrivals and endless elusion, the sentence that cannot end, always condemned to seek itself without recognition, the sentence that laments its own losing. What else can it do but leave itself forgotten in its own track, speaking to itself of itself, its first word already calling what is to come, and calling whatever follows back. The Canadian sentence is shaped to resume, yielding forever to the illusion of beginning, continually passing through that place, an end in itself. (62)

The first poem of *Apostrophes*, "Woman at a Piano," has an intriguing relation to one of F.R. Scott's best known poems, "Overture." Both poems register a listener's response to the music made by someone admired, at least for that ability. Scott's poem is about how neither the music nor his personal connection to it is enough; his similes work as much to undermine the beauty of a "Mozart sonata" as to describe it: "The bright / Clear notes fly like sparks through the air / And trace a flickering pattern of music there" (87). This description of the ineffable is necessary because the music must be placed in order to be refused. The poem is about the failure of art in a politicized world. "But how shall I hear old music?" the speaker asks, and answers that he can't because he is too busy listening to "overtures of an era being born." The Mozart "seems a trinket on a shelf, / A pretty octave played before a window / Beyond whose curtain grows a world crescendo." Like many of Scott's poems, "Overture" serves an consciously chosen political end, that of socialist (r)evolution.

Blodgett's poem is after something else, and the first sign of this is its refusal to offer grand similes for music. Rather, the poem seeks something like the condition of music, a fugue-like returning upon itself in which various words or themes repeat with variations, slowly assuming a presence far more resonant than any single instance could achieve. Tone becomes colour, colour becomes sound, all in the service of "the musicality of words, words you must speak because of the sheer joy of feeling them within the mouth" (Blodgett 1987, 22). Rather than a politics here, there is an erotics, an attempt to bring the body to bear, as music does, in the moment of perception—of listening or touching, as the last stanza of the poem declares. Here, as music falls, as the air fills with colours, as words slip their reification without losing touch with the thingness of the world, the poem declares its purpose: to hold us within its own ritual of art. And it does this in another of those long sinuous sentences that stretch across stanzas, enacting colour's engagement with light, sound's engagement with silence, touch's engagement with body, and arriving at that ending which cannot really conclude but only proffer a profound desire that reaches beyond the poem: "birds within the rituals of music begin to rise within the long going away / of blue. The woman sits. I tell you this: I want to open my mouth becoming / blue, becoming the dark, leaning into stillness, touch touching touch" (7). Not politics then, but that *ecstasis* Robin Blaser pointed to, an upwelling of desire that can only be enunciated in poetry, something akin to Rilke's cries to angels, and for much the same purpose.

Another way to put this is to say that *Apostrophes: Woman at a Piano* is a lover's discourse, a serial work addressed to the beloved while carefully refusing to identify her (and I only say her because the title of the first poem identifies the subject of its attention as a "Woman at a

Piano"). These poems of friendship and love are also brilliantly realized late twentieth-century hymns to the muse. Moreover, they are luminous examinations of the conditional quality of pronouns, a deliberately post-structural if not postmodern concern. Like those sinuous sentences "of endless arrivals and endless elusion" (62) Blodgett spoke of to Dunham, the pronouns in Blodgett's poetry refuse to stay fixed. They are not refer-ential, at least not beyond fulfilling what one critic called "Benveniste's carefully non-committal definition" of them as words that perform "the present instance of discourse containing the linguistic instance" of their utterance (Scobie 1989, 131). Because we cannot identify the I, the you, or the we of these poems with any certainty, all is cast into doubt, or, more accurately, into chance. There is a voice, there is an utterance, a spe-cial tone, but the poem directs its energies beyond lyric to something more complex and satisfying than the simple expression of personal emotion. Yet the feeling of love is present throughout.

❧

On the back cover of *Apostrophes: Woman at a Piano*, Blaser writes of how the "imagery of these poems, apparently repetitious—roses, rain, trees, winds, flowers, sea, and lake—is constantly flowing, wherein one may not step twice," utilizing Heraclitus to register Stein's point about repetition. I would only add that it's not so much the images but the words themselves that become, with each repetition, just slightly more loosened from their moorings in representation. Such indeterminacy grows throughout each book, and, as Hjartarson points out, "Blodgett composes *books* of poetry, rather than occasional poems" (xxi), and has perhaps been composing a single, extended, book throughout his career. Thus the poems swing toward a strangely thickened music that issues somewhere between statement and abstraction, oblique, opaque, and always inviting a new reading.

❧

The major poems of *Musical Offering* take up the challenge laid down by Adorno's famous statement, "to write a poem after Auschwitz is barbar-ic." Of these "fugues," "Fire Music" is the most stringently plangent, an elegy for losses so profound they cannot truly be named. Yet, this music of suffering must be written. As Blodgett puts it in "Dickinson's Dash," if Adorno does not "mean that we must return to silence," then the question must be asked: "does it mean something more difficult to bear?" (28). That difficulty is history itself, perhaps, and Blodgett desires to escape the reification of even Auschwitz that a simple naming can lead to. There is a kind of poetry, not the standard lyric, that might try to engage history but must do so as fiction, the discourse of which "aims at a content which is true, but independent of the verifiable" (29). Fiction here does not necessarily refer to narrative; rather it suggests an imaginative act of empathy, a layered set of temporal transparencies providing a vision of all the possibilities. "Fire Music," for example, creates a site in which Gabriela Mistral, a Chilean poet, Bach, and the lost women of Goethe and Celan meet—in the fires that destroyed Dresden. They are there in the poem precisely because they were not there in history: that is the fiction. This conjunction is also the act of grace that elegy can perform. History is argument, and the writing of it full of arguments. Poetry may collaborate with history, but it serves different ends: mystery (not mystification) that remains mystery. "To say this moves poetry radically away from the history it completes to the place that only poetry can reach, within language but possessed of a certain fear of the transgression it wants to make" (1987, 31). Smoke and music and intertexts and names swirl through the fugal verses of "Fire Music": the poem a chorus of destruction and loss. Even an imported children's verse can sing of death alone: "*Asche, Asche*, all fall down" (1986, 88). But even as the poem registers the "fall / of flesh unmeasurable and unrecovered // gods, the dust of Yahweh sifting through / the air, music of silence, Dresden and Bach // that signal in the night" (92), it also says it *No*. And there is the mystery—that the poem can still say:

> o, see the moon within
> the sun spelled, fire
> music, air for winds and tympanum. (93)

An accomplished lutenist, Blodgett plays and sings the music of such composer-poets as Campion. So it is only fitting that so much of his poetry could be titled *"Musical Offering."* The music of language is one of its saving graces for the poet, but also one of its dangers: "the musicality of words, words you must speak because of the sheer joy of feeling them within the mouth" (1987, 22). Did Blodgett take up the lute because he needed to play music in order to resist the temptation to use words for their music alone? Seeking their mystery and truth as well, with the artist's discipline he creates a stringent as well as a plangent music in his poems. There is restraint because there must be. Yet there is beauty too, whether the poems confront the results of hatred or of love. Dresden and all it represents cannot be ignored, but the moment of two people, "surrendered wholly to the earth / turning through the air" (1996, 70) is all the more precious for that dark knowledge. So the poet has come to that moment, and in some of his finest poems he has celebrated it again and again in his book of love. He seems to have moved into a form, that of the continuing short pieces that make up the ongoing *Apostrophes* series, that allows for a life-long sequence. There is such a complex, multitextured music in the languages he hears, a music that "is flesh / possessing in its passing immortality, the longing of / the trees in their humility" (1999, 35). It is such a humility, before words, before the world, the poet continues to practice.

ENDNOTES

[1] Blodgett insists that in *Take Away the Names* he was concerned with prepositions as "the key syntactic figure. The preposition prevents metaphor from taking place or inhibits the role of metaphor" (Dunham 29).

[2] See, for example, his collaborative Renga sequence, in both English and French, *Transfigurations*, with Jacques Brault.

[3] The closest he comes, perhaps, is in some lines from "Song of Silences": "But Mozart, but Lorca each in one grave / lies, and no one knows its place, a grave / of infinite numbers of bones, of all / who stood wherever the wrong side was—pauper, poet, / peasant, soldier—all bone / and white and cold and dumb" (1986, 60). There's a hint here that it is the right choice to stand "wherever the wrong side was."

Reading Roy Kiyooka's
transcanadaletters

Each of Roy Kiyooka's books makes its own particular demands and provides its own particular textual pleasures. It took me awhile to understand that, but by the time *transcanadaletters* appeared, I had a much better sense of Kiyooka's restless and always changing approach than when I read *Nevertheless These Eyes* in 1967. One of those gorgeous little productions Coach House Press graced us with in those days, it was a book I did not fully appreciate at the time. But *StoneDGloveS* (1971), and the traveling show of *StoneDGloveS* photographs at the University of Alberta Students' Union Gallery made me appreciate the unique cross-disciplinary artistry he seems always to have practiced.

So I was eager to read *transcanadaletters* when that large (unpaginated) collection of letters, applications, photos, notes, etc. appeared in 1975. Rereading it, I realize that it provokes many more questions than I noticed at the time, questions about discourses at odds, about genre breakdown and transgression, about the power of what bpNichol called "borderblur." That it does so is one more reason to be grateful it exists, and to look forward to the later *Pacific Rim Letters*, an edited version of which is planned. Kiyooka kept challenging limits right to the end, and he does so throughout *transcanadaletters* in a way that keeps us caught up in both the life that they inscribe and the various ways such inscription breaks conventional decorum more to cancel the conventions than just to upset decorum. There is a sly and impudent mind represented here, but also one that demonstrates concern on a number of personal and artistic levels. These pieces ask a number of tough and renewing questions, questions which other writing continues to ask today, and to which there are perhaps no firm answers: are these poems that might be letters, letters that are also poems, or simply a mixture of poems and letters? How is a life lived in writing, when it is also a life of art—of the making and teaching of art—yet is then "talked about," written into the various missives to various persons and institutions? How much do we believe a life written out, to individuals in dated notations of time spent doing what is now being written, about? How do the shifts of recipients change the writer, the writing? That is, does the writer create a series of "selves" to "correspond with" the many others to whom he delivers these goods? I am not sure what the answers to such questions will be. Nevertheless, these "I"s have much in common, and they believe in a communicative world, in which they live and write.

It is that world, in all its waywardness, that *transcanadaletters* offers us a glimpse into, and it does so in a way that consistently keeps us off guard, aware that we might be reading personal correspondence but that we are also reading a carefully edited collection that looks a bit like any collection of poetry—only "a bit" because the size of the pages, the insert of photosheets, the dates and place names, all remind us of its possibility as a collection of letters and other documents. But, of course, letters have existed almost since writing began; letter-writing came into being because people quickly learned and desired to use writing to talk to others they could not speak to in person. According to Bruce Redford, Virginia Woolf called correspondence "'the humane art,' the art 'which owes its origins to the love of friends' and its texture to the primacy of a conversational paradigm . . . [for] the voice of the letter-writer 'makes distance, presence'" (2). Redford goes on to argue that "the eighteenth-century familiar letter, like the eighteenth-century conversation, is a performance—an 'act' in the theatrical sense as well as a 'speech-act' in the linguistic" (2). And he later points out that "[e]very writer on the subject emphasized the importance of following rules designed to achieve an ideal of 'Civility'" (3). Many treatises stressed "the importance of 'an expressive, genteel, and easy Manner,' to be attained by methodizing Nature" (4). The lack of such conventions in our own time, although they may still have had some power even in Woolf's, means that it is much more difficult to "read" let alone "write" letters. This difficulty haunts all collections of letters by people of the later twentieth-century. Still, because letters are always, on some level, and in Kiyooka's case, on a very conscious level, works of artifice, devices and conventions there will be. This desire to make distance presence still haunts us, and it certainly animated Kiyooka. What *transcanadaletters* argues is the necessary uniqueness of correspondence, which is why he would not have cared a fig for those eighteenth-century treatises on the proprieties of the epistolary art.

Like the letter itself, the verse letter, or verse epistle as *The New Princeton Encyclopedia of Poetry and Poetics* puts it, is a long established form. According to Roger Hornsby and T.V.F. Brogan, it is a "poem addressed to a friend, lover, or patron, written in a familiar style," and "may be found as early as 146 B.C." They further argue that of the two types, "one on moral and philosophical subjects, which stems from Horace," and the other "on romantic and sentimental subjects, which stems from Ovid" (1351), the former had the greater effect on such writing from the Renaissance to the modern period, and they point to Auden's *New Year Letter* and MacNeice's *Letters from Iceland* as examples. But those two names bring up something of a problem: they represent precisely the kind of poetry against which Kiyooka, like many of his fellow Canadian poets, turned in their search for a contemporary and North American poetic. On the other hand, if certain traditional formalities go by the wayside in *transcanadaletters*, the essential desire to address a poem-as-letter "to a friend, lover, or patron, written in a familiar style" remains foremost, as the quickest perusal of the opening pages of *transcanadaletters* will show. The very first letter is addressed, in fact, to the nearest thing to a patron Canadian artists and writers have; it is, as titled, "an Intermin [sic] Report for the Canada Council," and it goes on, in a delightfully eccentric familiar style, to argue the case for sending this Canuck of Japanese ancestry to his forebears' homeland, not least by means of the list of "works" from various times and cultures all over the world that are to be found there. Then, at the end, he appends this:

> *p o s s i b i l i t i e s*
> HERE
> (or, Anywhere
> no larger than Everyman's Vision -
> has it ever been more
> than this?
> ALL THINGS SWIRL

making for whats possible

HERE/NOW

If the rest of this particular epistle is indeterminate in generic shape, what about these lines? Do they not announce themselves as postmodern verse? But, if they do, do they also alter our perception of the whole letter? What they do announce is a central aspect of the poetics grounding everything in the book, as does the epigraph facing this first letter:

> "The business of art is to live in the complete actual
> present, that is the complete actual present, and to
> completely express that complete actual present."
> (Gertrude Stein).

But to carry out such expression, even in part, and in "letters," is somehow to align oneself with both traditions of the verse epistle. It is not surprising then to find throughout this large volume much that is "romantic and sentimental" alongside much that is even "philosophical and moral," albeit in a highly specific and personal way. No Horace, Kiyooka would not want to suggest, in some broad philosophical manner, how other people should live; that, too, is one of the pleasures offered by the particular personality represented in these pieces.

The question that persists is how to read these letters. Kiyooka provides a deliberately indeterminate view in his 28 March, 1972 letter to Phyllis Webb:

> if you arent gonna make copies of our correspondence . . .
> i guess i have to save all of your letters. i mean to go right on
> making carbons of mine—i aint got scruples abt literary pro-
> prieties and do want to keep some sort of a record of my own
> thots viz letters. besides letters are the only things i write
> sometimes and they happen to be written out of the same con-
> cern i wld bring to bear if i were writing something else.

But what are these "letters" of his, and how do or should we read them?

Though we can certainly read the book as a part of Kiyooka's poetic oeuvre, *transcanadaletters* becomes more complex and compelling if read as a challenge to any single generic reading. In *On the Margins of Discourse*, Barbara Herrnstein Smith, always a challenger of narrow definitions, perhaps creates a too solid bifurcation of what she calls "natural" and "fictive" discourses (15), in which letters remain firmly fixed in the area of "natural discourse" and poems in the area of "fictive discourse." In her terms, "the text of any poem is to be interpreted, in the first place, as . . . a score or stage directions for the performance of a purely verbal act that exists only in being thus performed" (31) while the "context of a fictive utterance . . . is understood to be *historically indeterminate*" (33). But she sees a letter as a "natural utterance" which is historically bound and "cannot be exclusively identified or described independent of its context" (21). If this is so, how are we to read not just the obvious poems scattered throughout *transcanadaletters* but the embedded section of a letter dated "Spring '69? / Montreal Quebec," which, as its title, "To a Young Painter who wld be a Teacher," and first few pages imply, is written in the grand tradition of the didactic epistle? But, following the "lecture," the verse section takes a different tack, purporting to quote one of his earlier poems, even as it re-writes it, changing the first few lines, many of the line breaks, and deleting some words. I would argue that he has improved the original, but those who don't have *Nevertheless These Eyes* would never know that. The poem addresses "Gaston Lachaise," not the young painter, but a sculptor "who sang her praises in bronze" and "made bronze sing her orifices." "The figure of Her in the poems," Kiyooka argues at the end of *Nevertheless These Eyes* (1967, np), is the goddess, and belongs to no one, although her dance and song are the gift every artist seeks. This sense of, and attitude toward, the muse emerges in the next few lines: "and Gaston, add this, her tears will wash / the dirt from any man's eyes." The first half of the poem, then, "frm Nevertheless, These Eyes,"

> sez it one way
> there are other ways of saying it
> including yours. she has
> afterall a multitudeof faces: each

face an act of recognition.

KEEP IN TOUCH (also sez it .

On one level, this appears to be an instance of re-citing, and so we can read the act of quotation as a literary imposition upon the "natural utterance" of a letter. But, Kiyooka doesn't just re-cite, he re-writes his earlier poem, and then adds the final lines, which continue the poetic movement of the (mis)quoted lines. Even though we could interpret the rest of the letter solely in terms of its inscribed historical context, as offering advice to someone who asked for it, this interruption invites a less determined reading. The shift that occurs between sections of the book, and which makes it a kind of anthology of "natural" and "fictive" discourses, here occurs inside a section, thus disturbing its generic solidity. This happens more than once in *transcanadaletters*, and is one of the reasons it keeps its readers off balance.

Redford recognizes the importance of Smith's arguments, but he feels she "manages to ignore the letter-writer's power to create a context as well as to reflect it. When the writer does both, the resulting artifact straddles the barrier between 'fictive' and 'natural' discourse, between 'verbal artwork' and 'event in nature.' . . . The letters of a master thereby escape from their origins as reservoirs of fact: coherence replaces correspondence as the primary standard of judgment" (9). Although he is writing about eighteenth-century letters and letter-writers, Redford offers three criteria for judging whether or not letters achieve fictive status: "autonomy, fertility, and versatility" (9). While Kiyooka's *transcanadaletters* may not meet these criteria in eighteenth-century terms, I would argue that it does exemplify them for a late-twentieth-century artist. And, in doing so, it joins Redford's examples of an epistolary art that evades the exclusivity of Smith's two categories. "Instead it turns on the complex interplay between the natural and the fictive—between reflection and creation, history 'outside' and artifice 'within'" (13). Redford wants to define the familiar letter too specifically as a separate genre, while I want to keep Kiyooka's multiplex form hovering between genres, on the border-line. Still, his main point definitely applies to *transcanadaletters*: "The peculiar richness of the genre results from this very ambiguity of status. Like the Japanese poetic diary, we might say, the letter is 'at once related to fact and freed by art'; like the diary it moves between two poles, the historical and the artistic" (13). Redford's reference to the Japanese poetic diary, *utanikki*, is highly suggestive in the context of *transcanadaletters*, for it is a form that has entered contemporary Canadian poetry in many ways.[2] One of the things that becomes clear as we read through *transcanadaletters* is the way it maps a possible autobiography, in part through the record it offers of the many travels of its writer-protagonist, as well as his changing family life. Earl Miner's point that the Japanese have a "less rigid sense of what fiction is" than we do, and therefore tend to deny "the assumption that a work is divorced from its author or its circumstances" (6) speaks to the "borderblur" qualities of *transcanadaletters*, and suggests both how duplicitous it is and how duplicitous we must be in reading it. As a Japanese Canadian, a modern artist who comprehends the value of some pretty ancient conventions in a post-modern context, Kiyooka has created a new form that slips easily between genres in *transcanadaletters*. A carefully edited autobiographical writing in letters that are not always just letters, it is also a collection of separate missives addressed to particular individuals and angencies through various "I"s who answer to Roy Kiyooka but who are also in part personae created for particular occasions, and particular recipients.

William Dowling writes of the eighteenth-century verse epistle as "a gesture toward community in a world where some pre-existing order is threatened with decline or disintegration. The sense of epistolary tradition invoked by eighteenth-century verse epistle is one that remains perpetually mindful of the moment of loss or absence in which the letter originates, the movement toward dispersal or fragmentation that makes necessary an attempt to reconstitute community in alternative terms. This is the context in which epistolarity then becomes so often associated with a sense of imperiled community against a background of cultural decline" (36). In the eighteenth century, this shared sense of community among the great verse-epistolarists was a conservative one; in the late twentieth century, a Canadian artist like Kiyooka's shared sense of community, while centred among other artists, was likely a complex mixture of the conservative and the radical. Nevertheless, one can see the series of letters from Kyoto as not only "mindful of the moment of loss or absence in which the letter originates," but also as "an attempt to reconstitute community in alternative terms." Although Kiyooka's letters address a variety of friends back home, and cover a wide range of topics, clearly chosen for a particular correspondent (see "12/ 10/ '69," the hilarious rendering of a Japanese porno film for Phyllis Webb, for example), as a group they enact a gathering of specific community in terms of his sense of communion and communication with them all. Equally, an early verse letter, "late Autumn on 57th Street, N.Y./Montreal . '67," "for Max and Charlotte Bates at / the other edge of the continent-" speaks from "the San Paolo Bienniale" and the art revolution in New York in a desire to battle for his own cultural community against all forces of what he saw as cultural decline. He can make the necessary connection between "the layers of tin hovels" wherever he might be, and that fact that "theres no [sic] much difference between Art News or / Le Devoir when it comes to silly art reviews . you pays / yr dues and git yr name list'd among / A/rtists A/nonymous." But even as he notices what advertising means, and what's to be seen "on the last train to Brooklyn," he also recalls the meeting together of artists:

> i danced at the Dome :
>
> Claude sd he had a gun pull'd on him there .
>
> Emil the manager of the George Washington Hotel sent
>
> congratulations . his japanese wife
>
> Barnett Newman, Pat Martin Bates, Edwin Dickinson
>
> and Tim Deverell all showed up .
>
> too bad we couldn't get drunk together
>
> at Max's Kansas City .

The poem ranges widely, from his desire that his children and their generation "be the measure of my acts" to his desire that a black/ white/ yellow/ red or/ green Godess [sic] wld

abide in me and show me the secret colour of Mud

colours

dont lie . . .

Since he is writing to friends and fellow artists, he can shift from art talk to politics, from reminiscence to "Libidinous Dreams," and all the time he is thinking art, as the piece's conclusion insists:

The Red Yellow and Blue 'stains' of Paradise
+
to eat/ sleep/ love/ work/ and sing
what else is there
Orpheus? i believe in my feelings when
i feel like 'a song'

    +

    V e r m i c e l l i

    M a x

    - - - - - - - - - -

    H o w s y r

    D a f f o d i l s

    C h a r l o t t e ?

This is only one of many pieces whose form clearly identifies them as poems in the book. Like the little concrete pieces like "O / light," the sequence of poems on his missing finger tip, such titled poems as "Pacific Rim / Wake," "Four Frames," and the lengthy "marginalia" "o f S e a s o n a l P l e a s u r e s / a n d S m a l l H i n d r a n c e s," it moves as projective verse is meant to move. Perhaps it is closer to that New York practitioner of the mode, Paul Blackburn, than to Charles Olson, yet it clearly expresses Kiyooka's proprioceptive stance: the visual artist as writer. From the colours of "tin hovels" and surf, the "selections from the definitive collection of Graffiti," to "High embankments of primary colours / The Red Yellow and Blue 'stains' of Paradise," he includes in the poem what he has seen. At the same time, he allows various discourses to enter into the poem, if only by sarcastic allusion, as in the references to numerous publications, to politics, to various forms of PR, and to different dreams of art. About art and its difficult and compromised place in the world the letter assumes a collaborative understanding from its recipients, fellow artists far away from the urban complexities Kiyooka addresses. As well, there is a sure tone here, one of sardonic and intelligent awareness, which surfaces in many of the other letters to fellow artists, in whatever field. But it is a mixed tone, for it also conveys the assumption of a shared desire—here expressed in the references to Magick, the God[d]ess, Paradise, and Orpheus—for the glimpses of the transcendent art offers. This letter *is* a poem. Or this poem is also a letter, for, although almost everything about it signals its sure generic stance, it is specifically addressed to the Bateses, fellow artists. It is, therefore, a perfect example of how Kiyooka plays between the natural and the fictive, laying his texts in that borderline territory between genres, within a book whose generic claims also confound expectations.

Kiyooka's writing manifests many other tones, as the letters to intimate friends, to family members, and, in their different way, to various people associated with galleries or granting agencies, show. Although he never writes a conventional business letter, he does gather facts, costs, outlines of proposed projects like the "H A L I F A X / V A N C O U V E R : E X C H A N G E" of 1972. By including the letters of application, the advertisements of the happenings, and various personal letters to participants, Kiyooka provides a representational glimpse of the event as it progressed from idea to possibility to actual occurrence, and he thereby provides a view of one aspect of his life at that time. Letters around these addressed to close friends and to his children and divorcing wife add to his complex and complicating self-portrait, a processual autobiography that seems to leave in all the warts. The shifts from one kind of document to another remind readers of their own complicated lives and how they live many different roles at once. The different "I"s talk across each other, forming an inchoate, fictional and factual, chorus that leaves the decision as to which is which up to the readers.

Certainly, in such letters as those to his daughters, or those to particular friends, he achieves an intimacy and empathic rapport that is often deeply moving. Thus, in "Oxford St. Montreal/'68," he writes in compassionate and very specific terms to Carole, in response to her "birth-letter," which "continues haunting" him, not least because he "did not attend / the birth of even one of" his daughters. Yet he is able to add, "and i did not have any / feelings of guilt abt it. —from the very moment of / their births i have in my way attempted to celebrate— / their sheer presence on this our miraculous earth." Or, in "11/ '71," he writes "Gladfull all three of you made it" to George and Angela Bowering on the birth of their daughter, yet this time admits to "remorse" at missing his daughters' births even as he still insists he "wld nonetheless tell / of the sheer presence they have in the world." Nevertheless, that arrival of a new life reminds him that "hr by hr my brief whiff of a life seems / to be longer than memory's awe-fill'd HUG. . . ." To his daughters, in "Nov. '71," he is "your forlorn Pa" who "wonders abt you" and offers various kinds of advice and insight with an implied hug and no judging. And to lovers he is a person enjoying their rare presences and struggling to be with them as best he can. Letters or poems, they manifest the various roles we live in relation to all the people in our lives, and, sentimental as it may seem to say so, that appears to be one of the concepts behind the whole of *transcanadaletters*, one of the reasons Kiyooka put the book together the way he did.

Various small sub-narratives covering several letters, all part of the life being written, emerge throughout, like the grand tales of his time in Kyoto creating a sculpture for the Japanese Expo's Canadian pavilion or the "H A L I F A X / V A N C O U V E R : E X C H A N G E," the story of his young lover who leaves Halifax for a Zen retreat in the States and eventually goes home with her father, and the one about attempting to set up an artists' co-op in "a splendid 3 story / former POWER PLANT 2 miles north of Abbottsford BC." Redford's three criteria for judging whether or not letters achieve fictive status—"autonomy, fertility, and versatility"—are operative in all these letters, as well as in the more formally notated poems.

There are many more aspects of *transcanadaletters* than I have gone into here. In terms of its impact as a book, and the way it creates a sense of defamiliarization not found in conventional collections of letters by famous people (whether or not they are writers), there is, for example, the large portfolio of photographic prints about one-third of the way through. At one point Kiyooka discusses his photography, and the work he is doing on his contribution to *BC Almanac (H) C-B, The Eye in the Landscape,* but the portfolio here is something else, and its placement in *transcanadaletters* has a different effect because it is a part of the correspondence that inscribes a life. But then photography is a kind of inscription.

Although *transcanadaletters* works as an example of contemporary correspondence, in the tradition of "the humane art," the text refuses to stick to any single generic category, and especially seems to insist on being read also as a kind of serial poem constructed from one artist's life. In its own way, it serves as a prime example of what bpNichol called "borderblur," sliding as easily among genres as it does among the various personae its author adapts for the different correspondents he addresses. In the end, I tend to read it as a poem even as I am also fascinated by the contradictory artist and man it figures forth. It's a book, then, constructed as such, to be read whole and enjoyed on its terms, no others.

ENDNOTES

[1] At various points in *transcanadaletters,* Kiyooka alludes to other writing he is engaged upon, much of which only achieved publication in the posthumous *Pacific Windows: Collected Poems of Roy K. Kiyooka* (1997). Perhaps the "concern" out of which he writes the letters proved to be more important in that act than in others, and that is why he came to collect them for publication.

[2] See, for example., Ann Munton's essay, "The Long Poem as Poetic Diary," which specifically refers to a longer work of Kiyooka's, *Wheels a trip thru Honshu's Backcountry, '69,* then unpublished in its complete form but now available in *Pacific Windows.*

Some Thoughts on Poetry & Modernism in Australia

The whole question of modernism in Australian literature is a vexed one, but the example of poetry provides a number of interesting openings for exploration. As a Canadian, I am aware of how slowly certain aspects of literary modernism made their way into the literature of one settler colony. It seems many of the same pressures to resist modernist experimentation were at work in Australia, with the even greater distance from the imperial centre that was London working to keep what Julian Croft calls the "reaction against modernism . . . deep-seated and long-lasting" (409). The conservative tendency in twentieth-century Australian poetry, especially as regards formal innovation, appears to have maintained power longer than it did in North America, or even New Zealand.[1] Croft states that "Australian writers were promptly aware of what was going on in Europe from 1910 onwards, but they were slow to respond (World War I might have been one reason); nevertheless they did so in the second and third decade of the century in quite significant and distinct ways" (409). Some aspects of this response were negative, however: the artists grouped around the Sydney magazine, *Vision*, wished to repudiate the angst and pessimism they associated with European modernism, and they did so through a slaphappy (and essentially Georgian) importation of "classical" mythology to Australian environs. Nevertheless, modernity made itself felt, but while a poem like *The Wasteland* certainly had its effects, they tended not to be formal.

Croft compares developments in Australia and Brazil, another country physically isolated from Europe and given to a late-nineteenth century provincialism. He makes an interesting point about form: the new ideas in science and the humanities "circulated throughout Australia, and although style took some time to respond, the ideas themselves took vigourous root. In contrast to developments in Brazil, the modernism movement was not immediately apparent in stylistic experiments. However, its temperament—concentration on interior states, the depiction of alienated consciousness, a concern with the limitations of language, and the total uncertainty in an agnostic age—was clearly seen in novels and poems in the 1920s and the 1930s" (410-11). Croft's argument suggests that Australian writers responded to modernity, and to its tonal and emotional effects in European art of the time, but not to modernism. Generally, Australian poetry until well after World War II fails to take account of how the major modernists insisted, in their writing, on the indissolubility of form and content, which Pound's dictum, "Make it new," asserted.

This long-lasting formal conservatism is the first thing that strikes a reader coming to Australian poetry from the outside. A pair of anthologies for the *fin-de siècle* reveal, in very different ways, this conservatism, some of the forces that kept and keep it strong, and the slow resistance to that conservatism that built up in the second half of the century. Robert Gray and Geoffrey Lehmann's *Australian Poetry in the Twentieth Century* and John Tranter and Philip Mead's *The Penguin Book of Modern Australian Poetry* both appeared in 1991, but it is their oppositions that make a comparison between them so interesting.[2]

To anyone seeking some kind of map of twentieth century Australian poetry, these two anthologies demonstrate how widely charts of the field can vary. If nothing else, they provide a clear sense of how complex developments in poetry during the century have been, and they indicate, even if they do not fully elucidate, some of the major cultural conflicts those developments have engaged. It doesn't take long to discover selections, both of individual poets and of poems by the major poets neither volume could ignore, which reveal the differences between the "traditions" represented by them.[3] Whether or not the anthologists acknowledge them, such choices raise basic questions of taste, ideology, and poetics.

On the most basic level, *The Penguin Book of Modern Australian Poetry* offers much more: although it is only twenty-one pages longer, it contains eighty-six poets to *Twentieth Century*'s fifty-three, even though it covers a somewhat shorter time span. *Twentieth Century* begins at the opening of the century, with Christopher Brennan, an Australian symboliste (he corresponded with Mallarmé) who wrote from 1894 to 1913. It also includes five poets before Kenneth Slessor, the first entrant in *The*

Penguin Book. Slessor is widely considered to be the first genuinely modernist poet in Australia, namely, one who knew and learned something from the experiments of Eliot and Pound, albeit more in terms of tone and content than in terms of form. He has twelve poems in *Twentieth Century*, fourteen in *The Penguin Book*, but the anthologists choose different ones, except for the three almost every critic has posited as central to Australian poetry's development in this century: "The Night Ride," "Five Bells," his elegy for a long dead friend, and "Beach Burial."

With its stark evocation of an outback town, its strict realization of a place felt to exist, and its nevertheless savagely sardonic undermining of the optimistic Chamber of Commerce view of life in such places, "The Night Ride" catches the inevitable contradictions of life in what is still a colony in the first half of the century. Like the paintings of Russell Drysdale, it has a haunting power still.

> Gas flaring on the yellow platform; voices running up and down;
> Milk-tins in cold dented silver; half awake I stare,
> Pull up the blind, blink out—all sounds are drugged;
> The slow blowing of passengers asleep;
> Engines yawning; water on heavy drips;
> Black, sinister travellers, lumbering up the station,
> One moment in the window, hooked over bags;
> Hurrying, unknown faces—boxes with strange labels—
> All groping clumsily to mysterious ends,
> Out of the gaslight, dragged by private Fates.
> Their echoes die. The dark train shakes and plunges;
> Bells cry out; the night-ride starts again.
> Soon I shall look out into nothing but blackness,
> Pale, windy fields. The old roar and knock of the rails
> Melts in dull fury. Pull down the blind. Sleep. Sleep.
> Nothing but grey, rushing rivers of bush outside.
> Gaslight and milk-cans. Of Rapptown I recall nothing else.
> (PB 10)

With its mixture of contemporary details and speech, and its blank verse, this poem fits much more easily into Tranter and Mead's conflicted sense of poetic heritage than it does into Lehmann and Gray's more monolithic vision.

Still, the first poems of each book tend to set the thematic tone, and each in its different way strikes an attitude toward Europe and the various, confusing forms of cultural colonialism emanating from there. Lehmann and Gray choose a love poem by Brennan, much darker and more sardonic than its title suggests, followed by his "The Wanderer," and then a number of poems by other older poets that don't quite engage the Australian landscape and its history in any specific way. "Aubade" seems a good title to begin the anthology, as it suggests a dawning of poetic history that the anthology will reveal in the ever brightening light of the poems to follow. Or it would if it weren't for the poem itself:

> We woke together on a gusty dawn
> in the dim house amid the level waste
> and stared in anguish on the stretch of years
> filled with grey dawn and ever-weeping wind.
>
> For as the hour hung still 'twixt night and day
> we whom the dark had drawn so close together
> at that dead tide as strangers saw each other
> strangers divided by a sea of years.
>
> We might not weep out our passion of despair
> but in lorn trance we gazed upon each other
> and wonder'd what strange ways had brought our hands
> together in that chamber of the west.
>
> We felt the dumb compulsion of the hour
> to wander forth in spirit on the wind
> and drift far apart in undiscover'd realms
> of some blank world where dawn for ever wept. (*TC* 4)

This poem, like "The Wanderer," whose narrator tells us that "All night

I have walk'd and my heart was deep awake, / remembering ways I dream'd and that I chose, / remembering lucidly, and was not sad" (*TC* 5), digs deep into a Romantic yearning and sense of loss that seems more borrowed European than integrally Australian. Certainly, one does not get a sense of place at all in these poems: the landscape is symbolic, but not in the specifically located way that Slessor's train station will be a few decades later. Many critics consider Brennan to be the first modern Australian poet, and for his learning, his interest in the symbolistes, his awareness of something more than the bush ballads so popular at the time, he is. But he does not seem to be at home in his own country, not even to the extent of inscribing his uneasiness in that particular landscape in his poems. In fact, of the six poets before Slessor, only Shaw Neilson, and he only in a glancing fashion, seems to be writing about the country at all. Which is odd, because one of the things Lehmann and Gray seek to do with their anthology is uncover a mostly pastoral representation of an all-white Australia deeply rooted in its Anglo-Celtic inheritance.

Tranter and Mead do not begin with Slessor's "The Night Ride"; their choice of "Nuremberg," a poem about art, as the first poem in their anthology, also sets a thematic tone, in this case, asserting a modern, even anti-Romantic, sense of historical context. It also sets up a sequence of allusive connections among certain later poems that provides a fascinating subtext to the Introduction's statements about modern poetry in Australia. Although its form is conventional, and lines about how "wrought-pewter manticores . . . peering through / The rounds of glass, espied that sun-flushed room / With Dürer graving at intaglios" (*PB* 1) do not seem modern at all, it contrasts with Brennan's poem in illuminating ways. The poem consistently connects specific images of "green-scaled rows of metal" to "Albrecht Dürer and his plates of iron" (*PB* 1), implying a connection between Dürer's printmaking and poetry. Despite its Georgian formalities, it presents a clearly observed scene, and a commentary on it that insists on judgement. There is also a genial optimism at odds with the dark Romantic angst of the Brennan poems. Rather than an unseen but obscurely felt indebtedness to a particular stance, "Nuremberg" enunciates a deliberate sense of cultural heritage which will eventually be put to use in the new country, as the later "The Night Train," with its sharply etched representation of a specifically Australian scene, shows. Tranter and Mead intend that we should read it that way too, precisely because they place Slessor's early poems of large symbolic gesture first in order to show how they will be replaced by such specifically local poems as "The All-Night Taxi Stand," and "South Country."

One of the most interesting differences between these two anthologies shows up in their editors' introductions. Lehmann and Gray don't say much, and what they leave out is at least as interesting as what they include: "We have read again every poet of the period we could find, have chosen the poems we like most, and have let the proportional outcome amongst writers be as it may. We felt that by pleasing ourselves, and then each arguing against those choices that seemed to have been made out of private association or personal obsession, we had the best chance of pleasing others, and of arriving close to something objectively valid" (xi). It all sounds so reasonable, and perhaps if they had stopped with "pleasing others," it would be hard to dispute; but the argument of "arriving close to something objectively valid" raises far too many questions they refuse to engage. As does the following: "We have not tried to include poets on the basis of regional or any other prescriptive demands. It cannot be productive to pretend things are other than we have found them to be" (xi). The authoritative passive voice of that final sentence will brook no argument, yet it certainly raises a number of questions, not least about that lack of "prescriptive demands" they insist they adhered to, especially when the table of contents contains only twelve women and no aboriginals, even from the last few decades. Quality, it seems, remains assigned to white male inheritors of the English literary tradition. They give the game away about their sense of tradition when they say they "do not believe literary innovation is necessarily more admirable than an individual, revitalised use of tradition," and argue that "Philip Larkin proves for us how a major, unavoidable talent makes ludicrous all Hegelian, modernist contentions about literature having to 'progress' in a certain direction. Larkin has shown what the freedom of the writer in the modern western world really means" (xii).

Not that the Introduction to *The Penguin Book* doesn't have its problems too, raising at least a few questions it fails to answer, but the editors are aware such questions inhere in their project:

This book answers the need for a widely-representative and credible anthology of modern Australian poetry, as seen from the last decade of the twentieth century. The emphasis is on enjoyment. In our experience, poets don't write poems merely to be graded, studied or analysed; they write them, above all, to create for readers the enjoyment of a complex and intense aesthetic experience. In collecting these poems, we've kept that simple fact firmly in mind.

As well as presenting a generous selection of poems, this anthology also offers a guided tour of our modern poetry from around 1930, and by implication it gives tentative answers to some important questions: where does our modern poetry really begin? Of the mass of experimental work written in the 1940s, which poems still have something important to say to us today? What was going on under the surface in the conservative 1950s? What were the really significant discoveries of the late 1960s, and what was just shifting fashion? After the impact of feminism, multicultural writing and postmodern writing and reading strategies, where are we heading as the year 2000 rolls up on the calendar? (xxvii)

This at least strives to account for ideological presences Lehmann and Gray simply pretend do not exist, yet the reader wonders how close that "emphasis . . . on enjoyment" comes to their choosing "the poems we liked most." To be sure, while we might not trust editors who didn't at least like the works they included in their anthologies, we also want to know what factors influence their likes and dislikes. In that context, and granting that Tranter and Mead had no control over the title of their anthology, they present a more complex and interesting apologia than do Lehmann and Gray.

The major problem with *The Penguin Book* has more to do with its apparent attempt to construct a single, if broad, tradition of modernism, even as its editors admit that "the diversity of poetic activity over the last quarter-century convinced us we should avoid the kind of historical approach that tries to fit all this activity into a formula" (xxviii). They want to avoid the "repetitive and combative rhetoric" that has split that tradition into fragments: "modern versus anti-modern; international versus local; closed versus open form; traditional versus postmodern techniques; accessibility versus obscurity; humanist sermonising versus verbal abstraction" (xxviii)—not to mention feminism versus mateship. Assuming that "most of the argument based on these terms had faded by now into that muted region of past controversy" (xxviii), they assert "that modern Australian poetry needed to be looked at from a perspective that took in not only the issues of the 1960s, but those of the 1940s and the 1980s (now the 1990s) as well" (xxix). This sounds a note of reconciliation and inclusiveness the anthology itself does not quite live up to, as its very inclusiveness reveals some rather deep fissures in the poetic history it invokes. On the other hand, compared to Lehmann and Gray's selection, theirs does reveal a much broader cultural arena full of competing and collaborating traditions. And the premise does allow the editors to conclude that "[i]f the modern movement has a major theme, it must be the constant questioning of older ways of looking at things. This collection questions previous canons of modern Australian poetry" (xxix). But the term "modern" is still up for grabs, it seems.

The Penguin Book's bold claims for what it sets out to accomplish has provoked some complex and rigorous responses. John Forbes, a poet five years younger than Tranter, three years older than Mead, and undoubtedly one with his own position to promote, argues thus: "John Tranter doesn't have much luck with anthologies. At least with their Introductions." Suggesting that the Introduction is transparently political, seeking "to repudiate the idea that '68 represented any radical break in the development of Australian poetry," he adds that it "makes claims for the book that the selection of poems scarcely sustains" (129). Although treated rather well in The Penguin Book himself, Forbes argues that, in trying to establish a tradition of modernism running from Slessor right through to the present, Tranter and Mead must ignore not only certain poets who don't fit in but also good poems by the poets they do anthologize that fail to match their particular vision.[4] On the other hand, Martin Duwell suggests that having two editors allows for "a useful blending of positions, a mutual respect that bridges very different poetic backgrounds and practices" (145), and he praises the anthology for its "generosity" (145). These and other comments from Australian poets and critics have the advantage of me: these are people who know both the history of Australian poetry and its contemporary situation in a way an outsider cannot. Certainly they can mark the importance of those who are missing from *The Penguin Book* as I cannot.

The differing ideological casts of the Introductions signal the immense distance between the anthologies. Perhaps the clearest example of their dissimilarities is the way they invoke the infamous "Ern Malley" controversy. In 1944, two young and conservative poets, James McAuley and Harold Stewart, collaborated on a selection of what they called "deliberately concocted nonsense" (Harris and Murray-Smith 6), and sent it to *Angry Penguins*, where it was later published with a forceful encomium by the editor, Max Harris. The whole sorry tale of the hoax, and the even more comical and sinister trial for obscenity that followed, has been told many times, including in *The Poems of Ern Malley* (1988). An important aspect of the controversy was its public effect upon writing in Australia over the next twenty years, for it "did much to strengthen the anti-modernist forces in Australia" (Croft 410). How does the "Ern Malley" controversy play in these two anthologies? Lehmann and Gray include a sequence of haiku by Stewart and six poems by McAuley; they play up the collaborators' conviction that "modernist poetry of the irrational, obscurantist type arose from empty self-aggrandizing and was culturally destructive" (170); and they insist that the "Ern Malley" poems "are for the most part hyperbole and deliberate bathos" and that "[n]one of them have a formal wholeness or are works of art" (177). Tranter and Mead include poems by McAuley but none by Stewart. But, more importantly, they print "all the 'Ern Malley' poems" because they believe they are remarkable

> not as literary curiosities, but as an important work in their own right with an influential role in the poetic ferment of the 1940s, as James McAuley described it, and in the subsequent development of Australian poetry. Written while Roland Barthes was still in his twenties, Malley's poems speak of the death of the Author in a subtle, duplicitous voice and—as

McAuley himself prophesied—their enigmas and paradoxes still captivate new generations of young readers in a way that McAuley's or Harold Stewart's other work seems less able to do. . . . These unsettling works of the imagination may be seen as early examples of the postmodernist technique of *bricolage*, of knocking something together from whatever materials are close at hand. Beyond their satirical purpose McAuley and Stewart were tinkering about with textual bits and pieces as part of an experiment that, as with Victor Frankenstein and Dr Jekyll, would get out of their control. The poems they fabricated from many different sources— non-"poetic" ones often—survive as radical, intriguing challenges to traditional ways of writing and reading. (xxx)

Leaving aside the curious appeal to two central Gothic horror fictions and its unconscious implications concerning modernism, this statement defiantly stakes a claim for the "Ern Malley" poems as contributing to the development of modernism in Australian poetry.[5] Tranter and Mead's selection of McAuley's own poems is larger than Lehmann and Gray's, and only two poems overlap; according to *The Penguin Book*, McAuley is more of a modernist than he himself believed. With almost all the poets the anthologies share, especially the older ones, Tranter and Mead's selections are more daring and innovative.

The various antitheses between these two anthologies include the "continuing tension in Australian writing between groups which could loosely be called traditionalists and internationalists" (Tulip 480), the so-called Boeotian-Athenian, or country/city, opposition, which Les Murray first articulated in an essay on Peter Porter, and that between popular and high culture. Croft is not alone in pointing out that, until quite recently, "the poets turned their attention to the subjects of modernism but the forms and language they used were derived from the traditions of the previous age" (415). Certainly that formal conservatism strikes a Canadian reader, with A.D. Hope, in both his practice and his criticism, leading the rear-guard. Although internationally perceived as the major poet of his generation in Australia, Les Murray inhabits the Boeotian (pastoral) mode even as his poetry demonstrates a most sophisticated range of reference, both formally and thematically. His first book of poems was a co-publication with Geoffrey Lehmann, so it's probably not surprising that his spirit hovers over *Twentieth Century*.

On the whole, the choice of poems, not just of poets, in *Twentieth Century*, leans towards traditional forms and either philosophically and socially conservative or pastoral themes. The poetry of A.D. Hope, especially, represents a deep-seated formal and philosophical conservatism. Hope studied Pope and Swift, but seems to have learned more from the latter. All eight poems in *Twentieth Century* are extended, and usually satiric, meditations, with strong misogynistic undertones. In such poems as "Return from the Freudian Islands," Hope reveals a careful if distasteful study of modernity, but his powerfully nasty images do tend to concentrate upon a vision of women's bodies as images of disgust. "Logically" extending the popular idea that Freudianism called for casting off repression and going naked, the poem has people taking off their clothes, and then cutting away the skin and the outer musculature so as to show "The Ultimate Visceral Reality." This turns out to be "A bone-cage filled with female guts . . . / Tottering before them in the midday sun" (*TC* 81). This Swiftian vision concludes:

> And clear through gut and bowel the mashy chyme
> Churn downward; jelled in its transparent sheath
> The scowling foetus tethered, and the time-
> Bomb tumour set unguessed its budded death. (*TC* 82)

Other poems concern "The Martyrdom of St. Theresa," a self-regarding Susannah, the death of Pius the Twelfth, and Casserius's famous engraving of a dead pregnant woman cut open. They are chillingly brilliant, no doubt, but also strident refusals of democratizing movements of their own time.

Tranter and Mead choose equally brilliant, shorter poems, many of which speak more directly to the question of being an Australian who looks back to some classical culture elsewhere for whatever value civilization might offer. Thus, they include Hope's famous "Australia," with its (again interestingly misogynist) use of the land / woman trope:

They call her a young country, but they lie:
She is the last of lands, the emptiest,
A woman beyond her change of life, a breast
Still tender but within the womb is dry. (*PB* 16).

Its final lines sum up one view of what Australia stands for, or stood for, half a century ago, when it was written:

Such savage and scarlet as no green hills dare
Springs in that waste, some spirit which escapes
The learned doubt, the chatter of cultured apes
Which is called civilization over there. (*PB* 16)

Hope is generous with his scorn, a misanthrope too. By choosing as they do, Tranter and Mead seek to include Hope as a participant in the troubled conflicts of modern Australian poetry, rather than presenting him as somehow standing apart from them all. By also including "Imperial Adam," they point to the Hope who wrote all his life the kinds of poems Lehmann and Gray highlight, but their selection suggests that he is much more than that.

They perform the same service for other older poets, such as David Campbell and Judith Wright, both major figures since the 1940s. Lehmann and Gray choose well-known and generally pastoral poems by each, although they also include some light satiric pieces by Campbell and some deeply personal lyrics by Wright. Tranter and Mead go somewhat farther afield, and include some striking late formal experiments by each poet. In Campbell's case, this means including excerpts from the "Ku-Ring-Gai Rock Carvings" sequence:

Bora Ring

The kangaroo has a spear in his side. It was here
        Young men were initiated,
    Tied to a burning tree. Today
    Where are such cooling pools of water?

Baiame

Baiame, the All-father, is a big fellow with a big dong
    And the rayed crown of a god.
He looks at his Sunday children who snigger and drive
    Home to their home-units. The god is not surprised.

(PB 47-48)

Although closer to traditional *ekphrasis*, the whole series of minimalist mythic takes puts Campbell in the company of such "translators" of aboriginal writings as Jerome Rothenberg. In Wright's case, it means including some of her most recent work along with the famous poems of the forties and fifties. Where Lehmann and Gray take the trouble to point out that "considerable reservations have developed about her later work" (160), Tranter and Mead include four poems from *Phantom Dwelling* (1985), including a ghazal, which, in its assumption of a new form in English and self-reflexive play, represents a startling formal experiment for an older established poet.

Skins

This pair of skin gloves is sixty-six years old,
mended in places, worn thin across the knuckles.

Snakes get rid of their coverings all at once.
Even those empty cuticles trouble the passer-by.

Counting in seven-year rhythms I've lost nine skins
though their gradual flaking isn't so spectacular.

Holding a book or a pen I can't help seeing
how age crazes surfaces. Well, and interiors?

You ask me to read those poems I wrote in my thirties?
They dropped off several incarnations back. (*PB* 66)

Such choices signal Tranter and Mead's desire to include in their anthology formal innovation as a mark of modernism.

While there is much to admire about the Boeotian mode, as Porter himself admits in his witty response to Murray, it tends to be conservative politically, sexually, spiritually, as well as stylistically. On the whole, *Australian Poetry*'s choices tend that way, too. *The Penguin Book* addresses modernism and postmodernism in its selection of poets and poems from the late fifties through to the present in ways *Twentieth Century* simply refuses to do. Those reviewers who argue that *The Penguin Book* simply doesn't challenge the established canon as much as the editors say it does or as they want it to do seem not to allow for the fact that Tranter and Mead at least see fit to include such important poets as Robert Adamson, Jack Davis, Oodgeroo, David Malouf, Dimitris Tsaloumas, Dorothy Hewett, Vincent Buckley, Bruce Beaver, Fay Zwicky, Antigone Kefala, Tom Shapcott, Judith Rodriguez, Mudrooroo, J.S. Harry, Andrew Taylor, John A. Scott, Jennifer Maiden, Pamela Brown, Ania Walwicz, Robert Harris, Anthony Lawrence, Joanne Burns, and John Kinsella, whom Lehmann and Gray do not find "pleasing." If some of these choices seem more political than aesthetic, even in terms of *The Penguin Book*'s Introduction, I agree with its implicit suggestion that these writers are just too important to ignore. For example, I cannot imagine anyone attempting to understand Australian poetry over the past thirty years without confronting Beaver's extraordinary collections of the late sixties and early seventies, which, among other things, found a way to make American "confessional" poetry Australian.

Tranter and Mead could have been even more adventurous in highlighting formal innovation. Martin Duwell says that *The Penguin Book* "reminded [him] how wordy Australian poetry has been," and points to "a lack of silence," which reveals "that we do not have a tradition of minimalism, projectivism or a poetry of the silences between the lines" (149). Robert Adamson, (who is not even in *Twentieth Century*) has made a far finer and more discriminating Australian adaptation of the New American poetics than most poets of his generation or those since, and brought their lessons, including those alluded to by Duwell, to bear upon his writing. *The Penguin Book*'s generous selection of his poems provides at least some sense of his specific accomplishment. On the other hand, many late poems of David Campbell ignored by both anthologies demonstrate how fully he took the minimalist lessons of the sixties to heart.

Despite, or maybe because of, its editorial strategies, *Twentieth Century* includes the whole of Les Murray's "The Buladelah-Taree Holiday Song Cycle," perhaps the central poem exemplifying his Boeotian mythos, while *The Penguin Book* has only three of its thirteen sections. On the other hand, *The Penguin Book*'s selection gives a better sense of Murray's complexity of vision, what makes him, from Peter Porter's point of view, more of a city poet than he perhaps would like to admit. Tranter and Mead do choose some very pastoral poems (although in Murray's case, the mode is almost always ironized in one way or another), but they also include one of "The Sydney Highrise Variations," a definitive city sequence, and such discussion-poems as "Equanimity," a fervent Boeotian argument, yet one which could be found only in a city forum:

> Whatever its variants of meat-cuisine, worship, divorce,
> human order has at heart
> an equanimity. Quite different from inertia, it's a place
> where the churchman's not defensive, the indignant aren't on
> > the *qui vive*,
> the loser has lost interest, the accountant is truant to remorse,
> where the farmer has done enough struggling-to-survive
> for one day, and the artist rests from theory—
> where all are, in short, off the high comparative horse
> of their identity. (*PB* 222)

Their selection troubles both Murray's idealization of poetry and of his own poetics in ways that render him much more interesting as a major poet of contemporary Australia, with perhaps the largest international reputation.[6]

Once we get beyond Murray, there is far less to compare between the two anthologies, for *Twentieth Century* has few poets from this period, and even fewer in common with *The Penguin Book*. Of the four Tranter poems in *Twentieth Century*, three are from his most recent book at the time. Thus, though the editors admit that he "is the most prominent of a group of 'internationalist' Australian poets who emerged in the late 1960s and are oriented to the New York School" (359), they refuse to show us any of his early work. Tranter and Mead are, as should be expected, much fairer in their presentation of his work, with poems from early books right up to *Under Berlin* (1988). As a result, a reader comes away with a much better sense of Tranter's overall development, and of the power of his early work, which did, after all, propel him to a prominence even Lehmann and Gray admit he achieved. In the case of John Forbes, something similar occurs. Lehmann and Gray seem to have admitted him to the volume under some duress, if their editorial comments are to be believed: "He has published four individual volumes and a *Selected Poems*, which maintain his wittiness, bounce, and mockery of an intellectual manner, but show small range and little development" (430). They choose two poems that back up their complaints about his work while more or less fitting into their general schema. Tranter and Mead again cover the whole career, and thereby demonstrate both a much greater range and various developments in his work. Their selection demonstrates why Forbes is important, and leaves a reader wanting to track down more of his work.

But it is in the many poets they include whom Lehmann and Gray discard, that Tranter and Mead prove the superior quality of their anthology. Even just a few poems by such major aboriginal poets as Jack Davis, Mudrooroo, Oodgeroo, and younger ones like Archie Weller demonstrate the importance of recent aboriginal art in Australia. And the much wider selection of women poets, some of whom, like Ania Walwicz, are among the most innovative writers in Australia today, also speaks volumes about the changes that Australian culture has undergone since World War II. It is not only in its, possibly unconscious, code of mateship that *Twentieth Century* fails to move beyond the "little Australia" sensibility of the pre-War years, but also in its stunning refusal to admit any writers from the various ethnic groups that have expanded the definition of Australian in recent decades. Finally, as their choice of Philip Larkin as a presiding spirit suggests, although Lehmann and Gray want to offer a selection of "twentieth century" Australian poetry, they seem to want to do so in a way that will, as much as possible, keep the spectre of modernism at bay. However much Tranter and Mead's selection is biased toward only one kind of modernism, at least they seek to show both how modernism came to Australia and how it has slowly flourished there. In the end, despite the various ideological constructions that can be brought to bear upon both anthologies' editorial policies, *The Penguin Book of Modern Australian Poetry* offers a more complete view of how modernism works itself out in Australian poetry, more "news" (in Pound's sense), than does *Australian Poetry in the Twentieth Century*.

※

Recent work by three writers in *The Penguin Book of Modern Australian Poetry* and one other continues to extend the modernism(s) that anthology sought to exemplify. Of these three, only one, John Tranter, appears in *Twentieth Century*. These four books demonstrate the various ways the modernist heave continues to enter Australian poetry.

Robert Harris died too young, in 1997, just as he was beginning to achieve some recognition. *JANE, Interlinear & Other Poems* (1992) represents a definite formal push forward for him, and contains a number of formally interesting pieces. I was especially intrigued by the title poem, and the oddly provocative displacements of the couplets in most of its sections. As when reading some LANGUAGE poetry, I found the syntactic breakdown discovered in reading such lines as the following across rather than in two-line columns a raddled delight. Take, for example:

| the earth behaves | in thought. | the fish pond |
| like someone lost | Broken towers, | and the tilt yard. (36) |

I especially liked the notion of the earth behaving in thought and the fish pond behaving like someone lost, but soon the poem itself disabused me of such a misreading. What Harris is actually doing in this poem is closer to scholarly documentation, and as the documentary long poem is a highly popular form in Canada, I found his variation on the form fascinating. As he explains: "The artifice which controls the visual arrangement of [it] is mimetic of th[e] page design [of the *Interlinear Hebrew-Greek-English Bible*] and includes the idea of the events as a prior text from which the poems are 'translations'" (132).

This is still an intriguing artifice. If nothing else, the shift within the couplet from upper to lower line and back again at least slows readers down, and forces them to pay attention to the nuances of investigation over 450 years of the "coup which placed Lady Jane Dudley (Grey) on the English throne in July 1553[, which] is described by the *New Cambridge Modern History* as 'the most outrageous and hopeless conspiracy in a century filled with many handsome specimens'" (34). Perhaps one of the most fascinating aspects of the poem is the poet's presence in it, actively engaged not just in the writing, but rather driven in a quest for vision:

> I have sought out John's state a decade adrift
> the portraits. Master fiction, dynastic, infused with suppressed
> hysteria. . . .
>
>   thought about
>   I've   their politics: . . .
>
>   inclined to be droll?
>   . . . And Jane herself, I don't pity slender
> evidence, I search woman among stout face
> for this murdered these pigments. astray in time,
>
> her long neck Whoever she
> hidden in ermine. actually was, once. (53)

Despite my original small disappointment that it was not an experiment in breaking down narrative syntax, later readings of "JANE, Interlinear" confirm its value as a complex and moving exploration of an occluded moment in English history, and one that demonstrates a desire to achieve a modernist (even postmodernist) poetics. It is likely to be added to the line of major Australian long poems of this century.

Perhaps the best way to suggest the particular and peculiar power of John Tranter's *At the Florida* (1993) is to note that one of its central, and paradigmatic, poems, "North Woods," is dedicated to John Ashbery. As many critics have pointed out, Tranter has always been intrigued and perhaps influenced by the New York School of poets, which included Frank O'Hara, a figure whose light comic touch made him an obvious choice for comparisons, and Ashbery. Ashbery's advantage over O'Hara is that he has continued to live and write into the nineties, as, in comparison with another of the dedicatees in this volume, Michael Dransfield,[7] has Tranter: both poets have continued to develop their art, and their poetry has become simultaneously more grounded in the quotidian and less secured to our notions of how that quotidian actually enters our senses of it. Like Ashbery, Tranter has achieved a poetry of odd gracefulness, a poetry that seems to offer traditional effects but actually pulls the representational rug out from under its readers just when they might begin to believe in it. Mostly, the poems in the first two parts of *At the Florida* seem to be little narratives, much like many of the poems in his prize-winning *Under Berlin*; but even more than those poems they frustrate traditional narrative and swirl into a carefully articulated incoherence, a doubtful closure, a brilliant indeterminacy.

Tranter has always played these games, but there does seem to be a greater human, or social, awareness operating in his duplicitous fictions now. I was reminded, strangely (because these new poems are definitely not "light" in its manner), of that delightful and hokey joke, "Ode to Col Joye" in his *Selected Poems*; possibly because the new longish poems in *At the Florida* display a similar insouciant anti-narrative impulse. Take "North Woods," for example, a poem I believe to be a future anthology piece: it continually pulls us into a "story" only to shift characters, narrators, not to mention settings, while maintaining a tone that seems to suggest all these changing figures do belong together.

> The whirring projector flings this
> onto the screen: she tilts clockwise, leaves
> the view of the rocky river flowing out of focus
> tangled and white like laundry boiling, slowly
> turning her back and moving into the shadow
> of the porch, on a cloudy afternoon—the light
> tinted pearl, a naked toe bent and dipped
> into the water, that's what she's seen,
> it worries her sleep for weeks afterwards. (51)

Like almost all the figures of these poems, this woman is anonymous. Nevertheless, she seems at first to be the object of the gaze, the figure in the film, her actions the "this" flung "onto the screen." But by the end of the paragraph she seems to be the subject of that gaze we have been invited to share. Aside from Tranter's fine use of line breaks to keep nouns and verbs subtly out of touch of their modifiers, he demonstrates here how loosely syntax holds the world together. The next verse paragraph still seems to be about her for the first two lines, but suddenly changes the direction of its gaze: "Sitting on a ledge / high above the sky, a place for whispers, / you meet the question which had grown up / around the edges of the party" (51). What is "you" doing here? For one thing, "you" is about to find that at this party "she seems younger" and "looks into the depths of things, charming / some guests, frightening others." These shifts are exciting, they may be leading somewhere—and we are barely into the poem. What interests me is the way this particular poem manages to call attention to its fictionality, by referring not only to film but to novels, autobiographies, and, at one point, "the author," who "insists" "she'll be undaunted" (52). It also insists that it is really being enunciated by a "we," who may be the audience of the film, people at the party, or readers of the novel, not to mention a reflection of the readers of the poem. Tranter carefully makes the woman ever more fictional as the poem goes on, reminding us of the clichés she must live through. Yet he also manages to make of her a "character" apparently worthy of our reading as well as that of "we." It is an exhilarating high wire act, not least because it maintains a balance not only between narrative and its deconstruction but also between a satiric wit and a compassionate identification.

Indeed, it is that sense of balance, or tension, that powers most of the poems in the first two parts of this collection. Some might be read as personal poems, but most are obvious about their fictionality. Indeed, I tend to read most of his work as anything but "confessional," even in the most attenuated sense of the term, although I must admit that some poems, like "Lufthansa" and "Having Completed My Fortieth Year" in *Under Berlin* certainly play off the possibility. None of Tranter's "I"s are to be trusted, then, any more than the apparent stories they tell. Yet all these appearances are appealing, largely because they are so willing to deny themselves even as they tell their stories. There is also Tranter's fine craft, his use of a wide range of verse forms, some made-up, and his wonderfully apt vocabulary, an arcane mix of clichés and references, ideological tags, and all the rag ends of common speech that put all discourses to the question.

The final third of *At the Florida* is made up of a number of what we might call "reverse *Haibun*," twenty-line poems followed by a prose tag. Tranter has made this form his own, and it is entirely suited to his satiric wit. These poems do not seek the balance the anti-narratives do: they tend on the whole to be pushy and funny. Still, a poem like "Another Country" achieves a kind of simple nostalgia in its prose tag, but only after creating a complex critical distance in the verse's vision of Australia a generation ago. These poems, especially in the prose tags, push even further into indeterminacy by forcing syntax until it breaks. While in the poems in Parts 1 and 2 each sentence makes sense, and the poems only break down at the level of the paragraph or the statement, the "reverse *haibun*" perversely insist that even the simplest connections within the sentence can no longer be trusted, as "Bachelor Pad" demonstrates:

> tractable fidget hanker
> for joint discreet fire-
> side mature executive no
> stealth trollop, hey
> coach, love barefoot
> seaside video dreaming-
> swill venom, bitch! who
> married—cancel the writ
> portal hunch severing
> commitment my ill-behaved
> flight manager, prefer
> discreet reply, moonshine
> possible, bespectacled,
> mistress trim killer
> answer that passion
> prank, her chunky bulk
> deft in a disparate
> domicile, a walloping
> brouhaha, how stretched it
> grapples both ways

Sucks pencil for pencil read retractable pep ration bathroom cue—giveaway pizza shred fragments private eye spells predicate adjective "alone" no pets the old gang so soon chubby

grown fleshy damp towel pencil read applicant read light
shade for light read reading light insect nightfall. (89)

And yet, these poems cannot fully escape sense either. A playful linguistics is at work here, and even as meaning seems to recede, the material qualities of language are foregrounded through such elements as internal rime, assonance, consonance, over-the-top alliteration, and deliberate
utilization of cliché part-phrases. These poems force the reader to confront
language as material, as something we all manipulate even as it manipulates us. They resist all "natural" readings, insisting on what, in the
American context, Perloff would call their "radical artifice." As *At the
Florida* demonstrates, John Tranter belongs with the writers she places in
that new tradition. He continues to be one of the few poets in Australia
who consciously pushes poetic boundaries, an innovator whose influence
I hope will be felt.

Chris Mansell's *Day Easy Sunlight Fine* (1995) immediately
announces a writer interested in and intrigued by the ways language
betrays the hidden—agendas, ideologies, emotions. The four subtitles of
her collection further underline its political intent: "Poems to eat,"
"Poems with no breathing," "Poems for singing," and "Poems to say
while walking." Mansell plays with and off the cliché a lot, but she also
interrogates a number of specific jargons, holding them up in her poems
for our examination.

Her use of open forms, a lack of punctuation, and a witty punning
turn of line, bring some of these poems into the territory of what is often
called LANGUAGE poetry. Watch how the shifts of thought follow where
the words lead in "Phased in space":

stuffed to the gills
with religion and science
and numbers talk   language
and cigarettes   the smoke
                folds like an onion
one molecule at a time hitting
our topological

gnosis like a dance beautiful

mathematicians swimming in the dark   scared

scarred and sacred   like incense

we fold

in bland fractal

patterns trilling ever

lastingness song into sun each

day easy and sunlight fine

folding like envy

or intelligence touched like a sensitive

creature   clamming up

again

elegant abstract passionate

turning on a singular point

coming back to say

the world is our oyster

and we hardly know

where we are   weighty useless fishes

caught

uncomprehending in scales

we look out   through our time

our plot   the edges

twinkle twinkingly

how we wonder

what we do (125-26)

A note informs us that we may read up on fractals in any book on Chaos theory, but nowhere except here will we find the lovely subversive concept that "we fold / in bland fractal / patterns" in our spiritual and intellectual lives of desire. The "bland" is what does the job, especially after that slippage from "scared" to "sacred." There is an assured, if opaque, intellectual music to such lines.

Mansell, having found her own way to lyric/anti-lyric, is deliberately writing against conventional notions of the lyric. Even when her poems explore questions of friendship and love, she keeps easy lyric subjectivity out of it, in part by recognizing the ways in which contingent language so often creates the conventions by which we argue and feel. "Discussing it," for example, posits the problem and the possible escape: "the style state of the art thinking tricks / turning tricks falling back skills learnt in school / but your own silent voice differently signing" (128). Again, and again, especially in the later sections of her collection, Mansell's poems insist upon the intimate connection between political economy today and what the arts can accomplish, especially if too easily compromised:

> but to accept accepted it is accepted
> in the industry heavy undercapitalisation the normal
> the accepted . . .
> . . . .
> ensuring stability in the marketplace
> takeovers becoming more frequent the style
> the accepted style (132)

This is not standard lyric practice, but Mansell has found a way to make a rough and tough poetry out of the "accepted" phrases of the world-wide economy, and to tie them to questions of style that haunt all artists.

While not all the experiments in *Day Easy Sunlight Fine* work, the determination with which Mansell incorporates languages from areas like economic theory that tend conventionally to be out of bounds in Australian poetry is admirable. Reading *Day Easy Sunlight Fine* is an unsettling experience, as Chris Mansell continually produces unexpected juxtapositions, trills of exaggerated and off-balance music.

Long one of Australia's most important contemporary poets, Robert Adamson is perhaps a poet we would call postmodernist, as he has clearly chosen to learn from modernist and postmodernist writers outside Australia as well as those within, and his experiments have set him apart from all but a few of his contemporaries. His books cover a wide poetic range from the apparently confessional poems of *Swamp Riddles* (1974) and *Where I Come From* (1979) to the ecstatic visions of *Cross the Border* (1977). *The Clean Dark* (1989) is stunning in its classical purity. The poems were cleanly carved and full of a glowing chiaroscuro, moving from visions of fishing and prawning in his beloved Hawkesbury River to elegiac open form sonnets for Robert Duncan. It deservedly won most of Australia's major poetry awards, and set up great expectations for his later work, expectations he has more than met.

Waving to Hart Crane is the first brilliant result of his endeavours during the nineties, and is an even more direct challenge than his earlier work to an Australian poetics that has steadfastly remained formally conservative. Every culture needs what bpNichol called its researchers, and Robert Adamson, since at least the days of *Cross the Border* has been one of the most exciting of those in Australia. *Waving to Hart Crane* contains losenge poems in homage to Piet Mondrian, whose statement, "The light is coming," is the final "text" in the book. It's not the only one, for the poems therein are filled with allusions, quotations, translations, as well as addresses to various fellow poets and predecessors. Adamson interrogates and praises those he loves, not in the mode of Harold Bloom's Oedipal father-slayers but rather in a spirit of true homage, wherein he admits the presence of those he admires into his own poetics. Hart Crane is there, of course, and Robert Duncan, as well as other American influences, but also Brennan, Webb, and, in a deeply felt elegy, Robert Harris, all companions as Robin Blaser would put it.

The *fin de siècle* attitude of *Waving to Hart Crane* suggests we are also waving farewell to something as simple as voices on an old phone line. Instead,

> We enter the new
> century through glass,
> black oceans
>
> and black winds,
> thin fibre funnelling
> poetry out
> of existence.

No sonnet will survive
the fax on fire,
outsound that hash
of voices slung up

from the cable. (27)

If something other than the sonnet survives, it will be in poems like those
of *Waving to Hart Crane*. For they carry a weight of the unsaid, and even
the unsayable; and they present their necessary opacities with energy and
a passionate intensity attached to a vision of the best as well as an apprehension of the worst.

Adamson's elegy for Robert Harris, "Cornflowers," is an example of
a poem that beautifully renders conflicting emotions caught in the shifting skeins of memory. The subtle changes of speed, sound, and tone, are
especially admirable here: internal rhyme, assonance and consonance,
shifts from speech to elegiac memorialising. The deliberate pronominal
indeterminacy—"I just want to know who / owns the conversation"
(20)—insists upon both the loss of a friend and the refusal of that loss in
memory, and writing:

      our
hearts locked in their
cages of singing muscle;

it was concerning
this theme, he continued,
that I composed a tune

for the cornflowers
to sing, cut, sitting
on my table in an indigo jar. (21)

Many of the poems addressed to other artists fall into this mode,
but Adamson ranges further into experimentation in other poems, taking from the LANGUAGE poets what he wants for his own push into the

indeterminacies of language. This can be seen in the two lozenges, for instance, where every word stands apart from every other, demanding to be read in terms of its own history, and not just as part of a conventional syntactic unit. It's also true of the sly comedy to be found in "Percy Grainger Waltz," "The Australian Crawl," and the other poems of Part Four. They announce a world where "The silver we never used dancing / on the table like soft silver tadpoles // sequential meanings drift into meltdown" (74-5). In a world where "virtual poetry is being written / (or is that *done?*)" (70), these poems remind us, "We need some warmth, a long Charles / Olson breath, keep talking, / and don't stumble on the corpse" (71).

The final three sections of *Waving to Hart Crane* enter the games of language more forcefully than the earlier parts. The book thus leads its readers slowly into its intricacies as it goes along. Part Five is one long poem, "The Sugar Glider," in which the spirit of "Michael Palmer, / who writes new words" (80), is invoked, partly against such backward-looking poetics as Murray's. This American poet's work "becomes a chart / to map the margins" (80). And so this poem, in Palmer's spirit, looks back to Cook and

> the botany
> of colonisation, sentences
> handed out, breaking
> down—the pride-made savage
> English language. (80)

But Palmer's poetic offers an other possibility, one that

> Elegantly
> jumps through time
>
> into parts of speech
> that seem to glow; as
> poetry is stretched
> into life he writes in English

that would drive Cook

more insane than he
already was—this
is the joy of being
a modern poet, to skip time
and space

looking for the perfect
reader (80-81)

Adamson is willing to take that risk too, playfully addressing both the American and Australian poets he admires and resists, seeking not to copy but to utilize in the continuing exploration that is his own poetic.

Waving to Hart Crane has the depth, rhythmic intensity, and aural beauty that still signs "poetry" in the purist sense, yet it also continually throws up forms of resistance to conventional poetics. Experimental and divergent, it nevertheless still offers the traditional pleasures of the art. Adamson has the ability to incorporate a wide range of experiences into his writing, but he recognizes that one's reading is one of the most important experiences. His work is demanding, but it gives more in return than do most. It is a reminder to poets that much poetry derives from poetry. Adamson, like the other poets mentioned here, understands this; he also understands that the life will always be there, in the writing. In this, and in being able to dedicate his life to his art, he shares much with Canada's bpNichol.

There are many other poets and books I could invoke to demonstrate that Australian poetry is, at its best, as contemporary and inventive as that being written anywhere in English today. Like New Zealand poetry, it offers special and revelatory pleasures to a Canadian reader, whose colonial inheritance has much in common with those two countries and their cultural histories. If, in many ways, Australian poetry came to modernism late, and in the case of many writers with some resistance, as the anthologies reveal, it has achieved its own particular triumphs.

ENDNOTES

[1] One aspect that seems unique to Australia is the continuing popularity of "the bush ballad" well into the twentieth century. The ballad form, and the authority of the somewhat "Audenesque" A.D. Hope, with his insistence on traditional rhyme and metre, are among the forces resisting modernist tendencies.

[2] When quoting from these volumes I will use the following abbreviations, *TC* for *Australian Poetry in the Twentieth Century*; and *PB* for *The Penguin Book of Modern Australian Poetry*.

[3] One small example, which may have more to do with personal feelings than ideological stands: both Gray and Lehmann appear in the Penguin anthology, albeit with fewer poems than in their own; only Tranter appears in their anthology, again with fewer poems than in his and Mead's.

[4] "The trouble is that the anthology is far less radical than the Introduction would have us believe. This book is an Establishment anthology and like other contemporary establishments this one recreates the past in its own terms—in this case an imputed 'Modernism'—and structures the present in terms of its own self-image" (130). Given his animosity toward *The Penguin Book* (in which he has ten poems), I wonder what Forbes would have said about *Twentieth Century* (in which he has two)? Laurie Duggan provides a possible glimpse: "This afternoon, John Forbes visits / with his new Selected poems / . . . / —also a new Lehmann and Gray Anthology, / worse, if possible, than the first . . . / here my pen runs out of ink. / What better comment on this dire book" (13).

[5] The first "Ern Malley" poem joins a line of art poems beginning with Slessor's "Nuremberg." "Dürer: Innsbruck, 1495" exemplifies many of the aspects Tranter and Mead point to in their remarks:

> I had often, cowled in the slumberous heavy air,
> Closed my inanimate lids to find it real,
> As I knew it would be, the colourful spires
> And painted roofs, the high snows glimpsed at the back
> All reversed in the quiet reflecting waters—
> Not knowing then that Dürer perceived it too.
> Now I find that once more I have shrunk
> To an interloper, robber of dead men's dream,
> I had read in books that art is not easy
> But no one warned that the mind repeats
> In its ignorance the vision of others. I am still
> the black swan of trespass on alien waters. *PB* 86)

It is interesting to note how many phrases from the "Ern Malley" poems have become book and poem titles in recent years, "The Black Swan" being just one example.

[6] Murray's huge *The Rabbiter's Bounty: Collected Poems* was published in both the UK and the US, as have been all his later books.

[7] Dransfield (1948-73) is an icon of 1968, a year when many of the poets born in the forties began to make their mark. Although his poetic career was very short, he has been honoured with a large *Collected Poems*.

Sharon Thesen's and Bill Manhire's Apparently Lyric Poetry

When I first went to Christchurch in 1984, a Canadian with a background in the inherited canons of British and American literature, I was all too ignorant of the literatures of Australia and New Zealand. As I met and talked with writers and critics from both countries, I wanted to do something about that ignorance. In the poetry section of a local bookstore, I discovered Bill Manhire's *Good Looks* (1982). The poem I opened to was "Declining the Naked Horse."

> The naked horse came into the room.
> The naked horse comes into the room.
> The naked horse has come into the room.
> The naked horse will be coming into the room.
> The naked horse is coming into the room.
> The naked horse does come into the room.
> The naked horse had come into the room.
> The naked horse would of come into the room
> again if we hadn't of stopped it. (56)

At the time, Manhire was as unknown to me as any other New Zealand poet, yet here was a poet whose work I would read with great delight, as my friends can attest. At first, it was the "universal" qualities of this particular poem which captivated me, although I was also drawn to its playful questioning of the "'standard' version of the metropolitan language as the norm [which] marginalizes all 'variants' as impurities" (Ashcroft et.al. 7).

Manhire's work addressed my own concerns about writing and language. Though his other poems were darker, deeper, and perhaps more complex in their relations with the reader, all had that duplicitous unwillingness to guarantee anything which to me is one of the basic signs of a contemporary poetry that knows how high the stakes are in the representational game as it is played today. I get the same kind of enjoyment, and for the same reasons, when I read the poetry of Sharon Thesen. In comparing the two, I find that readings which attempt to go beyond my personal responses are at best contingent. Still, in order to suggest something beyond my own particular taste, I can make a few points. Both poets live near the ocean, in English-speaking countries of the Pacific Rim that only became self-conscious about their post-colonial status during the period when they began to write. Given their geographical and cultural contexts, they share a sense of potential transformation based on their visceral knowledge of the shifting boundaries between land and sea, the literal dissipation of margin they observe twice a day. Nothing is fixed at the tide-line, nor in the poetry of Bill Manhire and Sharon Thesen. Perhaps there is a similarity in the dark valences and sly wit I encounter in the texts of each of them. They share the experience of writing on imperial margins, though Thesen has the extra marginality of being a woman writing in a patriarchal culture. More specifically, they both have inherited and resisted the necessities of The Great Tradition. While finding similarities is seductive, despite the differences of gender, country, and national literary traditions, I really do not know how far their commonality goes. Yet, both born in 1946, each is a representative figure of a generation of writers in New Zealand and Canada who have confronted the rich inheritance of international Modernism, the particular requirements of their own times and places, and the increasingly contingent sense of the representational powers of language which these underwrite. They are exemplary figures in the postcolonial attempt to deconstruct the traditional lyric from within: they keep the lyric's strengths, its music, its directness of tone, its suddenness, yet push against its thematic constraints in variously successful ways.

During this century mature national literatures have emerged in both Canada and New Zealand. Many writers and critics have insisted that poetry in its largest sense explore the best ways by which to represent the reality of the new country to its citizens and others. In his "Introduction" to *The Penguin Book of New Zealand Verse* (1960), Allen Curnow celebrates "an adventure, or series of adventures, in search of reality," apparently a single "reality" waiting to be discovered and represented by the proper words and phrases. He adds, "Reality must be local and special at the point where we pick up the traces" (17). Similarly, Margaret Atwood argues, in her extremely popular if also critically superficial and narrowly focused *Survival* (1972), that "Literature is not only a mirror [into which a reader looks 'and sees not the writer but himself; and behind his own image in the foreground, a reflection of the world he lives in' (15)]; it is also a map" (18). She further explains that Canadian short stories she read in high school "felt real to me in a way that Charles Dickens, much as I enjoyed him, did not" (31). All of us read this way at times, and in at least the first half of this century, many, if not most, of our writers wrote to be read this way: they were "realists" and they believed they were "representing" their countries in their actuality. While acknowledging the validity of this as one approach to language and literature, recent writers, seeing it as only one of a number of possible approaches, have begun to question and subvert the conventions of realism even as they use them in a spirit of mixed nostalgic love and witty satire. Sharon Thesen and Bill Manhire share an awareness of the end of the imperial hegemony of the traditional "realism" of lyric poetry; as well, they live the writing life of members of post-colonial nations. For these reasons, I look at them together.

Both writers are best known for their collections of shorter poems, although Manhire has published collections of short fiction and Thesen has explored the long poem. Their poetry has been critiqued as part of the lyric tradition even though one has to bend the conventional meaning of lyric to fit them into that category. I would argue that what they write, with wit and determination, is lyric/anti-lyric. Yet both achieve what Fred Wah, in speaking of Thesen's writing, calls "cadence" (114). "I believe it is important," Wah argues, "to see the use of cadence as being the concrete evidence and notation of the lyrical sub-language, the urge for the song . . . [and] her poems are exemplary of [this kind of] contemporary lyric" (121), which I interpret as post-Olson lyric, lyric written against traditional lyric conventions. Such writing consistently displays a scepticism about the trustworthiness of the only material the writer has to trust, language itself.

As well, critics have often pointed to the private nature of their poetics, the specifically personal discourses, especially intimate speech and thought, they tend to represent in their poems. When Iain Sharp says of Manhire, "His is a private voice" (238), he could be speaking of Thesen. This privacy has something to do with the way lyric "distinguishes itself from narrative as being primarily cadential" (Wah 114), but it also has to do with the fact that their poems tend to ask questions rather than make statements.

Poets of "personal and private emotion, sensation, interior, physiology, and proprioception" (Wah 114), neither has an "interest in jeremiads, vatic pronouncements, social prophecies, political campaigning, or moralising from above on topical issues" (Sharp 238); yet, as we well know, there is no such thing as non-political writing, and even these writers have been goaded upon occasion to write poems which self-consciously address the politics of New Zealand or British Columbia. When they do, it is from a personal perspective, and it is the misuse of language they attack: the brutish violence of political banality, the exploitation of language as part of an economic scam to purchase power, the extravagance of spectacle used to seduce belief. Both Thesen's "Woman Reading" (1987, 31-32) and Manhire's "Wellington" (1984, 57) render sardonic, subversive political speech, not the speeches that get made at rallies but their opposite, the small talk of those who don't belong to or share in power.

Thesen observes one example of how politics and business mix, watching fireworks at Vancouver's World Exposition "mutter banalities of profit and loss / like a dumb king":

The pronouncements collapse
into swirls of pale smoke
and another blossoms
red and another green
then a long concluding space of dark. (31)

Manhire observes a more mundane collaboration "down on Lambton Quay," where

. . . the boys from Muldoon Real Estate

are breaking someone's arm.
They don't mean harm, really, it's
nobody's business, mainly free
instructive entertainment,
especially if you don't get close
but keep well back like
all the distant figures in the crowd. (57)

If Manhire seems to play more fully with demotic speech, both speakers stand back in the crowd, not willing to be won over by the "instructive entertainment" put on by the leaders of their respective governments. Thesen segues into comic dismissal in a subtly muted couplet, with its perfect timing on the line break: "They are quite beautiful / the way kings used to be" (31). Then she turns to a personal image of art's more insistent attraction before returning to the ugly spectacle of the Social Credit political convention on TV. There, "cruel professional optimists / are counting the votes" while "we" can only project "our hunger / into utter nonsense" (32).

Manhire also uses his line breaks for maximum effect: "nobody's business" is probably all that's "mainly free" in the world of the poem. He holds us ("you") in the crowd, trying to look innocuous, pretending "to inspect with interest instead / the photographs of desirable private / properties" (57). He finishes the poem, and the reader, off with grim humour:

The question is, do you put your hands
above your head or keep them
in your pockets. Do you want a place
without a garage, could you manage
all those steps. The answer is
the man would simply like you off the streets.
You haven't even got a window
and his is full of houses. (57)

Perhaps it's because they address the politics of their times and places that these poems come closer to conventional referentiality than do other works by these writers. But does it matter finally if we identify such signs as "Muldoon" (former New Zealand prime minister and "pragmatic" leader of the National Party) or "Social Credit" (which was electing as its leader and B.C. premier Bill Vander Zalm, owner and operator of Fantasy Gardens)? Perhaps we need only recognize the general political referents as such. The wit of the poems works for the reader whether or not she knows who or what those names stand for. Yet, these poems, however effective as protesting utterances, are unusual in their specific address to contemporary political events. Most of Thesen's and Manhire's poems are both more private and more rigorously duplicitous about representation.

※

In either of these postcolonial nations it is impossible to write outside the English Literary Tradition, no matter how much one might wish to write beyond it. Manhire and Thesen are aware of the past, and their comic sensibilities serve them well when dealing head-on with that famous tradition. Manhire, in "The Poetry Reading," plays straight man to his own discourse (or so it appears, but how can it "really" be "his"?):

> The green fields. The green fields.
> How beautiful they are.
> How beautiful they are.
>
> This next poem is about the green fields
> Which are to be found in England.
> They contain certain small animals
> Which have chosen to make their life there.
>
> The public has constant access to them.
> Not to the animals, as you might
> Understandably think, but to the green fields
> In which they have chosen to make their homes. (1984, 21)

It seems England is the only place poetic "green fields" can exist. But who "really" exists in "England," given the further deflation of the human to the animal, when that lovely hesitant phrase "as you might / Understandably think" slides signifier under signifier until we cannot tell if it's the animals or the public which "have chosen to make their homes" in those "green fields"? Or is it in the traditional green-fields-poem; and which public, then, is making that choice, England's or New Zealand's? The poem becomes even more ironic in the light of Mark Williams's citation of Manhire's apt comment "that Pound's line, 'Dawn enters with little feet like a gilded Pavlova' makes it inadvisable in this country to strive too earnestly after a cosmopolitan poetics" (16), which perhaps only those who have eaten dessert in New Zealand (or Australia) can fully appreciate.

Sharon Thesen's past is different but similar. Evoking an other aspect of colonial culture-cringe, she utilizes the particularly Canadian icon of the Canadian Broadcasting Corporation to present it. "Getting On With It" appears to be a conventional lyric cry: there is pain, there must be loss, and certainly the subject of the poem is suffering and self-centred. Yet the conventional responses dissolve in the sharp solvent of laughter:

> The word
> Shakespeare
> reaches upstairs from CBC
> I shiver, don't feel
> so good. Poetry,
> 4:50 PM & this
> curtained light.
> Shakespeare
> drag yr mouldy old bones
> up these stairs & tell me
> what you died of,
> I think
> I've got it
> too. (1980, 33)

If this poem invokes the great tradition of which Shakespeare's sonnets are a central jewel, it does so only to suggest that sticking too close to such a tradition may be no more than a kind of necrophilia, or at least a disease best avoided if one is to live, and write, free. There's a subtle restraint here, partly conveyed through the hesitations of the short lines; and in the laconic demotic speech of the poem I hear a definite Canadian accent.

※

More than one critic has suggested that "Sharon Thesen is brilliant with titles" (Sullivan 32). Full of witty contradictions, the title of her first book, *Artemis Hates Romance* (1980), calls into question a number of patriarchal conventions about both women and literature. This was followed by *Holding the Pose* (1983), which once again plays with the contradictory demands made on women, especially women artists. Then came *The Beginning of the Long Dash* (1987), a title to which, as Stephen Scobie says, "Writers all across Canada . . . reacted with a delight that was not unmixed with envy: why didn't *I* think of that first?!" (1989, 45). Scobie explains:

> The phrase is instantly recognizable; we hear it every morning on the CBC, the National Research Council Official Time Signal. "At the beginning of the long dash, following ten seconds of silence, it will be precisely ten o'clock, Pacific Standard Time." Thus it carries with it the complex intertext of Canadian nationality: of transcontinental time zones (half an hour earlier in Newfoundland), of our country's vast distances and fragile unity. A single signifier, it yet signifies different times in different parts of the country.
>
> Yet its use as a title shows that the phrase is also purely detachable: quotable, citable, re-citable. On its own, it takes on a life of its own. (45)

Scobie spends a whole essay demonstrating the truth of his final two sentences here, but the point is, once again, how richly ambiguous the phrase becomes as a title. The title of her Selected Poems, *The Pangs of Sunday* (1990), quotes Jane Austen, and it too has its scattered intertexts. All these titles, intriguing in themselves, become even more so in the context of the various poems they preface. Although *Aurora* (1995) looks quite plain in comparison, it still manages to play the Canadian Northern Lights off against a romanticized poetic archaism.

Bill Manhire is also brilliant with titles. His first collection, *The Elaboration* (1972), introduces a writing which both enacts and demands from its readers more of what its title says. *How to Take Off Your Clothes at the Picnic* (1977) sets itself up against European art history in much the same way as *Artemis Hates Romance* does against traditional romantic mythology; they demonstrate an irony both postmodern and postcolonial in impetus. *Good Looks* is nicely double-minded, inviting in what it promises yet possibly distancing in its (albeit self-deprecatory) boasting. An ironic distance is something these texts seem to insist upon. *Zoetropes: Poems 1972-82* (1984), has a title at least as duplicitously intertextual as any of Thesen's, with its images from and specific reference to "the *Zoetrope* or *Wheel of Life* [, whose] images produced the illusion of movement," as the back cover copy has it. As Roger Storrocks points out, "today its images have lost their naturalness and only a cartoon cuteness remains. Many of Manhire's phrases are clichés used in a be-mused way. . . . The reader is encouraged to think of descriptions as approximate or hypothetical" (1983, 116). This remains true for *Milky Way Bar* (1991), whose title poem pushes possible reference far beyond an internationally recognized American treat. I'd argue that Thesen plays with clichés in a similar manner, although the clichés she deconstructs are as likely to be sexist as Euro-centrist. Both writers take on the banal and the conventional with the verve, humour, and implied admission of complicity which is present in their titles. Indeed, Manhire and Thesen share a love of, and an ability to play with, various inherited discourses: the lyric tradition, demotic speech, the generalizations of art, of business, of teaching, of domesticity, and of love. It's how they mix and match these within individual poems that sets their writing apart.

🦋

One aspect of postcolonial writing is its answering-back to the cultural icons of the imperial past. In "The Landlord's Tiger Lilies," Thesen takes on Rilke, one of the last great Romantic writers, one of the first great moderns. She begins with domestic detail, the detail Rilke would have ignored, at least in the *Duino Elegies*:

> A lost thing was found
> on a shiny day we didn't know
> was lost. Airplanes
> pull tin foil off the roll of the sky
> & a wandering dog
> gilds the landlord's tiger lilies.

But even as this slippery ordinariness seems to be the point, the poem slides into analysis, or something like analysis:

> For the barren reach
> of modern desire
> there must be better forms
> than this—
> something cool,
> intimate as a restaurant.

In both stanzas, signifiers slide away from ordinary reference: is it the thing or the day that was lost? The line break insists on both. And what form would ever match the intimacy of a restaurant; and what does "this" refer to, anyway? Still, as readers, we might think we knew who the "I" of this poem was, and so we would read the first line of the next stanza as belonging to it, until the next line pulled us back to an historical longshot:

> If I thought you would answer me
> Rilke called to the angels,
> If I thought
> you would answer me.

Rilke's angels evoke a massive European Romantic tradition. So too does Thesen's allusion to Bliss Carman's "Low Tide on Grand Pré," whose "barren reaches" reveal a pre-modern, all-too-Romantic desire (Scobie

1989, 48). The repetition dissipates the possibility of any singular speech act here; the line break in the second version calling attention to the artist's will while simultaneously calling it into question. At the end, the personal returns, with a twist of bathos in the last line, to be heard against the high discourse of the Great Poem, the woman writing today undercutting that tradition from her own perspective as both implied writer and mother:

> Even so, he was wrong
> not to go to his daughter's wedding
> & hurting people's feelings. (1987, 16)

Manhire's tone is somewhat sharper than Thesen's, at least when he takes on the British tradition of poetic uplift, as in what one commentator calls his "excoriation of poor Matthew Arnold ('The Buried Life'), 'The Buried Soap'" (Alcock 241). Manhire's target is both Arnold's poem and the transcendent inner truth it seeks to evoke: "turn those limpid eyes on mine, / And let me read there, love! thy inmost soul" (Arnold 245). Of course, Arnold's poem goes on to suggest that we rarely achieve a "lost pulse of feeling" in which "the heart lies plain," and that only "When a belovéd hand is laid in ours" (Arnold 247). Still, it is what we desire, surely. Yet Manhire's text turns away from such metaphysics of the heart: "Matthew Arnold's big / silver lips // puff out / their tiny stars: // one there, / one there, // one there / above the cars" (1984, 49-50). This is the modern world with a vengeance where connections once felt are lost, whether they be between the signifiers or their wished-for signifieds. Although this "I" can "simply / stay at home" asking an anonymous "her / to caress me," all that he gets is "a little pain / and pleasure" which will soon be "gone again" (50). Or he can, again "simply," wash himself "with all this buried // soap"; but what will he cleanse himself of? A friend begs him not to "give / up beauty / love and peace nor // yet all hope, / we hope (50-51). We are and we are not in Arnold's company here; these very short lines, their breaking syntax, both plead for and deny any transcendent truth. "Well, " says today's man, "I could sit // among these loud / white flowers // my friend / possibly for // hours / and endless //

hours on end" (51), but to what end? Arnold's text allows that in such meditation, when "the eye sinks inward, . . . what we mean, we say, and what we would, we know" (247). Manhire's allows no more than the "slashing indecorum" (Alcock 241) of a drugged vision:

'So first
it was the trees

went purple then
went green.' Dis-

gusting, how
obscene. I think

that's just a wicked
thing to want

to say, Charlene. (51)

Bathos, comedy of deflation. What kind of (literary) anger brings a writer to such games? An earlier poem, "On Originality," offers some clues. There the speaker wants to follow poets "out of the forest into the city / or out of the city into the forest" (1984, 24). After describing his killing of three poets, each time taking a weapon from the dead man, this poetic follower insists he has made progress:

Now I slide a gun into the gun
and go out looking.

It is a difficult world.
Each word is another bruise.

This is my nest of weapons.
This is my lyrical foliage. (24-25)

This "I" lives in the margin, in between, yet that is where he can "slide a gun into the gun" and go *on* looking, go on writing. A savagely comic view of Harold Bloom's Oedipal theory of influence, this poem resists it by the black comedy of its narrative. And yet, it seems these poems consciously "address the issues of language, reality, and their inherited and now troubling epistemological assumptions," as they call into question "European preconceptions about the relation between language and reality" and "the assumed universality of their theoretical bases" (Ashcroft *et.al.* 138). And perhaps that is where we can leave these three poems, as they challenge, in their various ways, the tyranny of the imperial centre.

In their most recent books, *Aurora* and *Milky Way Bar*, both Thesen and Manhire continue to write the sly lyric/anti-lyric poems they are best known for, but they are not simply repeating themselves. In "Dangerous," for example, Thesen continues a process of opening the poem to other characters, other speakers as she argues that "A love poem is a dangerous poem":

> How, possibly, to kill this
> or that, or leave here,
> leave her. Just
> drive down to California, if
> it takes all night you can pull
> over, sleep, or not: just go. (1995, 21)

These are simply instructions for the unwary, perhaps. But the tone is interesting in its complicity with what the poem fears, perhaps even hates. That complicity is further complicated at the end:

> But it's too late, I'm, he's
> old to be going anywhere else.
> But sit here on its haunches
> on the train to Alexandria
> watching the sumac blur by
> as a maroon haze in ditches
> of broken stone & flexing branch. (22)

Here we find, again, those shifting pronouns which complicate feeling as well as reference.

The long sequence, "Gala Roses," is something new for Thesen, however, with its long lines, broken syntax, repetitions, and collage effects. This is the kind of poem one expects from a poet fully engaged with contemporary poetic theory, yet Thesen has written essays attacking such theorists. I think the poet knows better than the essayist here. The thirteen sections of "Gala Roses" are part of an ongoing argument with self, poetry, and contemporary life and, although carefully set apart, they are part of a single poem. One section will suggest its new and defamiliarizing flavour:

Tone is something to take in the lake whose arms
embrace peninsula of trees teepees canoes and strings
of hung smoked fishes all in the museum The Museum
of Love and What Is Pretty, purchases from abroad *foreign*
merchandise sd the American grandma from her wing chair 93
pushed the plate-glass door to early bird sitting
open herself expecting to find things
not to her liking: the tune on the player piano.
On her dictionary flyleaf in blue ink *nostalgia*
arthritis recluse royal expanse of lawn out the window
should have been peacocks too but their cries hurt she
never stopped loving her third husband the one
who looked like Spencer Tracy (72)

The shorter poems in *Milky Way Bar* seem to play the same games of wit and irony as before, but Manhire too has explored extended forms, even if, in his case, that only means a short series. In part, he is deliberately finding comic ways of taking on the colonial history of New Zealand, as in "Allen Curnow Meets Judge Dredd," which begins "How pleased we were, wedged solid, / exhausted forty years ago. Was that / perhaps part of our appeal?" (1991, 39). This could be alluding to Curnow's early post-war attempts to find somehow a historical New Zealand anthology of poetry. But, as the poem later says, "more than / one poet //

got lost in thought / in time long past, perhaps wedged solid" (39). The nine part poem, "Life with Madame Rosa," takes the children's toy crystal ball seriously enough to predict a magic number of possibilities for it or through it. The final three poems, "Hirohito," "Brazil," and "Phar Lap," all take on history in one guise or another. They play with the variety of media-constructed images of all three in Manhire's own version of collage, what he calls in "Phar Lap" "Unlikely combinations" (68). Once again, his witty sense of the colonial disjunctions—those mis-readings, mis-apprehensions that occur to both perception and its language in new spaces—creates a dispassionate irony throughout these poems. "Brazil," for example, plays off movies, adventure tales, and I suspect the poems of Elizabeth Bishop:

> 3.
> Papers on a desk, a river,
> and around each bend in the river
> Brazil replaced Brazil.
> It was a funny idea, she thought:
> tampons in the jungle.
>
> Papers on a desk safeguarded the desk.
> You sat in a chair while the man there
> told you his problems: no village,
> no machinery, no available women. (61)

There is nothing here quite so new for the poet as "Gala Roses" is for Thesen, but there is a quiet maturity of vision at work which invites a similarly thoughtful response. While entertaining, these new poems subtly ask some tough questions.

❧

Throughout their careers, Thesen and Manhire have entered lyric discourse in order to mine its conventional twists and turns of emotional logic. They have sought to go beyond lyric: Thesen by writing musical serial poems of various lengths ("Parts of Speech," "Radio New France

Radio," "Long Distance: An Octave," *Confabulations*, "Marine Life, 1970," "Being Adults," "The Beginning of the Long Dash," "Six," and now the more experimental "Gala Roses"); Manhire by turning to prose (the comically strange choose-your-own-adventure style *The Brain of Katherine Mansfield*, and the various short stories collected in *The New Land A Picture Book*) and extending the philosophic reach of his recent longer poems. But it is their ability to play the lyric fool I have concentrated on here, and I want to conclude with an example of sustained lyric invention and deconstruction by each of them.

Sharon Thesen's "Pensatrice," the very title of which evokes a dissolving semblance, gives and takes away with the same gesture: there is representation and naming, there is, she insists, an "outside world," but there are denials hard-won, as well, and nothing remains absolutely solid, not syntax, not the words themselves. The line breaks and the punctuation refuse to pin things down, allowing reference full play. It is a marvelous performance, and a deeply moving one, and that is both its power and its charm:

> Is there anything
> you can do you ask
> without the question mark
> & I shake my head No
> I say, It's okay. Cry
> me a river of some old
> old suffering, then return
> to my book so frivolous
> a biography, Chanel's affairs
> with officers and the way
> she insulted Jean Cocteau.
> It was either that or
> cruelty or boredom,
> Shackleton dragging his ship
> across the icy wastes
> or the baroque concealments
> of Henry James. Your new book

reminds me of *Orlando*
I meant to say to Michael—
the scene of the skaters
& the lights telling stories
of the outside world
and I insist it *is*
outside us. My tears wetted
my husband's night shirt
but he didn't mind. By not using
the word 'trace'
I keep the salt in,
the part that stains—
as aurora borealis stains
the skies of night
by quick turns of her
absolute mirror,
her salt & chewy hair. (1987, 82)

Manhire's "Water, A Stopping Place," creates something of the same effect. It is a beautifully modulated narrative of changing perspectives on both "the given" and the language in which "it" is given. Roger Storrocks devotes a number of pages to opening up its many complexities in all their rich duplicity, but he finally thinks it is not quite the "open text" Lyn Hejinian has called for because "its final lines usher us back to our seats . . . for the lyrical finale" (122). I disagree: the final lines refuse closure as language falls away into simple sound. This poem manages the difficult feat of creating a deliberately vague sense of both insecurity in and acceptance of the world. Like Thesen's lyric, it names and unnames in the same breath.

There are places named for
other places, ones where
a word survives whatever happened

which it once referred to. And there are
names for the places water comes and touches,

but nothing for the whole. A world

released from reference
is travelling away. Its monotones of swell
surround the modest island nation

where a man and woman
lie together by a stream
on a blanket anchored to the grass

by stones. She has turned a radio on
and as their passion comes to rest
she hears the first commercial break

which advertises cereals, then tractors.
Later she walks down
to fill a bottle from the stream

and stands, bare feet on gravel,
meaning to scoop water out of water,
her dress tucked up. It is late

to be changing the topic of a conversation
but she is searching for a word,
something to tell him why he something huge

about devotion, some other sound beyond
this small dark gargle from the past,
not vowel, not consonant, not either. (1984, 74)

Let these two poems stand for the lyric/anti-lyric music both these poets
achieve in their best work. In them I hear a sound of the present listening
to and arguing with the past.

Some New Zealand Poets in Europe / Europe in Some New Zealand Poems

Allen Curnow, C.K. Stead, Jenny Bornholdt

꼴꼴 One of the many possibly haunting questions in the so-called New World is: Where does our culture come from? When we speak of culture, of course,—especially when we speak as poets, we speak of language. Language, with all its varied cultural baggage, in-forms writing, and, for those of us whose inheritance is European, that luggage is "an ancient slang *and* a modern" we have slowly learned to speak on our own terms (cf. Jones 1970, 163). From Europe, vision moves outward, a centrifugal push. From Britain as a part of Europe, the push is the same. Problems of dissemination. And settlement. Sediment: the theory of layering in language that we build upon. Whoever we are. Wherever we are. How it happens.

When I travel to New Zealand from Canada, I have to go through the USA. Similarly, if I send books to or order books from New Zealand, they will travel through the USA. It was not always thus; and once, not just Canadian writing but even US writing had to travel through the centre of empire, through London, to reach New Zealand. Today, Britain is becoming ever more enmeshed in the European Union, but for most of its colonizing history it has stood apart, and New Zealand, like Australia and Canada, participated in the imperial enterprise run from London. New Zealanders reached Europe through London; Europe reached New Zealanders through London; London therefore had some control over the version of Europe New Zealand knew. While this is no longer necessarily the case, even now when New Zealand poets travel to Europe, they tend to travel via Singapore, India, etc., to London, and then on to the European mainland. A Canadian, I go East to Europe or I go West to New Zealand. Yet when I find Europe in New Zealand writing I recognize a distanced view, a way of seeing it, that reminds me of home: a Canadian might see it that way, or a way like that, too. The term "Europe," of course, is open to question. First of all, it stands here for its various "parts," different countries that have produced certain aspects of "high culture," "origin," "colonization," etc.. "Europe," then, is not only, say, France, Germany, Denmark, or Austria. It also encompasses the ways they interact with each other culturally, economically, politically, and emotionally. It is a continuing issue, as Tom Nairn argues, quoting Etienne Balibar: "'we have to ask ourselves what this word "Europe" means and what it will signify tomorrow . . . In reality we are here discovering the *truth* of the earlier situation, which explodes the representation that we used to have of it. Europe is not something that is "constructed" at a slower or faster pace, with greater or less ease; it is a historical problem without any pre-established solution'" (6). Nairn's and Balibar's speculations about nationalism touch on matters the poets discussed here tend to slide around, but the tenor of this quotation should remind us that "Europe" is anything but a monolithic concept.

As early as 1924, R.A.K. Mason, the first major New Zealand poet, "placed" self and people out on the borderlands in one of his best known poems. "Sonnet of Brotherhood" reveals its modern vision in the way it creates, through the whole of its fourteen lines, an image of humanity alone against all odds on the far edge of the universe that may also be read as an image of pakeha, or white, New Zealand (as Curnow, Stead, Evans, and others have pointed out):

> Garrisons pent up in a little fort
> with foes who do but wait on every side
> knowing the time soon comes when they shall ride
> triumphant over those trapped and make sport
> of them: when those within know very short
> is now their hour and no aid can betide:
> such men as these not quarrel and divide
> but friend and foe are friends in their hard sort
> And if these things be so oh men then what
> of these beleaguered victims this our race
> betrayed alike by Fate's gigantic plot
> here in this far-pitched perilous hostile place
> this solitary hard-assaulted plot
> fixed at the friendless outer edge of space. (35)

The concept of margin that can be read here relates to Europe that "originary" place a hemisphere and half a world away. Although Canadians of Mason's generation shared Europe's hemisphere, they would, I think, have had no difficulty identifying with the sensibility inherent in this poem. Indeed, the first word of the poem, "Garrisons," calls to mind Northrop Frye's famous theory of a "garrison mentality" (225-26).

Allen Curnow, C.K. Stead, and Jenny Bornholdt are interesting not only because they have entered Europe and allowed Europe to enter their work in one way or another, but because they represent three different generations of New Zealand writing. Having published poetry since the early thirties, Curnow is now the grand old man of New Zealand poetry, and considered by many to be one of the major poets writing in English today. He is also, in many ways, the architect of modern New Zealand poetry, especially through his influential editing of, first, *A Book of New Zealand Verse 1923-45* (1945), and then *The Penguin Book of New Zealand Verse* (1960). Stead is a member of the middle generation of poets, following upon the generation of which James K. Baxter is the most famous representative; he is also clearly a modernist as opposed to simply modern poet. Bornholdt is one of many fine younger poets born in the sixties and seventies, following that exciting and revolutionary generation who started publishing in the late sixties, and which includes Bill Manhire, Elizabeth Smither, and Ian Wedde, among others.

I want to approach the three poets via a somewhat roundabout route, most specifically through some of the insights in Roger Storrocks's series of essays on New Zealand culture and writing. For Storrocks, Curnow is the major twentieth century fabricator of New Zealand as a literary site. In "The Invention of New Zealand," he subtly argues that Curnow's famous vision of "realism" is a central myth of twentieth century New Zealand cultural criticism, pointing out that "Allen Curnow has had a long career as a magician, a maker of fictions, yet always in the language of 'reality' or 'truth'" (1983, 9). "Curnow as *homo faber*" (10) interests Storrocks more than Curnow as simple representational poet of place. Yet, as he points out, "[t]he best magicians are so subtle they are taken for realists—they seem to be merely pointing to what is there, to powers inherent in things" (11). Storrocks shows how Curnow shaped an attitude towards New Zealand as place, and as rooted home-to-be, by the way he shaped *The Penguin Book of New Zealand Verse*. The "reality" Curnow sought, according to Storrocks, was a myth, of absences essentially, especially the absences of British and European inherited culture, a reminder, to Canadians, of Robert Kroetsch's much later, and much more self-reflexive, presentation of absence in the epic list of European absences, mixed with erotic ones, on the Canadian prairies, in *Seed Catalogue*. In Curnow's editorial endeavour (surely his poetic one too), "Palgravian fountains and dragons [signs of a fantastic Europe of cultural nostalgia] were playfully conjured up only to see them transformed by the magic word 'reality'" (11). Insofar as that "reality" invokes Europe, it does so only as it imperially impinged on the locale he was striving to make his own, his home. "Landfall in Unknown Seas," where a first murder sealed the islands' fate, imagines the power of this "realist" Europe, as it balances false celebrations 300 years on against a deeper, darker truth: "The stain of blood that writes an island story" (Curnow 1982, 75).

Recalling his own response to the Penguin anthology, Storrocks deliberately invokes a period now long past for both New Zealand poetry and for Curnow himself. But he also inquires into the art-in-fact of a central artifact, *The Penguin Book of New Zealand Verse* itself, which influenced the next generations of both poets and critics. Curnow's early statement that "some not insubstantial poems have sprung from those very anxieties about our footing on our own soil, our standing in the world, which must continue to inhibit us as a people" (1987, 74) speaks directly to a Canadian reader of a shared colonial heritage. But does it speak the only "reality"? Storrocks is not entirely sure, although, as a teenager, he was moved by the way the *Penguin Book* brought such a concept home to its readers: "Certainly this is true of many of the poems in the *Penguin Book*—they have 'grown' from a sense of suffering, anxiety, and absence ('what great gloom / . . . in a land of settlers / With never a soul at home'" (1983, 27).[1] The anxiety is, of course, the settler colonists' anxiety that any art made "here" cannot match that made "back home," "there"; and besides, as Frye once put it for Canadians, "Where is *here*" anyway (220)?[2] However much the criticism of Storrocks and others questions the ways in which Curnow fabricated a myth of the real New Zealand through his poetry and editing, that fabrication helped him find his own answer to Frye's question. What is interesting is that Curnow doesn't seem to have been able to write in Europe, nor to write Europe into his poems, until he felt "at home" in New Zealand, and that didn't happen until after he had written his many poems and edited his two anthologies of discovery and settlement. Although their mode may still be essentially realistic, the poems in *An Incorrigible Music* (1979) reveal that in the seventies Curnow felt sufficiently "at home" to be able to go "away" and write of Europe (or "a" Europe), secure in the knowledge that he had solid ground, his own, from which to construct his vision.

In "No Theory Permitted on These Premises," Storrocks writes of how the concept of "theory," in all its various forms, has long been seen in New Zealand as something imposed from outside—Britain, the USA, Europe (especially with the New French Theory, as it tends to be mono-lithically perceived). Again, a tough and pragmatic "realism," embodied in "our no-nonsense culture" (1984a, 129), was proposed to stand against it. Writers, especially of Curnow's generation, Storrocks explains: "have to be on their toes to address a community that barely welcomes them—they can't afford to waste words, they'd better have something solid, something bloody important to say . . ." (129). This need to have "something bloody important to say" would seem to apply to Curnow's poetic approaches to the European given: history as violent enactment within leading to violent exploitation without, as "Landfall in Unknown Seas" and other poems of that ilk suggest. For the pakeha New Zealand poet of the thirties to fifties, the first sense of Europe as an idea points to its violent appropriation of the place, and so of his own ambivalent presence there as inheritor of that violent act.

It does not seem surprising, then, that when he eventually turns to European subjects, Curnow sticks, quite literally, to "something *bloody* important to say," in shaping fragmented narratives out of two assassinations, one historical and one as close as 1978's newspapers. And although his later poems are brilliant displays of competing discourses, ironic interrogations of the various languages and ideologies competing in the sites which are human lives, the poems still appear realist, and gesture to the older ideal of realism Stead remarks as Curnow's generation's literary inheritance from the Auden generation in Britain (1981, 139-159). Although Curnow has never stopped growing as a poet, and has learned a great deal from the Modernists as well as the moderns, the two sequences, "In the Duomo" and "Moro Assassinato," although definitely the work of Storrocks's "magician," seem meant to be read as realist, as dealing with "the facts of the matter."

The poems of *An Incorrigible Music* are angry, sardonic, humanist, even bleakly mystical. The volume is a kind of Job's complaint with no necessary sense that God may ever return answer. And although the two sequences are its centrepieces, it opens and closes with poems that underline the sense of being no more than a fish to be caught and killed in the world, as it is. "Canst Thou Draw out Leviathan with an Hook?" invokes the Bible only to step beyond its categories into a fishing stream in New Zealand, where a local fish serves as illustration—but of what precisely? "A rockpool catches the blood, / so that in a red cloud of itself / the kawahai lies white belly uppermost" (1982, 198): this image of so-called natural death will return to haunt the sequences. Meanwhile, in this very poem, human replaces kawahai, "God" replaces fisherman,

> and you're caught, mate, you're caught,
> the harder you pull it
> the worse it hurts, and it makes
> no sense whatever in the air
> or the seas or the rocks
> how you kick or cry, or sleeplessly
> dream as you drown.
> A big one! a big one! (199)

At the end of the book, the other framing poem, the title poem, returns to "nature" to count losses, but finds only that counting, even a small group of herons, never ends: "punctually the picture completes itself / and is never complete" (235). If the herons' music is incorrigible, so is the poet's, as *An Incorrigible Music* demonstrates. But to be incorrigible is to be, necessarily, wrong; the poet warns us, once again, to distrust the very reality he has worked so hard to represent: "There's only one book in the world, and that's the one / everyone accurately misquotes. // *A big one! A big one!*" (236)—such a proud, such a sardonic and pitiful cry. But just who is hooked here anyway?

"In the Duomo" turns back in time to "26 APRIL 1478" (206), to the assassination of Giuliano de' Medici. The cathedral, as the opening "RECITATIVE" puts it, "is the rock where you cast your barbed wishes. / That is the clifftop where you hang by the eyes. / Here is where Leviathan lives" (202). The ancient art of the building is invoked only to point out that "'of such' is the highly / esteemed 'kingdom of heaven', what else?" (202). The voice of the poem, aloof yet interested, slips forward to indicate the mass, which "serves up to Messer Domeneddio god and lord / the recycled eternity of his butchered son, / this mouthful of himself alive and warm," and then adds, almost as if it didn't count, "this is the cup / to catch and keep him in, this is where he floats / in a red cloud of himself" (203), a sharp reminder of the kawahai that becomes the image of the murdered Giuliano as well as of Aldo Moro.

"In the Duomo" evokes an earlier Italy of blood feuds and murder, in which even the sanctuary of the church wasn't safe from assassination, invoking the images of sacrifice—of fish for human food, of Christ for human salvation—only to demonstrate how ineffective the ideal of sacrifice is in a world where realpolitik rules in all its pragmatic cynicism. As the poem offers views of "A PROFESSIONAL SOLDIER" (203-05) who finally says no, and of the "two priests / for the cathedral job" (206), it traverses past and present to hold both up to a kind of philosophical ridicule in which the church, especially, appears as bad as anyone. "26 APRIL 1478" sharply and clearly narrates the assassination attempt, including Lorenzo's escape as his brother "bled where he had to bleed," the church filled with "the strong bestial smell / of dissolving clay." The corpse is, after all, the assassins' "offering to the oldest god / that holiest day" (207). The image of Giuliano's dying "where he had to die" recalls that kawahai, but, while the terms in which the death is represented seem to imply a sacrifice the rimes and the flattened Biblical allusions sardonically undercut such a reading. As Edward Burman points out, the concept of "sacrifice" can be found throughout Curnow's earlier work (23-31); but if in the earlier poems, "sacrifice was perceived as an essential part of the attempt to create a New Jerusalem in New Zealand," the encounter with Europe both past and present recorded in *An Incorrigible Music* leads to the recognition "that sacrifice does not necessarily lead to the success which Job's sacrifice achieved: it is merely an inevitable part of the human condition, with no sense of progress implied" (35).

"Moro Assassinato," especially, reaches this recognition. As Curnow's note on *An Incorrigible Music* says, "[t]he character of the book was decided, and most of the poems written, some months earlier than the kidnapping of Aldo Moro," but "[i]t was impossible to live in Italy from early April through June, reading the newspapers, catching the mood from chance remarks or no remarks at all, and not be affected" (1982, 241). Affected, he affects a range of narrative stances—the auto-biographical, the documentary, the fictional—to get at the meaning, or perhaps the meaninglessness, of the kidnapping and assassination. And to do so, he begins at home, for from that perspective, as "The Traveller," he can argue the common humanity he shares with the dead man in Europe: "All seas are one sea, / the blood one blood / and the hands one hand" (220). Is this simply the tourist's hope? I think it is more than that, as the poem insists on the connections felt between visiting poet and local people. The rest of the sequence, making use of the documents available, enters the voices of terrorists, of Moro himself, and of a kind of "objective" commentator who oversees it all, remarking the various responses within and without the act. The "event" is the core of the poem, and its Italian setting is far less important, although it is clear that Curnow would not have written it had he not been there.

The text manages to make a fictional foray into the very minds of the figures involved, often through documentary use of such sources as an interview with a German terrorist, yet it also maintains enough distance to display the faultlines in their discourses. Here, for example, is "An Urban Guerilla":

> the faces that came and went,
> the seven of us comrades

like the days of the week repeating
themselves, themselves,
it was cleaning your gun ten times
a day, taking time
washing your cock, no love
lost, aimlessly fondling
the things that think faster than fingers,
trigger friggers, gunsuckers. (222)

The first few lines almost invoke our sympathy, but the slow descent into a mechanized vision of both the communal and the personal body under-cuts that and replaces it with a sense of sociopathic dehumanization. Any connection we might feel has been cut off from the other side, yet the poem speaks from there: this is brilliantly realized modern satire, the more pow-erfully antagonistic for its cool refusal of obvious anger. But the black comedy of the guerillas' representation of their acts does the satirist's job of showing us that battles like this are finally battles of language. Their voice manages to boast and complain at once from "the Prison of the People" (226), the very name of which the poet clearly recognizes as a per-fect example of revolutionary "newspeak" that requires no comment as it enters into the dialogic continuum of the poem. That prison

was a tight squeeze, how long
would it take to squeeze the brain
till the fuses blew?
Not that we gave it a thought,
wasn't the State on the block
and the front page yelling rape,
and the cameras in at the fuck
and the dirtiest pants scared off
the arses of the Bourses,
when we took him alive and we left
five dead in the street? (226)

I think the antipodean term for this sort of thing is "whinging."

The poems on Moro himself have all the empathy the poems on the guerillas lack, yet they too recognize their own fictionality, a fictionality that even applies to "The Letters," for example, the real ones published in the newspapers then and not just the poem of that title which asks the central question: "How can we know / who it is that speaks?" (228). The poem slides from the investigator's necessary skepticism to the letter writer's increasingly desperate desire to be recognized: "But I am, you would say, / not I but another who is not to be," where the line break reinforces the loss of self in which the whole poem implicates terrorism and realpolitik, "taken seriously" (229). But the "Moro" of the poem comes to recognize that loss and to rebel against it too, as his final words show:

I repeat, I do not accept
the unjust, ungrateful judgement of the party.
I absolve, I excuse nobody.
My cry is the cry of my family, wounded to death.
I request that at my funeral, nobody
representing the State, nor men of the Party,
take part, I ask to be followed by the few
who have truly wished me well and are therefore worthy
to go with me in their prayers, and in their love. (230)

This is powerful rhetoric, but like all rhetoric it falls before a fusillade, which "The Executioners" describes all too fully, even to their vision of Moro as a kind of *liebestod* Molly Bloom saying "yes" to all eleven shots (232). Dead, Moro joins the other ghosts; though mourned now, he becomes as they are, and

They are all dead as nineteen hundred
years or the moment after.
They do not live in memory or imagination
or history, or any other
of death's entertainments. Poems
don't work any more. (232)

"Moro Assassinato" concludes on a note slightly more hopeful than that, but not by much. "The poor publish their grief / on doors and door-ways," an announcement they all understand of "the day's news, *Death was here*" (233). But what the poem says, finally, is that such an announcement does nothing, changes nothing:

> Dreamlessly nonna nods
>
> into her ninetieth year,
> where she sits, catching the sun
>
> at the dark doorway;
> over her, in black and white
>
> run off at the tipografia
> round the corner, which is always busy
>
> _____
>
> **per Aldo Moro**
>
> _____
>
> strikes off one more. (233-34)

This is closure with a vengeance, and to a purpose both formal and the-matic. The traveler has seen, and seen clearly, "something *bloody* impor-tant to say" in a Europe whose reality, historically and culturally, all too clearly reinforces the knowledge he brought with him to it. Which is to say, perhaps, only that Curnow's "realism" has become a satirist's sar-donic vision of a world speeding towards its self-made hell. And that the Europe he encountered in Italy in 1978 embodied that vision.

It's possible that this reading ignores important aspects of Curnow's work as a whole, but I can only register my feeling that his poetry since 1972 has generally been both energetic and increasingly angry. C.K. Stead, in a 1963 article on Curnow, says of his poems that, "for all the anguish which lies somewhere behind their achieved irony, [they] are engaged in affirming life and a world which is real"; and he adds, that "[w]hat emerges from [Curnow's] struggle ["to meet and encompass the contraries" of our world] is a kind of affirmation Yeats called 'tragic joy'" (1981, 205). As the poems of *An Incorrigible Music* and later volumes demonstrate, such an oxymoronic achievement is exhilarating but not easy, for the writer or the reader. Curnow's Europe, as inscribed in "In the Duomo" and "Moro Assassinato," is a stark and scandalous icon of savage civilization, another oxymoron his poetry has investigated both at home and abroad.

⬚

The Europe of later New Zealand poets is not so harsh a place, but it is equally complex. It is also much more a sign system and a system of discourses. In part, this may be because they approach it through what Stead, in "From Wystan to Carlos," would call modernist "open form" perspectives (139-59). It may also have to do with their ages, and the relatively greater ease with which they take their place in the world, in New Zealand. Stead, for example, went to England as a graduate student, and his first book was the well-received study of literary modernism, *The New Poetic: Yeats to Eliot* (1964).

In 1964 Stead also published his first book of poetry, *Whether the Will is Free*, whose "Pictures in a Gallery Undersea" (1964, 52-56), had already appeared in *The Penguin Book of New Zealand Verse*. That poem stands in interesting relation to *The New Poetic*, as it mixes quotations and historical references to build a prototypic archaeological "dig" of literary London. Formally, it owes much to *The Wasteland*, but thematically it is a "wild colonial boy's" delighted leap into the literary fray. Dreaming encounters with Wilde, Hueffer, Pound, Eliot, and others, he also confronts his Scandinavian grandfather, "who asked me / Directions to the dock; and later departed, / Bearing me with him in his northern potency / South" (53). If the poem pays too much homage to its predecessors, if its capitalized left-hand margins imply a youthful insecurity in open form, it nevertheless argues its subject's southern potency as he eagerly returns to join the grand tradition:

It was winter, the year '58,
And many were dead. But into the same heart and out

> Through channels of stone and light, the blood still
>   pulsed—
> Carried me with it down New Oxford Street
> Through Soho to the whirling clock of the Circus,
> Then down, on to the bridge. (55-56)

It's the insouciant sense of belonging there that separates this poem from its New Zealand context, Mason's "Song of Allegiance," in which, however ironically, the subject is only "bringing up the rear" (45).

During the seventies, both Stead's theory and practice move away from the Yeats-Eliot tradition toward the Pound one. In poetry, this leads to sequences and long poems, the inevitable outcome, it now seems, of the thinking about open form that resulted in "From Wystan to Carlos." And in the eighties, due to both the changes in his own poetic and his travels to Europe, Stead writes two sequences in which "Europe" looms large: "Yes, T.S.," a round-the-world travelogue, and *Paris*, a comical study in cultural semiotics. Both poems serve the ideals of openness Stead explicated in his essay, while displaying a sensibility happily at home in the indeterminate. In "Yes, T.S.," the subject insists upon his autobiographical presence even if the writing reveals that he is no more than a written figure in a text: "Je est une auto / elle suis Rimbaud" (1982, 47). In *Paris*, however, everything is up for grabs, and the "I" of the poem is as fragmented an inscription as every other piece of its ironic bricolage.

"Yes, T.S." is a collage of sorts, but it is most of all a series of intelligent and witty glimpses of places noticed in passing (through). So the poem catches images and texts of Singapore and London on the way to Paris, Dijon, Munich, and Amsterdam, and then on to San Francisco before returning to Auckland. The passage which gives it its title sets its tone:

> Yes t.s.
>
>   it's
>
> (it is)
> still
>
>   whirling away
>   a world

```
                    it's London
calling
the Clash      /       dreadlocks
toilets
                    and thanks
for the anagram
            to Rosie Allpress)
                        flush
(t.s.)
                    aux etoiles.
                    (1982, 28-29)
```

This, as much as anything in the poem, demonstrates how far the writer has traveled both formally and thematically from "Pictures in a Gallery Undersea." The same good humour, complicated by delicious pseudo self-deprecation, marks the stance of an archetypically naive tourist in Paris: "All these French live in France speak French / all the time such as the infants even speak it / better than I can making each word come out / clear as a little bell" (39). Even the cute little girls, all called Natalie, "speak French / from morning to night / du matin à nuit / sans cesse and without any mistakes." The pleasure here is a self-conscious pleasure of the cultural text. The subject playfully engages languages and cultural givens while accepting the tourist's role with wit and grace. The formal lessons on collage-text he has assimilated from Pound give him leave to refuse the temptation to appropriate a history he doesn't know: it's the now of travel, of sighting and citing what he encounters, that the poem processes. This now contains the past, of course, especially the always present past of art. So it's not surprising to find references to poetry and painting, like the playful repetitive run at Matisse (43-4) or the commentary on "Verlaine's / roses: absolute red / his ivy: absolute black // tout rouge les roses / tout noirs les lierres // and isn't that also / la poésie du fait?" (41). This is a poetry of fact: it may sound something like Curnow's realism but it's not. Formally, Stead's text is more generously welcoming to all sorts of discourses. If "Moro Assassinato" achieves some dialogism in its dramatic presentation of its story, "Yes T.S." becomes a bazaar of babel in which every sign imaginable has its moment, even as its significcation slips the handcuffs of historical and cultural meaning.

In its play with other tongues, but also in its reprinting of excerpts from books, "Notices in the Lavatory, 1st floor, / Hotel Richelieu (one star)" (46), overheard conversations, quotations, an interview with a Jew in Amsterdam that carefully refuses commentary or any "poetic" addition to his memories of the war, the note on "Correspondences" (50-51) from Stead's journal, and even a German translation of one of his earlier poems, "Yes T.S." achieves a witty intensity of surface. But then, its meaning may be that surface is all that it, or we, can encounter in travel. It is at ease with this prospect, and that may be the major sign of its author's cultural security in New Zealand and the world. To the subject of "Yes T.S.," Europe simply is; it's neither symbolic cultural weight to be borne nor historic enterprise to be refused. The pleasure of its text is a measure of the pleasure of exploration back to that ground no longer weighted with any specific significance to the antipodean world traveler.

Paris, a poem in ten parts, confronts a problem "Yes T.S." merely brushed against but which faces everyone from outside writing about Europe. Europe has been overwritten to the extreme; and so it seems there is no way to say anything new about Paris, for example. Stead is too intelligent not to know this, so he confronts the problem head-on, a sly sabotaging bricoleur. *Paris* parades its happy heteroglossia, as it cobbles together clichés, famous images, and fragments of other texts from Rimbaud through Henry Miller to the latest travel advertisements. In its insouciant playfulness the text is both postmodern and postcolonial: this Paris is marked as the desired, beloved, singular place, but the vision is anything but misty-eyed (except of course parodically). After all, written from the country of the Rainbow Warrior, it knows the dark forces at work in the City of Light.

Paris is the sign of the desired Other to romantics everywhere, whether they compare it with Kansas City, Victoria, Brisbane, or Palmerston North. One long apostrophe, the poem begins in dream, with a prayer: "Paris, summon me to your table. / I invite myself to your board, I accept your invitation / and my defeat. Paris, put yourself in the picture" (1984, #1).[3] But to be "in the picture" is to be framed, whether by the texts of art, photography, and film, or by this text, and the rest of the poem slips from one "take" to another, never letting one take precedence, continually reveling in the way each view further undermines any single determinate sense of the city or its people. Indeed, as an outsider, the poem's equally indeterminate subject is especially well placed to say "Paris, you don't know yourself" (#2), before beginning to slap the various pieces of his particular collage onto the "canvas" of his text. Names of places and famous people float across its surface, but so do images and phrases we have heard before, the languages by which Paris has become known as "Paris."

In an acute and playful example of cultural appropriation (but is it that when directed back against the self-designated cultural centre?), *Paris* turns to cinema: "Here's Catherine Deneuve she's walking under klieg lights / . . . —hesitates, lights cigarette, / walks on. The cameras love her and so do you" (#5). Who is this "you"? Pronominal uncertainty reigns throughout *Paris*, further fragmenting the subject at play within it, as the end of this passage shows:

> You feel yourself drifting away
> over traffic, through the jostle of falling leaves,
> above the cold shoulder of a statue staring down whitely
> at a girl on a bench in the Luxembourg Gardens weeping
> at the thought of Catherine Deneuve. Your name may be
> > > Truffaut
> but there's no end in sight. This Paris is like a disease. (#5)

Paris also turns to art, and images of and out of Picasso, Matisse, Bonnard, Gauguin, Manet, Magritte, and Chagall suddenly appear. Sometimes they are simply signposts to the city of the mind the poem is constructing; sometimes they perform a more ironic function, as when, in its lightly satirical jab at French politics, *Paris* offers this juxtaposition:

> In Le Déjeuner sur l'Herbe of Manet only the lady is naked.
> In the eyes of the President are tears for the love of France
> while he pours the wine. Nor will the franc be devalued. (#8)

Paris is finally a poem about dreams, about the ways an economics of culture can influence the cultural economy by which we live and dream. When advertising and tourism occupy the sites where poetry and art once wrestled with their angels, mere technology cheapens and replaces imagination:

> Showing at the cinema on the far side of the square
> is your movie with Catherine Deneuve—yes already it's made.
> She kisses you in a mirror and the cats on the mansard
> quote Rimbaud at the moon, which answers in French. (#10)

Perhaps. But *Paris* the poem isn't absolutely sure, just as it isn't absolutely pure. In a textual space finally full of nameless figures, the poem closes with this opening addressed to all possible tourists and dreamers: "do not neglect to dictate these informal strictures / with all their whims of glass, their glosses on lust, / to the Paris of Paris that's nobody's dream but your own" (#10).

These poems suggest that a postcolonial vision can now encounter Europe with a clarity similar to, if still different from, the European, and perhaps with a comic perspicacity that only comes from the outside. The casual confidence of Stead's writings reveals a culture come of age. The work of younger writers, whatever direction it takes, is equally confident, not in the self necessarily but in the self's ability to engage the materials of both the craft and the encountered other. For them, at least, Europe is simply there, now, a place to be entered, a place to be written, up.

※

Since Jenny Bornholdt's *This Big Face* appeared in 1988, she has achieved a significant presence in New Zealand poetry, as the reference to her in Evans's *Penguin History* indicates: "Jenny Bornholdt (1960) seems completely original in much of what she writes, and her long poem 'Sophie Travels Backwards on the Train' . . . represents a genuinely experimental talent" (255). With wit and passion, her poems assert the power of a vision informed by feminine, perhaps even feminist, concerns. Her first two books are centred in New Zealand, and, as in the "Sophie" poem, they often concentrate on character studies and explorations of home territory. When Europe does enter these early poems, it does so ironically, as, for example, in "Spring," where in a lover's dream, "I am always pale and / we are in Paris / which is just off the / end of Te Awamutu" (1989, 23). In the dream anything can happen: she can even "say pain au chocolat / which somehow reminds / me of pain of death / —biting into soft / tragedies going for the / sweet centre which / confounds the plot" (23).

But in *Waiting Shelter*, a book of travel, the poems enter the real Europe, partly to explore the roots of family. But because a real Europe almost always becomes an artistic sign before it is anything else to those from without, it is fitting that the book opens with a wittily temporal "reading/writing" of Cézanne's *Les Grandes Baigneuses*. In its recognition of Impressionism's engagement with people as well as landscape, "The Bathers" sets the tone for the poems to follow. It is also a fine study of the way art works on and in the mind, as it infers the painted bodies' delight that "Cézanne / abandoned them in such a / pleasurable landscape" (1991, 9).

> Bodies slanted towards trees,
> water, a dog asleep on the
> ground. They sighed, over those
> eight years, talked amongst
> themselves quietly, each morning
> a small *ah* of pleasure
> at the day, wondering if
> *today* . . . for eight years
> until the trees grew thick
> with colour, the lake
> darkened and their bodies'
> cool formation fixed
> beside the admiring water. (9)

Even before the subject leaves to travel to Europe, Europe has traveled to her, and not just in the reproductions of artbooks: "My parents send post-cards / saying . . . that the sky here / is the bluest they have run / their eyes across" (14). Those postcards would seem to fix that "here" in Europe, but the rest of the poem allows it to slip the bonds of reference: in a post-colonial world, Frye's question can be directed anywhere. "Tourists Often Stop," the first sequence in *Waiting Shelter*, uses the prose poem, a European invention, to comment on the behavior of tourists from various "theres" when they visit "here," New Zealand. The title sequence is a narrative about family, in the third rather than first person. Once again, *word* of Europe enters, but it undercuts expectations, it isn't different enough: "Her father rings from Austria, says / it is all Mozart and the Sound of / Music" (35). No wonder he "is depressed / because the whole world is the same" (35). He almost has to be "Astonished and at the same time / blinded by what he sees" (35), and that is the point.

In the section titled "Le Nom," Bornholdt begins to juxtapose her text to all those other texts that make up Europe in our minds. Like Stead, she knows the impossibility of seeing Europe with "innocent eyes." So the lightly comic "Overseas" begins with other peoples' talk, and suggests the way that speech becomes or is a kind of writing, finally a kind of "experience":

> For years, over dinner, someone has been saying *St Peter's Square* and everyone at the table has nodded. After some years she also began to nod because the square and other places had become so familiar she felt she had been there. She could now recount her own stories of overseas. When someone said 'that cafe in Paris, the one painted red inside, to the left of the Arc de Triomphe' she could chip in, with all confidence, saying 'no, no, it's on the right, two down from the place that sells the wonderful bagels.' (41)

Photos, novels, pop magazines: these are the sources of knowledge, all of which could lead toward cynicism. Although the comedy of preparation, desire, and travel is not ignored, "Overseas" is generous enough to contradict itself. In the end, by imagination or by plane, she gets "there," and the comedy stays human, humane: alone, she enters the facsimiles of other's vacations, and "[f]amilies all over the world have her in their holiday / snaps" (44).

I was sure we only had three children, couples say to
each other. Who is this? friends of families all over
the world ask. Oh, that's just someone we met, they say:
my sister's stepdaughter from her husband's third marriage,
the mother of Brian's illegitimate children. That, they
say, is the daughter we never had. We found her in Florence
and she recognized us instantly. (45)

"You approach the world / with open arms and hope / it wants you"
(46): "The Visit" wittily offers the traveler's prayer and acceptance of
how things are. Then a number of small poems respond to places, people,
art, the signs of elsewhere, with delicate wit and irony, especially as they
register the responses (essentially cliché) of the subject as well as other
tourists. As "Poland," a longish series of verbal snapshots, shows,
Bornholdt has a genuine knack for catching change, possibility, and
glimpses and sounds of actual life on the run. "Le Nom" itself comes to
Paris, invoked as a place name full of names: first of places, of art, then a
list of flower names that speak of ongoing cultural exchange even at the
heart of Europe's supposedly fixed cultural capital. A final list of translated street names asserts Paris as a place of places whose names are
magic passages to imagination's possibilities, stories waiting to be told. So
texts and pretexts are rendered as part of the palimpsest reality any
"where" (but especially Europe?) has become, and Bornholdt's wryly
witty "samplings" of speech, behavior, and artistic expression combine to
form a generously comic bricolage.

"We Will, We Do" is something else, an attempt to trace family back
to its history in Europe, where it came "[f]rom behind the curtains / of
Germany" (69). Although her parents met and wed in New Zealand, their
families remain scattered across both countries: "The long arms of the
family rest / along the shoulders of the world" (77). The poem imagina-
tively enters the passing of the family back and forth from Europe to New
Zealand, through conversation, documentation, dreams. A final imperative connects present and past in a vision of forbears rowing a boat across
the sea off New Zealand: "You wave and / wave they raise / a hand" (78).

Bornholdt's Europe is, then, a place first known by its various images: it reaches the New Zealander (and the Canadian, the Australian, too) as a massive and complex simulation. But it is also an actual place, even if when there, as all these poems demonstrate, it seems one only comes to know it through already given texts. Europe, then, is nothing if not palimpsestic. She can see this, and she can say it. In their different ways, it is what Curnow and Stead also say. It is, perhaps, all any of us can say. But it is our pleasure in their texts' particular way of saying this that marks their poems as important documents of the slowly maturing ability of postcolonial writing in New Zealand and elsewhere to make new what it makes us see.

Meanwhile, although New Zealand still sits out on "the outer edge of space" (Mason 35), the poems I have looked at here would seem to argue that later writers have moved beyond R.A.K. Mason's concept of margin. The title poem of Bill Manhire's 1991 collection, *Milky Way Bar*, demonstrates how postmodernist attitude affects the postcolonial stance. As a closing parenthesis to the opening parenthesis of Mason's sonnet, it alludes to Mason's poem only to undermine its alienation. While admitting the tragi-farcical cultural effects of the technologies of communication and capital's demeaning use of them for advertising, its comic subject still finds pleasure in a world where supposedly "marginal" New Zealand and "central" Europe are so intertwined they are one in the view from the lunar lander, a different gift of technology:

> I live at the edge of the universe,
> like everybody else. Sometimes I think
> congratulations are in order:
> I look out at the stars
> and my eye merely blinks a little,
> my voice settles for a sigh.
> But my whole pleasure is the inconspicuous;
> I love the unimportant thing.
> I go down to the Twilight Arcade
> and watch the Martian invaders,

already appalled by our language,

pointing at what they want. (19)

ENDNOTES

[1] The quotation is from "House and Land" (1982, 39-40), one of Curnow's best known early poems.

[2] Ian Wedde reiterates this point, in reference to New Zealand poetry, and with a specific nod to Frye's comments, in his "Introduction" to *The Penguin Book of New Zealand Verse* (29-31).

[3] *Paris* is unpaginated, so all references are to the section numbers.

A Short Note on Dinah Hawken and Michele Leggott

What does it mean to write as both a feminist and a postmodernist? This is a question with as many answers as there are writers. In Canada, for example, many poets have been called, or call themselves feminists who have very little else in common. It would be difficult to find more dissimilar poetics than those practiced by Daphne Marlatt and Lorna Crozier, to name two well-known writers with substantially different audiences. At such a point, one's personal tastes and interests come into play: I read Marlatt (and Tostevin, Webb, and others) more than I read Crozier, but I recognize that both have deservedly important reputations in Canadian poetry.

In New Zealand, certain kinds of innovation, drawing energy from the poetics of Williams and such later writers as Creeley and Olson, have been part of the poetic scene since at least the early sixties, and can be observed, in different ways, in the books of two of the more interesting poets to emerge in the late eighties and early nineties. Both of them have spent time in North America, which may have something to do with their choice of influences. Michele Leggott pursued a Ph.D. at the University of British Columbia, where she studied the poetry of Louis Zukofsky, and has since published a well-received study of his *80 Flowers*. Dinah Hawken lived in New York for a period in the early eighties. Their first books appeared within a year of each other in 1987 and 1988. So did their third volumes, and it is these that I wish to discuss. Although very different poets in many ways, each of them has found new and intertextually complex ways to create work that speaks to both the heart and the head.

We can write heart poems, the ones that take breath away or make tears and laughter come. Or they release the little zing that is desire. You want to write bits down, hear it again, play it again (that's hunger). You keep them by you, within reach (sufficiency). Sometimes they ride around with you for days at a time. Sometimes they step from the shadows when you were thinking of something else entirely. You ignore the tearing sound at your peril; they always have something to say. We work in the dark, they say, we do what we can. We give what we have. Our doubt is our passion. Our passion is our task. The rest is the madness of art. You can quote me. (Leggott 61)

Leggott's argument here, in both its sharp evocations and its humour, is one that George Bowering, Daphne Marlatt, bpNichol, or Phyllis Webb, to name just a few Canadian poets, would respond to with recognition. Although not altogether dismissive of lyric, Leggott seeks something beyond the lyric in her work, and her practice leads to something very close to what Robert Kroetsch called, with reference to Webb, "a being compelled out of lyric by lyric" (118).

In her first two volumes, Leggott explored lyric sound and the possibilities of extension. *DIA* pushes at generic boundaries with even greater excess. Explaining the context of longer poems that make up *DIA* (an interesting word, as a prefix it stands for "through," "across," "transversely," and "apart," according to the *OED*), she adds:

I want heart but I want scope too. Big projects for poetry, like raiding and rewriting its androcentric history. I am not interested in the one-page poem unless it is a constituent of something bigger, unless its brevity is a training ground so I can read to marathon length. This is where complexity comes in, and I welcome it. Complexity is about endurance, about surviving over time and distance to ask old questions in new places. What I have written mixes up these things because it is both lyrical and investigative. Some of the time it investigates lyricism, using lyric poetry to find out who writes it, and why, and why that should be so. (61-2)

The theory here is as much feminist as deconstructive, but the effects are equally an attempt to achieve *ostraenie*, or what Brecht referred to as "estrangement," without, at least in her case, entirely eschewing the effects that lyric can attain: there is "heart" in these poems, but it often appears off to the side, or in a slippery glance we can't be sure actually occurred. At the same time, *DIA*'s poems call attention to their material being. Indeed, a few are highly concrete in their visual presence, especially the wonderful pair of inscribed lips, "Micromelismata." In an example of what Perloff has called "radical artifice," one is made up of "x"s, the other of words exactly matching the first in terms of displaying the same number of letters in the same places on the page.

"Where exactly are we?" is a "ribbon text," which first appeared on the walls of the Wellington City Art Gallery, where the strung-together words from various discourses invited viewers and readers to make their own connections. Like "Micromelismata," it focuses on its materiality and on the (f)act of its production, encouraging us to "see" poetry in different frames from those in which we usually receive it. The book's use of large caps, some bold, some in outline, some shadowed in parts or in whole, forces us to see the words and phrases as both advertising and art simultaneously, while still insisting that we read them in their fragmented agonistic engagement with various discourses of power. The other three pieces in *DIA*, "Blue Irises," "Circle" and "Keeping Warm," appear more ordinary, but all challenge conventional lyric reading.

"Blue Irises" is a serial bricolage of the love lyric, with subtitled sections, "dia," "honeybee," "ladies mile," "seven from nine," and "boat of heaven," stretched beyond whatever the tradition has outlined for both writer and reader. Yet, as poetry and desire, or as a poetry of desire, it enacts its very first line: "i want to mouth you all over" (10). The typesetting is important, for every line is a separate stanza in terms of vertical spacing. Sometimes the syntax connects, sometimes it refuses connection. Each separate page is numbered, although the discourse often seems to run over the page breaks. The writing here ignores obvious formal rules, demanding that we read on in explorative mode. Leggott offers one clue to its variety when she states, "It has a big cast, so many voices having their say, but ultimately the cast-list is just seven: I, you, he, she, we, you (all), and they. Moving the seven around history makes the voices speak again in new contexts, and often they are extremely beautiful, or moving, or both" (62). Who speaks here is the question, and the answer is a beast of many backs emerging from a forest of many texts: "For him // the language is a woman's body and she // will stand out in the rain a hundred years // running it back at him   Hast 'ou seen the rose // in the steeldust (or swansdown ever?)" (14). One of the grand articulated beauties of "Blue Irises" is the way it uses all seven pronouns to create a site of desire from which gender is dis-articulated. Desire, the heart of the lyric, speaks strongly here, but it resists any placing, especially the usual one of androcentric tradition. The body in the poem cannot be identified, except as a body. This is both jarring and strangely pleasurable, as it invites each reader into a collaborative and open representation.

To give some sense of how fully this pleasure lies in the play of language's own body, here is one complete section:

> We could all go some more we could go down
> for it ourselves and come back on the Cream Run
> one quay at a time, mangos bagels wisdom
> from the markets where you lean on one elbow
> after making love and begin to make
> the universe dooby doux to a tune that suits
> your ripening sense of history
> Going out for the makings, staying in to eat
> mouth to mouth, why was it lost most
> when we needed that contagion in the telling?
> There is still a special place on her head
> where they touch her for more of the story
> while back in bed a sleep of hands and hearts
> is airing nectar in all the generous mouths (18)

The playful mood of the whole comes through here; it is love play, and the love is for language itself, as a body, of history, knowledge, speech, touch; the polymorphous perversity of linguistic desire energizes the whole sequence.[1]

"Circle" is a long poem in which Leggott pays homage to earlier New

Zealand women poets, practicing "a mind of ventriloquism, picking out white-hot lines from" their poems "and recombining them with an ear for the heart, complexity, and engagement with which they were written" (62).

> the heart in its cage stands up
> desiring fine instruments   what
>   shall we play?
> laughter startles the sublime lyric
> *c'est le pays du désir*
>   and I
>   its best
>   gesture
> wake in tears (42)

She works her pronouns with vigour here, bringing "she" and "you" together in the desire to make these voices heard. The poem moves through many quotations "in extremis" to a vision of hope and desire: "*when I close my eyes* / you are there when I open them you are marvelling / at the woman in the firelight who has stopped singing // to smile at your approach" (53).

In the very short lines and three line stanzas of "Keeping Warm," Leggott writes of love to "you there at / the long end / of my arm" (56), who can and will and does transform the poem into being. The poem delightedly seeks an other from which desire comes and to whom (or which) it is given. It ends with "your bridge to / where I stand // laughing at / it already / written in // big glittering / letters: let's / go out there // and do the poem" (59). Which is what this book has been asking readers to do all the way through. These are poems that break out of lyric egocentricity by their desiring demand that we participate in their making. There are many ways to do this, and *DIA* finds a number of thoroughly engaging ones.

✄

Dinah Hawken, also "[p]ondering the death of the lyric poem" (50), takes a different tack from that of Leggott. In *Water, Leaves, Stones*, she pursues a minimalist clarity found in such objects, paring her language down while tightening its metaphysical bite as taut as possible. These often small poems (although there is a striking sequence at the centre of the book that stretches out) use simple language but they also engage with complex questions about language. The result is a poetry that resists paraphrase as it insists on a meditative response. Early in the book, "Small Poem" asks, "how can I bear / . . . even the word / hope with its wide-eyed unbroken o / held on either side / by soft consonants / each slightly and distinctly / different from the other" (13). The question is startling enough, and lovely in its linguistic bareness, but rather than an answer, we find another question, which lifts this poem into the mystic, at least for me:

Does everything
depend on the fierce e
staying here with all its might
but in silence
daring a poem to breathe? (13)

What Hawken does, over and over again, in these short anti-lyrics, is create the silent gaps in which her poems dare to breathe. There is a seeming simplicity enveloping them which a discerning reader must move beyond, for even the smallest hold our attention the way the things of the title do They are objects of contemplation, as is, for example, "Earth":

How does the earth do it

how are we

not falling down? (23)

There is a gentle, if somewhat cliffhanging, humour at work here; and there is that respect for words and letters as material things, which Leggott also invokes, albeit, with a different formal approach.

Part Two of *Water, Leaves, Stones* is a sequence of what Phyllis Webb would call "anti ghazals," and this is no accident, for Hawken specifically pays homage to Webb's *Water and Light* in both the poem and her notes.[2] "Water, Women and Birds Gather" is a twenty-nine poem sequence, playing off Webb's originals, aspects of desire in language, love, and the physicality of New Zealand's landscape. The line on "the death of the lyric poem" comes from section 22, but the whole sequence has been pondering what to do with lyric desire in an age when the lyric has been made moribund in the hands of so many of its practitioners. Section 4 reminds us that "Lesbos is a long wide way from here," and adds that we might only "play the lyre badly" trying to "fill the distances ourselves" (32). But both we and she do, that is the point: "She always does emerge. Let me tell you this, she'll say, / someone in some future time will think of us" (32), and that "us" is so inclusive it takes in every poet who has ever listened to Sappho's song, and all her readers, in whatever language, too.

Hawken pays graceful tribute to the later woman poet from whom she's borrowed her form by relating her words (and birds) to uniquely New Zealand ones:

> I have a new presence inside me.
> You. It is a pale day.
>
> The tuis are really here,
> I have seen them, three of them.
>
> Thrush, tui—which is more mellifluous?
> A word I learned from Phyllis Webb.
>
> 'Drunken and amatory, illogical, stoned, mellifluous
> journey of the ten lines.' If I could sing
>
> like you, like her, tui, like spring water and
> far off a rock falling. (33)

Not only homage, this also focuses attention on the ghazal form, and what Webb called the anti-ghazal, as translated into English in the second half of the twentieth century. Webb worked her anti-ghazals out from under the weight of centuries of patriarchal tradition; Hawken continues Webb's efforts, not least by siting desire in a polymorphous pronominal play that undermines gender fixity. "Water, Women and Birds Gather" pays its homage most clearly by living up to its progenitor.

There are poems of travel, love and contemplation in this book. They all share a "naked" quality that reminds me of another great Webb title, *Naked Poems*. It's interesting to see this kind of cross-cultural reading and writing in action between Canadian and New Zealand poetry, especially when it happens at the formal level. *Water, Leaves, Stones* denies the conventional enjoyment of lyric by pushing lyric so intensely it reinvents itself as something newly thought and felt. Along with Leggott's *DIA*, it explores some of the possibilities of lyric/anti-lyric. These poets deserve an audience far beyond the islands of their present location.

ENDNOTES

[1] It is interesting to note that something like influence moves back and forth across the ocean now, for if Dinah Hawken borrows Phyllis Webb's anti-ghazals for her book, Sharon Thesen has clearly borrowed the form of "Blue Irises" for her sequence, "Gala Roses,' in *Aurora* (1995), where she specifically includes *DIA* in her "Bibliography, discography" ([4]).

[2] In her "Author's Note," she says: "The sequence 'Water, Women and Birds Gather' has been strongly influenced by Phyllis Webb's wonderful book *Water and Light, Ghazals and Anti Ghazals* (Coach House Press, Toronto, 1984). I read *Water and Light* over and over again during the period I was writing 'Water, Women and Birds Gather' . . ." (79).

Susan Howe:
Language/Writing/History
Notes around a resistant articulation

> *A writer will find that the more precisely, conscientiously,*
> *appropriately he expresses himself, the more obscure the literary*
> *result is thought, whereas a loose and irresponsible formulation*
> *is at once rewarded with certain understanding.*
>
> Theodor Adorno (101)

To read Susan Howe's driven and resistant work is to confront, with a mixture of awe and delight, one of a small number of recent American poets whose writing engages the complex history of her country with an equal complexity of form.

Of Irish-American ancestry, she knows her Yeats; at least, she has produced a body of work, each part of which provides context for every other part, much as Yeats's poetry does. Hugh Kenner first made this point many years ago, his comment on Yeats fitting Howe's situation as well: "the two regnant presuppositions of the mid-twentieth century—the old one, that poems reflect lives and announce doctrines, the new one, that poems are self-contained or else imperfect—are rendered helpless by Yeats' most radical, most casual, and most characteristic maneuver: he was an architect, not a decorator; he didn't accumulate poems, he wrote books" (1958, 13-14). I might want to drop the term "casual" in reference to Howe's writing, but even more clearly than Yeats, partly because she emerges from a U.S. line of poetic inheritance including Pound and Olson, among others, she writes books that demand to be read whole. Her work, associated with LANGUAGE writing's refusal to "privilege any single mode" (Bernstein 1986, 239), does not yield easily to conventional interpretation or explication. Thus, her engagements with history, especially what she calls "the dark side of history, voices that are anonymous, slighted—inarticulate" (1990a:14) demand a tentative approach. Coming at her work in little slanting forays, noting what I can glancingly, I will attempt to indicate why I return to a writing that stringently refuses to offer its readers the conventional invitations. Thus, notes: a series of takes on aspects of Howe's work.

Susan Howe has by now achieved a certain eminence, at least among those who care to look for her work. Like most of the other so-called LANGUAGE writers, she was completely marginalized in her early career, her early volumes were published by very small presses. Her recent books, often collections of some of those very fugitive volumes, published by such recognized presses as Wesleyan University Press and New Directions, have begun to reach a wider readership, and to receive some critical attention outside the little group of journals dedicated to LANGUAGE writing. Nevertheless, the academy still tends to ignore her. Major anthologies, like *The Norton Anthology of Modern Poetry*, by which the contemporary canon in the universities is constructed, still refuse to publish Jack Spicer, let alone any of the LANGUAGE writers. By the mid-nineties, they appeared in such anthologies as *Postmodern American Poetry* (1994) and *From the Other Side of the Century: A New American Poetry 1960-1990* (1994), but by that very fact they remain outside the mainstream. I think many of them may be quite satisfied to remain there, as their appearance in something like *The Norton Anthology* would be a sign that their oppositional poetics had failed or at least been appropriated by those it was meant to oppose. The fact remains that their work is less widely read than that of many poets consistently reviewed in the literary magazines of both the United States and Britain. In the United States, for example, poets dealing with history in more conventionally narrative modes, such as Robert Lowell, John Berryman, or Gary Holthaus, are more likely than Howe to be reviewed in the mainstream press and taught in university, as is the case, in Britain, with Seamus Heaney compared to Basil Bunting. All of which means that Howe still does her work in a semi-obscurity that allows her freedom even as it denies her a larger audience.

✖

Poetry, then, means lyric, and by lyric, Clausen evidently refers to a short verse utterance (or sequence of such utterances) in

*which a single speaker expresses, in figurative language, his sub-
jective vision of "the truths of moments, situations, relationships," a vision culminating in a "unique insight" or epiphany
that unites poet and reader.*

Marjorie Perloff (1985, 173-4)

In an interesting essay, Peter Middleton calls Howe "one of the most original and thoughtful American poets to have emerged in the past twenty
years" (81). Whether or not it's a typo, the first sentence of his essay actually clarifies the difficulty associated with trying to categorize her writing:
"In her recent book *on* poetry, *Articulation of Sound Forms in Time*, the
American poet Susan Howe offers what appears to be a series of neat
rhetorical paradigms for philosophy and theory" (81; emphasis added). In
fact, *Articulation* was published as a book *of* poetry. Yet Middleton is
quite right to quote some of its fragmented statements, such as the "enigmatic couplet" "Algorithms bravadoes jetsam / All Wisdom's plethora pattern," as "a direct poetic intervention within the very forms of recent theory that have had most to say about such poetic strategies as this" (81).
Although her "work appears consciously postmodern in its formal disruption of what she calls the 'visible surface of discourse' . . . its interest in the
possibility of truth and history makes it sit uneasily within that category"
(81). Indeed, one of her writing's major strengths is that "it is hard to place
within any existing category although her poetry would seem to offer itself
as a paradigm of that kind of formal literary experiment which uses linguistic disruption to challenge the existing symbolic order" (81-2).

Challenge. Disruption. Truth and history. That these do not always
exist together in the same writing suggests the singularity of Howe's project, a project she has carried out in all her writings, no matter how readers
and critics might categorize them. She articulates something of the complex
and personal aspects of this project in a piece that first appeared as a "dramatic biographical statement" (Reinfeld 121) on her poetics, and later as
the preface to *The Europe of Trusts*, a single volume collection of three of
her books of poetry. There she suggests why truth and history mean so
much to her and why her writing, however fragmented and disruptive it
might appear, never seeks to deny the power, if not always the truth, of referentiality. She first writes of how her consciousness and conscience were

formed by the documentation of World War II she encountered as a child:

> From 1939 until 1946 in news photographs, day after day I saw signs of culture exploding into murder. Shots of children being herded into trucks by hideous helmeted conquerors— shots of children who were orphaned and lost—shots of the emaciated bodies of Jews dumped into mass graves on top of more emaciated bodies—nameless numberless men women and children, uprooted in a world almost demented. God had abandoned them to history's sovereign Necessity.

> If to see is to *have* at a distance, I had so many dead Innocents distance was abolished. Substance broke loose from the domain of time and obedient intention. I became part of the ruin. In the blank skies over Europe I was Strife represented. (1990a, 11-12)

"Language surrounds Chaos," she says, but it doesn't necessarily control it. Moreover, a writing which fails to articulate something of chaos may also fail to acknowledge its power and presence in the world of her earliest memories. These childhood encounters with the world already inscribed in letters from her father and the daily newspapers, themselves inscribed now in a dense prose that simultaneously renders the child's imaginative grasp and the adult writer's complex awareness of its limitations, lead her to argue: "This is my historical consciousness. I have no choice in it. In my poetry, time and again, questions of assigning *the cause* of history dictate the sound of what is thought" (13). "Poetry," she insists, "brings similitude and representation to configurations waiting from forever to be spoken. North Americans have tended to confuse human fate with their own salvation. In this I am North American. . . . I write to break out into perfect primeval Consent. I wish I could tenderly lift from the dark side of history, voices that are anonymous, slighted—inarticulate" (14).

This preface, whose title, "There are not leaves enough to crown to cover to crown to cover," should be warning enough not to read it as transparent prose argument, is a good example of how Howe slides from genre to genre within a single piece of writing. Containing fragments from her own poetry, at least one couplet from a folksong, a line the Union troops sang at Gettysburg, and many private and public allusions, it is at least something more than autobiography, personal essay, or simple introduction. Although Howe can write the clearest of straight sentences, many here are deliberately dark and gnomic. All her writing serves history by refusing to deny its confusion and essential darkness: "History gathers in the missing" (1996, 1). As she says elsewhere, in a kind of hopeful despair: "Words are the only clues we have. What if they fail us?" (1993a, 178). Words are the only clues we have in the documents she so often turns to, but they almost have to fail us because so much, of context, in all its possibilities, has either been lost or overdetermined. This may be why she deploys them so often in paratactic fragments, whose meaning is unclear but whose implications feel resonant:

Lost intellectual structures

records of the Conquerors

Into grit glooming

Thrown something

Indignant barbarity

animal kingdom of necessity

restoration of Order

collective north night of a murder

Obsessional snatched away

nameless and a changeling

scornbite stray ("Bride's Day," 1990a, 144)

They may be disconnected, yet these lines limn an almost mythic tale of conquest, loss, and violence. They do so, as other poets and critics have pointed out, by virtue of their rhythmic intensity, alliteration, assonance

and consonance, and by the allusive quality of almost every line.[1] We feel
we can almost recognize the source; in fact, it does not matter if we do,
so long as we feel that we might.

※

> *Not only ballad, not only epic, not only genres affiliated with*
> *heavily gendered griefs, but*
>
> *a feminist appropriation of*
>
> *every genre large and small.*
>
> Rachel Blau DuPlessis (130)

Susan Howe's works challenge traditional definitions of poetry; more
specifically, they challenge traditional definitions of genre. Whatever any
one appears to be, they all belong to a single and singular writing which
seeks to uncover something of what was left unsaid in "the record of winners," that history whose "[d]ocuments were written by the Masters"
(1990a, 11). Howe is an assiduous researcher, and has spent much time
in the archives, especially those of early American documents. What she
derives from them enters into what is published as poetry and as prose,
but, again, these publishing categories tend to separate works out from
what is a single project.

Howe has many times registered her debt to Charles Olson, but she is
well read in all the major modernists, including Pound as well as Stein.
Perloff suggests what she would have learned from the works of those
men. As she points out, for the English-speaking world, "the pivotal figure
in the transformation of the Romantic (and Modernistic) lyric into what
we now think of as postmodern poetry is surely Ezra Pound" (1985, 181).
Referring to Michael Bernstein's statement, in *The Tale of the Tribe, Ezra
Pound and the Modern Verse Epic*, that the *Cantos* shows, "for the first
time in over a century, that poetry can actually *incorporate* prose," and
that the mixing of various forms of prose document and lyric song "*without privileging either medium*, represents one of the decisive turning-points
in modern poetics, opening for verse the capacity to include domains of
experience long since considered alien territory" (40), she adds:

Without privileging either medium, lyric poem or "prose instruction"—this has, more and more come to be our own poetic domain. A corollary, equally important for postmodernism, is that the lyric voice gives way to multiple voices or voice fragments . . .

The mode, in other words, is that of *collage*, the setting side by side or juxtaposition of disparate materials without commitment to explicit syntactical relations between elements. (1985, 183)

Furthermore, in such writing the lyric-speaking subject dissipates if it doesn't disappear entirely. This dispersal, an important aspect of postmodern poetry, is already there in the *Cantos*, as Bernstein argues, when he writes that its speaking subject functions as an "unspoken marginal presence which silently articulates (makes sense out of) the gaps in the printed text, a voice we only really discover in the process of 'speaking it' ourselves" (1986, 170). One difference between Pound and Howe is that the latter no longer thinks it possible to make sense out of the gaps, but does feel it necessary to inscribe each and every gap she discovers. This is true both of the "poessays" and the poems, although they deal with their materials somewhat differently. Indeed, to get at what she calls, after Olson, "the stutter in American literature" (1993a, 181) and history, she turns back to Emily Dickinson, where she finds what she needs poetically:

Oneness and scattering.
Marginal notes. Irretrievable indirection—
Uncertainty extends to the heart of replication. Meaning is scattered at the limit of concentration. The other of meaning is indecipherable variation. (1993a, 148)

This quotation takes us into Howe's poetics of response, how her "poessays" work. These phrases, paying homage to Dickinson's "networks of signs and discontinuities" (1993a, 143) by replying to them in kind, come from "These Flames and Generosities of the Heart: Emily Dickinson and the Illogic of Sumptuary Values." The essays in *The Birth-mark: unset-*

tling the wilderness in American literary history carry further the explorations begun in *My Emily Dickinson*, a book Perloff quite correctly associates with such precursors as "William Carlos Williams's *In the American Grain*, Charles Olson's *Call Me Ishmael*, and Robert Duncan's *H.D. Book*—texts in which one poet meditates so intensely on the work of another that the two voices imperceptibly merge" (1990, 36). Such books, and especially Howe's, approach a form of "poet's prose," or "associative rhythm—the rhythm equidistant from both verse and prose, whose unit is the abrupt, discontinuous, repetitive, heavily accented phrase" (1985, 189) which insists upon precisely the "illogic" of both the writing and reading experience. Howe, however, can be marvelously logical when she wants to be, as her arguments with the editors of Dickinson about the need, which they dismiss, to print her work exactly as it is written, show. But then, they flow from her utter, and passionate rather than logical, immersion in Dickinson's texts.

My Emily Dickinson is a very good place to begin reading Howe, for, while it is full of sudden turns not usually associated with criticism, it reveals Howe's intense and wide-ranging learning in such a way as to convince the reader that her interpretation of Dickinson's learning as well as her poems is valid. Her Emily Dickinson chose to live as she did in order to write, and she reveals in every hesitation, every odd turn of phrase, every resistance to the adulterated norm of lady's poetry of the time, her drive to mastery. Recalling that "Wallace Stevens said that 'Poetry is a scholar's art'" (1985, 15), Howe demonstrates her own astonishing scholarship by uncovering Dickinson's. Essentially, *My Emily Dickinson* explores "My Life had stood—a Loaded Gun—" in great detail, reading it through Dickinson's reading and the United States' tangled Puritan history, of which Dickinson, like Howe, is one of the pretty pure products. Howe is able to enter into Dickinson's poetic work by dint of an imaginative labour rooted in her own poetic. This intense appropriation of another's soul leads to moments like this, one complete paragraph (or should I say stanza?):

On this heath wrecked from Genesis, nerve endings quicken. Naked sensibility at the extremist periphery.

Narrative expanding contracting dissolving. Nearer to know less before afterward schism in sum. No hierarchy, no notion of polarity. Perception of an object means loosing and losing it. Quests end in failure, no victory and sham questor. One answer undoes another and fiction is real. Trust absence, allegory, mystery—the setting not the rising sun is Beauty. No titles or numbers for the poems. That would force order. No titles for the packets she sewed the poems into. No manufactured print. No outside editor/"robber." Conventional punctuation was abolished not to add "soigné stitchery"[2] but to subtract arbitrary authority. Dashes drew liberty of interruption inside the structure of each poem. Hush and hesitation for breath and for breathing. Empirical domain of revolution and revelation where words are in danger, dissolving . . . only Mutability certain. (1985, 23)

This is definitely associative prose, a poet's prose in flight. Alliteration, consonance & assonance, quotation and allusion: all serve a vision that emerges as much from the language followed as from an already chosen argument. Yet the argument, if we so call it, is woven—no "soigné stichery" here either—intimately through the whole text.

The other chapters of *The Birth-mark* work in much the same way. Just their titles announce something other than comforting conventional essays: "*Submarginalia*," "Incloser," "Quasi-marginalia" (this a single page note), "The Captivity and Restoration of Mrs. Mary Rowlandson," (there is also a "*Talisman* Interview"). All are, as the sub-title to the book indicates, explorations of the continuing unsettling of the wilderness, how its original un-settlement throws traces from the first books written in America across everything written since. "The Captivity and Restoration of Mrs. Mary Rowlandson" first appeared in the experimental journal *Temblor: Contemporary Poets*. In the context of *The Birth-mark* as a whole, it takes on deeper hues, but still stands out as a stunning example of scholarship as an utterly poetic art. It is a collage of many voices, especially those of Rowlandson herself, her minister husband (editor of her manuscript), the Mathers, Emerson, and too many others to note here.

Often their texts are quoted at length in order that Howe's text might unravel what they desire so much to hide, but the overall effect is not so much simple analysis as charged confrontation. Howe's writing here weaves "together narrative and lyric, scholarship and historical speculation, found text and pure invention," as Perloff says on the back cover, to create a prose work that offers many of the same pleasures of the modern epic as are found in the *Cantos, Paterson, The Anathemata*, or *The Maximus Poems*.

If we accept with Howe that "The break with the Old World was a rupture into contraries" (1993a, 90), then all the juxtaposed fragments of history and vision will accumulate to make not a wholly coherent argument but a carefully articulated collection of ruins, the none-too-solid plinth upon which the Republic would eventually be erected. But the "poessay" mostly seeks to read through the surrounding walls of early editing and scholarship to the profoundly ambivalent wilderness within the writing of a woman never meant to have a voice. Howe thus discovers a line descending from Rowlandson through Dickinson, H.D., Stein, and many others, to herself. Rowlandson's narrative had to tell of God's gifts to her, especially when she was restored to "civilization" from captivity and despite the losses of children along the way, all part of King Philip's War, and all part, as Cotton Mather would later say, of a divine plan. Still, there's the rupture:

> In the first chapter of the first published narrative written by an Anglo-American woman, ostensibly to serve as a reminder of God's Providence, guns fire, houses burn, a father, mother, and sucking child are killed by blows to the head. Two children are carried off alive. Two more adults are clubbed to death. . . . The victims are nameless. Specificity is unnecessary in whiplash confrontation. Only monotone enumeration.
>
> In the first chapter of the first published narrative written by an Anglo-American woman, ostensibly to serve as a reminder of God's Providence, twelve Christians are killed by Indians. The author and her youngest daughter are wounded by bullets. The author's brother-in-law is killed while defend-

ing her garrison. . . . Finally, the author's two other children (aged fifteen and ten) are pulled away from her sight.

In the first chapter of the first published narrative written by an Anglo-American woman, ostensibly to serve as a reminder of God's Providence, Native Americans are called "murderous wretches," "bloody heathen," "hell-hounds," "ravenous bears," "wolves." (1993a, 95)

Howe has found the means by which to enter into Rowlandson's plight as inscribed, while carefully demonstrating its essential configuration as inscription: anaphora. But Rowlandson, in Howe's telling, is now trapped in narrative: she must tell more, must journey "as prisoner and slave" with these Others "for eleven weeks and five days" through "'several Removes we had up and down the Wilderness'" (95). "Out in a gap in the shadows" is exactly where Howe's text pursues her, "elided, tribeless, lost" (95), but not without apprehension; and for Howe, "Rowlandson's apprehension of nature is an endless ambiguous enclosure" (96).

That ambiguity is at the core of all American writing, Howe believes, and she brings all her scholarship to bear upon that point. Since there's no copy of the first edition of Mary Rowlandson's *Narrative*, "[a]ll of the editions we have now depend on the text of a 'Second Addition Corrected and Emended' printed during the same year as the first. Future distortions, exaggerations, modifications, corrections and emendations may endow a text with meanings it never formed" (97). Howe argues that most likely Rowlandson's reverend husband supervised the "addition" (and how like her work elsewhere to copy so carefully the misprints for their diverse information) of "scriptural parallels and referents that would support and censor her narrative at the same time that they entwined the telling in a becoming Christological corporate pattern" (97). But what actually happened, and what did Rowlandson have to tell? "A woman is hiking through the Republic's corporate eschatology, carrying her dying daughter Sarah" (97). That daughter will be buried in an unmarked grave; that woman will journey with her captors deeper into the wilderness, and Howe must ask, What is the nature of that wilderness? What happened to Rowlandson there? What was she able to articulate of her experience when she was restored? And the answers, carefully scattered throughout, entwined with a vast array of other writings from then and later, are wholly of the profound ambivalence that lies at the heart of the American settler experience. "Here is the way of contradiction" (99), says Howe, noting how Rowlandson hates the aborigines, and exclaims upon their fallen ways, yet can't help "noting their frequent acts of kindness to her" (98). And it is in that contradiction that the poet seeks her way through the wilderness of words thrown up supposedly to form the necessary garrison against the wilderness these early Puritan settlers thought was outside themselves.

Howe notes how Rowlandson "interrupts the homeward direction of her impending restoration with a list of specific criticisms of colonial policies toward her captors. 'Before I go any further, I would take leave to mention . . .'; then she stops her slide into Reason's ruin by pushing her readers back to the imperatives of Wonder-Working Providence" (100-101). Her own essay then slides off to explore the writings of John Winthrop and other early men, the poems of Anne Bradstreet, and later interpretations, all gathered into a collective voicing of pioneer failure to escape contradiction. Returning to Rowlandson, the essay demonstrates how "First she hated them then she joined them now she remembers to hate them again" (124), and through its crafty quotations it makes her alienation and ambivalence relevant once more. Leading up to one of the moments of crisis in the text, Howe shows us the narrator "narrating something about the recalcitrant beast in Everywoman. In this wild place every human has a bait she must bite" (125), and quotes Rowlandson's tale of being given raw liver to eat, with suitable Biblical quotation attached. "There she stands, blood about her mouth, savoring the taste of raw horse liver. God's seal of ratification spills from her lips or from her husband's pen" (126). "The trick of her text is its mix" (127), says Howe, pointing to the trick of her own texts as well. That mix calls out to a reader/writer like Howe, who would consciously inscribe it into her own writing as well as her readings. Her final word on Rowlandson feels true, not only to the *Narrative* but also to the almost silent, nearly silenced, project she discovers throughout American literature, inscribed within the works of authors such as Dickinson, no matter what their editors might do to them or how they might be marginalized or misread. Mary Rowlandson is still important, says Howe, because "she saw what she did not see said what she did not say" (128).

〔image glyph〕

> EF: *Well, how then are poems related to history?*
> SH: *I think the poet opens herself as Spicer says. You open your-self and let language enter, let it lead you somewhere. I never start with an intention for the subject of a poem. I sit quietly at my desk and let various things—memories, fragments, bits, pieces, scraps, sounds—let them all work into something. This has to do with changing order and abolishing categories. It has to do with sounds in silence. It has to do with peace.*
>
> Susan Howe (1993a, 164)

A "'poem including history.'" An interesting phrase, every term contest-ed; at least in the work of Howe, not to mention Williams's *Paterson*, Olson's *Maximus Poems* or much of Charles Reznikov's work, parts of Louis Zukofsky's *A*, Robert Duncan's *Passages*, all of which owe some-thing to the preliminary work of the *Cantos*. But, as I have intimated above, Howe does not share the faith of Pound, and perhaps of Williams and Olson, that the poem can include history in such a way as to fill in the gaps. Hers is a bleaker view, yet she still feels the need for poetry to do what it can. Admitting that she feels history as an actuality, she argues: "Of course, I know that history can be falsified, has been falsi-fied. Still, there are archives and new ways of interpreting their uncom-promising details. I am naive enough to hope the truth will out. . . . If you are a woman, archives hold perpetual ironies. Because the gaps and silences are where you find yourself" (1993a, 158). Later, she adds: "Poets aren't reliable. But poetry may be. I don't think you can divorce poetry from history and culture" (163). So, "poem" can be *My Emily Dickinson* or the sections of *The Birth-mark* as well as *Articulation of Sound Forms in Time* or *Defenestration of Prague* or *The Liberties*; "including" can mean allusion, incorporation of documents, legendary and mythical imaging, specific reference, use of visuals, and combina-tions of these; "history" will include both the "record written by winners"

(158) and every implication of what has been silenced the writer can find ways to render. All of which explains the many different ways Howe's texts will take to inscribe the very loss each exploration of the archives uncovers, all those gaps, printer's errors, deliberate destruction of texts, and invented or imagined irruptions that explode any coherent story into an expanding cloud of linguistic data.

The Liberties, for example, concerns Stella, Hester (Esther) Johnson, Jonathan Swift's longtime companion. In her introductory note, "Fragments of a Liquidation," Howe points out that "No authentic portrait exists" (1990a 152).[3] What she offers is no more authentic than any previous "portraits," whether drawn or painted, or written, as were the poems and journals of Swift and others of his acquaintance, but this book does seek to speak from within the woman's silence rather than from the outer articulation of the masculine gaze under which she spent her life. As is the case in many of Howe's "poems including history," *The Liberties* opens with a prose exploration of the facts as scholarship has been able to manifest them. Howe demonstrates remarkable powers of compression here, gathering only the most relevant details into a significant suggestion of a narrative. What follows unravels. It is an encounter with the unknown, the unstated. Swift's *Journal* remains. "None of Stella's letters have been saved" (1990a, 152).

What is the poetry Howe can make from all this? Here is the first page:

her diary soared above her house

over heads of

those clouds
are billows below
spume
white
tossed this way
or that
wild geese in a stammered place
athwart and sundered

for the sea rose and sheets clapped at sky
and sleep a straggler led the predator away
(Say, *Stella*, feel you no Content
Reflecting on a Life well spent?)
Bedeikke bedl
bedevilled by a printer's error
the sight of a dead page filled her with terror
garbled version
page in her coffin. . . .
do those dots mean that the speaker lapsed
into silence?

Often I hear Romans murmuring
I think of them lying dead in their graves. (1990a, 158)

Beginning with an image of the burned letters it segues into an invitation
to speculate on the loss of Esther's words, perhaps to wonder about her
journey across the sea to Ireland (or is it Swift's journey back to England,
from whence the letters making up his *Journal* would come?). But whose
sleep and what predator arrives in that heavily metrical and alliterative
line? The next couplet is Swift's, from his Birth-Day verse of 1726-7
(1967, 32), a poem full of apprehension of sickness, decay, and fear that
she will die and leave him bereft of her comfort and care. Then print fails,
and documentation falters: the "dead page" of history terrorizes, but
whom? Now the floating and dissipated subject of the text slides among
pronominal sites. Death is all we can know, of them.

Still, this is pretty straightforward stuff. "THEIR / *Book of Stella*,"
which follows, soon breaks discourse further down. Thus in "my dispeo-
pled kingdom," a voice speaks of "famine   pestilence / there in me
them in me   I / halted   I heard footsteps" (1990a, 160). It becomes
less and less simple to assign the subject of these articulations. But the
intensity of the poet's meditation insists that the subject will be both
writer and written figure(s). This "I" slips simple reference to become
Stella and Susan, not to mention Cordelia, another silent woman, who
soon enters *The Liberties* in dialogue with Stella.

> The real plot was invisible
>   everything possible
>   was the attempt for the finest thing
>   was the attempt
> him over the bridge into the water
> her some sort of daughter
>   events now led to a region
> returned in a fictional direction
>   I asked where that road to the left lay
>   and they named the place
> Predestination
>   automaton whose veiled face
>   growing wings
>   or taking up arms
>   must always undo or sever
>   HALLUCINATION OF THE MIRROR (1990a, 169)

Cordelia is but a ghostly presence here, "some sort of daughter" like
Stella in her relation with Swift; but the very next page she gets her own
book, "WHITE FOOLSCAP / *Book of Cordelia*," in which, by turning back
yet further in time, a deeper discursive breakdown occurs. Throughout,
the dispersed narrating subject creates "a poetic collage, made up largely
of citations from Renaissance and eighteenth-century texts, in which
Stella, Cordelia and the poet herself come together" (Perloff 1990, 37) in
the hallucination of the mirror (the tip of the hat to Jacques Lacan is
deliberate). Indeed, the pages assume a more and more hallucinatory
aspect, yet the fragmented phrases and words resonate ever more complexly with what readers may or may not recall:

>   Running rings
>   of light
>   we'll hunt
>   the wren
>   calling to a catch of thorn
>   crying to announce a want
> along a bank

carried her child

    hovered among the ruins

        of the game

            when the Queen spins

            round

                Once again

            we'll hunt the wren

              says Richard to Robin

        we'll hunt the wren

says everyone.

                    I can re

                    trac

                    my steps

                    Iwho

                    crawl

                    between thwarts

Do not come down the ladder

ifor I

haveaten

it a

way (1990a: 179-80)

Folksongs, children's games, and desires neither Stella nor Cordelia could speak play across these carefully designed pages, as does a singular homage to Samuel Beckett. As Linda Reinfeld points out, the second part of this section, the thin ladder-like fall of words, recalls both a line from *Murphy*, "'Do not come down the ladder, they have taken it away,'" and that Howe "was formally educated as a painter" (127). Indeed, "she always places her words on the page with painterly awareness" (127). But in her usual fashion, Howe has eaten away the solid structure of words in which even the young Beckett grounded his writing. This "I" is insecure, caught "between thwarts" without a complete "trac" to follow. On that ladder (and there are many potential allusions in it), an insubstantial subject of discourse, "ifor I," is not taking the subject in discourse away but swallowing it. Subjectivity disperses; what's outer becomes inner, and the text encompasses (composes) all "we" have—here I recall Howe's comment that "If to see is to have at a distance, I had so many dead Innocents distance was abolished" [1990a, 12]).

Part II of *The Liberties*, "God's Spies," brings Stella and Cordelia together on a phantasmagoric stage, where a rather Beckettian play ensues. Paradoxes, puns, poems and songs find their way into the text. At one point Stella speaks the whole of "Stella to Dr. Swift on his Birth-Day, November 30, 1721," one of the few extant texts by Esther Johnson, the ending of which—"Late dying may you cast a Shred / Of your rich mantle o'er my Head; / To bear with dignity my Sorrow, / One Day alone, then die Tomorrow" (Swift 1967, 38; Howe 1990a, 191)—the editor of *Stella's Birth-Days* commends thus: "Many tributes were paid to the Dean by his literary friends; none ever equalled the last four lines of Stella's poem" (Swift 1967, 36). As they spend a week together in the wilderness of their abandonment, Stella and Cordelia move to an imagined peace of their forgetting—"A dream. Not a trace. We are at peace—pathless" (1990a, 199)—perhaps. This drama of history and myth fragmenting ends with an all too ambivalent stage direction: "Darkness. Silence. Gunshot. Silence" (1990a, 199).

What follows that shot in Part III is an even greater breakdown of discourse, words scattered across the page in painterly blocks:

		S			
		rebuke	boyne		
	churn	alpha	bet	a	keep
1727	expose	blade	blade	hid	
pierce	hang	sum			
clear	hester	quay	Liberties	46	
tense	whisper	here	libel	foam	
print	pen	dot	i	still	
	hole	yew	skip	1.	

(1990a, 206)

As Butterick points out (318), this recalls the opening and closing pages of Robert Duncan's "The Fire   Passages 13" (40, 45), with their single words carefully blocked across and down the page space. This "strew of words" (1990a, 212) in *The Liberties* creates what Peter Quartermain calls an "[u]nparaphraseable" text, whose "lines seem to register a process of perception and thought subject perpetually and continuously to re-casting, re-seeing, re-vision" (187). The dispersed "I" of the writer is present, a "semblance / of irish susans" (1992a, 213) redistributed throughout. To Butterick, "it is Howe's remarkable ability to absent herself, to shed herself, from her lines that allows them to stand with such authority." Yet, she does appear, but only as a linguistic construct, a dialogically and geographically dispersed subject that has nothing in common with the sad "I"-ed subjects of "confessional poetry," but rather occurs as the grammatical subject of a riddle, that ancient poetic game:

> I am composed of nine letters.
> 1 is the subject of a proposition in logic.
> 2 is a female sheep, or tree.
> 3 is equal to one.
> 4 is a beginning.
> 5 & 7 are nothing.
> 6 7 & 8 are a question, or salutation.
> 6 7 8 & 9 are deep, a depression.

THE KEY

> e n i g m a s t i f e m i a t e d c r y p t o a t h
> a b c d e f g h i j k l m n o p q r s t u v w x y
>   z or zed
>   graphy
>   reland
>   I   (1993a, 209)

"Confession is not her purpose, although revelation is" (Butterick 314). It is, perhaps, something akin to the revelation found in Rothko's late paintings.

The page is not neutral. Not blank, and not neutral. It is a territory.

Rachel Blau DuPlessis (131)

In a fascinating essay both celebrating and challenging Olson, Howe says: "The spatial expressiveness of much of Olson's writing is seldom emphasized enough. . . . This feeling for seeing in a poem, is Olson's innovation. Acute visual sensitivity separates *The Maximus Poems* from *The Cantos* [sic] and *Paterson*" (1987b, 5). As is so often the case in a poet's criticism, she could be talking about her own work: "At his best, Olson lets words and groups of words, even letter arrangements and spelling accidentals shoot suggestions at each other, as if each page were a canvas and the motion of words—reality across surface. Optical effects, seemingly chance encounters of letters, are a BRIDGE. Through a screen of juxtaposition one dynamic image may be visible" (5-6). Howe approaches the page as a field, across the whole of which language can be deployed for both visual and aural effects. Her more recent work has taken to playing the visual aspects of type and typesetting for maximum effect, as in parts of *Articulation of Sound Forms in Time* and, especially, *A Bibliography of the King's Book or, Eikon Basilike*.

If possible, one should read the first of these in its original publication, where each section is carefully placed in the large white space of a single page. The hidden narrative from which these fragments of savagely cropped discourse derive has to do with a militia attack on natives in the Connecticut River valley in May 1676. During the retreat, the ambiguously named minister, Hope Atherton, was separated from his companions, met Indians who neither killed nor helped him "'thinking it was the Englishman's God, etc. etc.,'" as the *"EXTRACT from a LETTER (dated June 8th, 1781,) of Stephen Williams to President Styles"* has it (1990b, 5), somehow crossed the river, and eventually wandered back to Hadley. With this as context, not only does Howe "frequently decompose, transpose, and refigure the word . . .; she consistently breaks down or . . . 'demilitarizes' the syntax of her verbal units. [Thus, r]eading the poem . . . one is never sure what subject pronoun goes with what verb, what object follows a given preposition, which of two nouns a participle is modifying, what phrases a conjunctive connects, and so on" (Perloff 1990, 303-304). In the almost primeval world where a Hope of European conquest has "this borderline, half-wilderness, half-Indian, insanity-sanity experience," somehow living through "the point chaos enters cosmos" (Howe 1993a, 167, 173), these poems render a collapse of language back toward its etymological roots. Nothing is secure here. The sequence begins with twelve, increasingly broken, small poems, full of lines like "Otherworld light into fable / Best plays are secret plays" (1990b, 11), and ending with a passage that can almost be read as analysis:

> Impulsion of a myth of beginning
> The figure of a far-off Wanderer
>
> Grail face of bronze or brass
> Grass and weeds cover the face
>
> Colonnades of rigorous Americanism
> Portents of lonely destructivism
>
> Knowledge narrowly fixed knowledge
> Whose bounds in theories slay
>
> Talismanic stepping-stone children
> brawl over pebble and shallow
>
> Marching and counter marching
> Danger of roaming the woods at random
>
> Men whet their scythes go out to mow
> Nets tackle weir birchbark
>
> Mowing salt marshes and sedge meadows   (1990b, 12)

This almost seems to be a kind of explanation, perhaps a rather easy one, but the grammatical slippages, the little games, undermine too simple a response. Rather, the passage calls attention to its artifice, with internal rhyme and alliteration, as well as such small jokes as "in theories slay" where the last word evades the expected banality and calls our attention to the ideologies in contest here.

After this beginning, three visuals similar to those in *The Liberties* appear, but with an even greater inscribed sense of disconnection (meant, perhaps, to mime the dissociation experienced by the reverend Hope Atherton):

Body perception thought of perceiving (half-thought

chaotic architext repudiate line Q confine lie link realm

circle a euclidean curtail theme theme toll function coda

severity whey crayon so distant grain scalp gnat carol

omen Cur cornice zed primitive shad sac stone fur bray

tub epoch too tall fum alter rude recess emblem sixty key

Epithets young in a box told as you fly (1990b, 13)

Only then does the text offer a fragmented version of Hope Atherton's sermon upon his return, almost an explanation of what has preceded it:

. . . .
We are a small remnant
of signal escapes wonderful in themselves
. . . .
We must not worry
how few we are and fall from each other
More than language can express (1990b: 16)

In the second half of the book, "Taking the Forest," a series of highly compressed verses open up "the possibilities for difference, for the 'presentiment of rupture / Voicing desire no more from here'" (Perloff, 1990, 310). The writing here, "Threadbare evergreen season / Mother and maiden," and "Keen woes centuries slacken / woe long wars endurance bear"

(1990b, 24), for example, implodes traditional lyric to create what Perloff calls "meditations" (1990, 309). One page of this meditation demonstrates how Howe constructs anti-lyric *in extremis* as part of a larger work:

> Freedom's dominion of possible
>
> Ear to parable
> lilies spin glory
>
> Adamant glides architrave front
>
> Path to blest vanishing
> kindled oracle vanishing
>
> Stripped of metaphysical proof
> Stoop to gather chaff
>
> Face to fringe of itself
> forseen form from far off
>
> Homeward hollow zodiac core
>
> omen cold path to goal
>
> End of the world as trial or possible
> trail (1990b, 27)

The Biblical allusions seen before reappear here; they must, for they are the ground of the language the Puritans spoke and wrote. The fragmentation, however, serves to undermine whatever faith in what they say might still remain. Hope, of course, remains (as the subject of the earlier half of the text); charity perhaps emerges in the gaps, or in that strange turn on two letters in the final couplet. Meanwhile, even as they resist both explanation and closure, the lines do sing, especially in an Anglo-Saxon kind of way through increasing alliteration. The final page offers this bleak couplet: "Archaic presentiment of rupture / Voicing desire no more from here" (1990b, 38); but the poem as a whole never stops voicing desire, if only in an ecstasy of ruin.

A Bibliography of the King's Book or, Eikon Basilike is a fascinating work, in which the silenced past is the king himself, that is King Charles the First, on the day of whose beheading "*The Eikon Basilike, The Pourtraicture of His Sacred Majestie in his Solitude and Sufferings,* was published and widely distributed throughout England, despite the best efforts of government censors to get rid of it" (1993b, 47). Howe, in her usual thorough manner, provides a poetic but also scholarly introduction to the bibliographical battles over this changeable and politically combustible text, before playing with what type has left us: "All those apophthegms / Civil and Sacred / torn among fragments" (1993b, 60). It is in this book that her debt to Olson's "spatial expressiveness" is most marked. Although she obviously has pages from *The Maximus Poems: Volume Three* in mind (for example, Olson 1983, 438, 498, 499), it appears she has laid out the field of certain pages (1993b, 56-7, 79) specifically to emblematize the continuing struggle over the king's performance, power, and presence in both the world of politics and the world of letters. Although the first two of these pages forces a reader to turn the book around physically while reading, they do provide lines which can be read aloud for strangely poetic aural effects. The third one is much more purely visual, forcing the reading away from the ear and toward the abstracting power of the eye.

The Nonconformist's Memorial contains four longer poems, of which *A Bibliography of the King's Book or, Eikon Basilike* is one. Most of the pages throughout this large volume are fairly standard, at least for Howe. They insist upon their individuality and indivisibility, but they are to be read, in their fragmented manner, from top left to bottom right of each poetic column. Still, all but one of the longer poems contain pages in which the irruptive force of visual abstraction is brought to bear. The lesson for poetry that Howe derived from Olson's practice in the late *Maximus Poems* remains important to her project.

꧁

Two dangers never cease threatening in the world: order and disorder.

Lyn Hejinian (653)

Continually grappling with these two dangers, Howe explains her practice:

> So I start in a place with fragments, lines and marks, stops and gaps, and then I have more ordered sections, and then things break up again. That's how I begin most of my books. I think it's what we were talking about in history as well, that the outsidedness—these sounds, these pieces of words—comes into the chaos of life, and then you try to order them and to explain something, and the explanation breaks free of itself. I think a lot of my work is about breaking free: starting free and being captured and breaking free and being captured again. (1993a, 166)

She writes her fragmented and singular works because she must, then: "History has happened. The narrator is disobedient. A return is necessary, a way for women to go. Because we are in the stutter. We were expelled from the Garden of the Mythology of the American Frontier. The drama's done. We are the wilderness. We have come on to the stage stammering" (1993a, 181). Her stammer is her poetic, and it speaks volumes.

Charles Bernstein argues that "poetry is beyond compare," and "any mapping of poetic terrain is at the same time a mismapping" (1992: 162). If I began by wanting to explain, to myself at any rate, how Howe's poetry works, I end with feeling that such explanation is by the way. Her "mysteries," what Butterick calls a poetry "of scratched continuity, space-invaded units, nonsemantic trace occurrences, where a sense of erasure is more powerful than of closure" (318-19), are their own reason to be. The deep encounter of associative reading they invite is enough. As with Yeats, but in her own way, all her writing feeds all the rest, and the more you read the more it makes not so much sense as a continually opening pattern of possibility. Finally, one major difference between Susan Howe and those early figures she rescues into inscription with such linguistic passion is this: unlike them, she knows precisely how and why "she saw what she did not see said what she did not say."

ENDNOTES

[1] What such writing does, it does differently for every reader. I, for example, read "Into grit glooming" and hear echoes of Pound (Canto XI: "In the gloom, the gold gathers the light against it" [1970, 51]) and Olson ("having descried the nation / to write a Republic / in gloom on Watch-House Point" [1983, 377]), among others.

[2] The phrase is quoted from Gilbert and Gubar's *The Madwoman in the Attic* (1979), a passage from which Howe had angrily disagreed with a few pages earlier.

[3] As Howe's original small press editions are hard to find, I give page references to the later collections.

Works Cited

Adamson, Robert. *Waving to Hart Crane*. Sydney: Angus and Robertson, 1994.

Adorno, Theodor. *Minima Moralia: Reflections from Damaged Life*. Trans. E.F.N. Jephcott. London: New Left Books, 1974.

Ahmad, Aijaz, ed. *Ghazals of Ghalib*. New York: Columbia University Press, 1971.

Alcock, Peter. "Review of Bill Manhire's *Zoetropes* ." *Landfall 154* (June 1995): 240-244.

Arnason, David, Dennis Cooley, and Robert Enright. "Interview with Eli Mandel, March 16/78." *Essays on Canadian Writing* 18/19 (Summer/Fall 1980): 70-89.

Arnold, Matthew. *The Poetical Works of Matthew Arnold*. Ed. C.B. Tinker and H.F. Lowry. London: Oxford, 1950.

Ashcroft , Bill, Gareth Griffiths, and Helen Tiffin. *The Empire Writes Back: Theory and Practice in Post-colonial Literatures*. London: Routledge, 1989.

Atwood, Margaret, ed. *The New Oxford Book of Canadian Verse in English*. Toronto: Oxford University Press, 1982.

_____ *The Journals of Susanna Moodie*. Toronto: Oxford University Press, 1970.

Auden, W. H. *The Collected Poetry of W.H. Auden*. New York: Random House, 1945.

Bakhtin, M.M. *The Dialogic Imagination*. Ed. Michael Holquist. Trans. Caryl Emerson and Michael Holquist. Austin: University of Texas Press, 1981.

Barbour, Douglas. *Michael Ondaatje*. New York: Twayne Publishers, 1993.

Barnard, Mary, trans. *Sappho: a new translation*. Berkeley: University of California Press, 1958.

Bernstein, Charles. *Content's Dream: Essays 1975-1984*. Los Angeles: Sun and Moon Press, 1994 (1986).

_____ *A Poetics*. Cambridge and London: Harvard University Press, 1992.

Bernstein, Michael. *The Tale of the Tribe: Ezra Pound and the Modern Verse Epic*. Princeton: Princeton University Press, 1980.

Blaser, Robin. "The Fire." *The Poetics of The New American Poetry*. Ed. Donald Allen and Warren Tallman. New York: Grove Press, 1973. 235-246.

_____ "The Moth Poem." *The Holy Forest*. Toronto: Coach House Press, 1993. 37-58. Also in Ondaatje (1979): 159-179.

_____ "Statement." In Ondaatje (1979): 323-325.

Blodgett, E.D. *Take Away the Names*. Toronto: Coach House Press, 1975.

_____ *Sounding*. Edmonton: Tree Frog Press, 1977.

_____ *Beast Gate*. Edmonton: NeWest Press, 1980.

_____ *Arché/Elegies*. Edmonton: Longspoon Press, 1983.

_____ "The Book, Its Discourse, and the Lyric: Notes on Robert Kroetsch's *Field Notes*." *Open Letter* 5: 8-9 (Summer-Fall 1984): 195-205.

_____ *Musical Offering*. Toronto: Coach House Press, 1986.

_____ "Dickinson's Dash: An *Apologia* for Poetry." *Open Letter* 6:7 (Spring 1987): 21-34.

_____ *Da Capo: The Selected Poems of E.D. Blodgett*. Ed. Paul Hjartarson. Edmonton: NeWest Press, 1990.

_____ *Apostrophes: woman at a piano*. Ottawa: Buschek Books, 1996.

_____ *Apostrophes II: through you I*. Edmonton: University of Alberta Press, 1997.

_____ and Jacques Brault. *Transfigurations*. Saint-Hippolyte: Éditions du Noroit / Ottawa: Buschek Books, 1998.

_____ *Apostrophes III: alone upon the earth*. Ottawa: Buschek Books, 1999.

Bly, Robert. *Leaping Poetry*. Boston: Beacon Press, 1975.

Bornholdt, Jenny. *This Big Face*. Wellington: Victoria University Press, 1998.

_____ *Moving House*. Wellington: Victoria University Press, 1989.

_____ *Waiting Shelter*. Wellington: Victoria University Press, 1991.

Bowering, George. *Imaginary Hand*. Edmonton: NeWest Press, 1988.

Branston, Brian. *The Lost Gods of England*. London: Thames and Hudson, 1957.

Brown, Cheryl L. and Karen Olson, eds. *Feminist Criticism: Essays on Theory, Poetry and Prose*. Metuchen, NJ: The Scarecrow Press, 1978.

Brydon, Diana. "Introduction: Reading Postcoloniality, Reading Canada." In Brydon, Diana, ed. *Testing the Limits: Postcolonial Theories and Canadian Literature Essays on Canadian Writing 56* (Fall 1995[b]): 1-19.

Burman, Edward. "The Culminating Sacrifice: An Interpretation of Allen Curnow's 'Moro Assassinato'." *Landfall 153* (March 1985), 22-36.

Butling, Pauline. "Paradox and play in the poetry of Phyllis Webb." In Neuman and Kamboureli (1986): 191-204.

Butterick, George F. "The Mysterious Vision of Susan Howe." *North Dakota Quarterly*, 55:4 (Fall 1987). 312-321.

Chamberlin, J.E. "Let There Be Commerce Between Us: The Poetry of Michael Ondaatje." In Solecki (1985): 31-41.

Cirlot, J.E. *A Dictionary of Symbols.*, 2nd Ed. Trans. Jack Sage. London: Routledge and Kegan Paul, 1971.

Clark, Kenneth, Colin MacInnes, and Bryan Robertson. *Sidney Nolan*. London: Thames and Hudson, 1961.

Cogswell, Fred. "Eros or Narcissus? The Male Canadian Poet." *Mosaic*, 1:2 (January 1968): 103-111.

Coldwell, Joan. "Anne Wilkinson." *The Oxford Companion to Canadian Literature*. Ed. William Toye. Toronto: Oxford University Press, 1983. 831-832.

Crawford, Isabella Valancy. *Collected Poems*. Introduction by James Reaney. Toronto: University of Toronto Press, 1972.

Creeley, Robert. *The Collected Poems of Robert Creeley 1945-1975*. Berkeley and Los Angeles: University of California Press, 1983.

Croft, Julian. "Responses to Modernism, 1915-1965." In *The Penguin New Literary History of Australia*. Ed. Laurie Hergenhan, et. al. Ringwood, Victoria: Penguin, 1988. 409-429.

Culler, Jonathan. *On Deconstruction*. Ithaca, NY: Cornell University Press, 1982.

Curnow, Allen, ed. *The Penguin Book of New Zealand Verse*. Harmondsworth, Middlesex: Penguin, 1960.

_____ *Selected Poems*. Auckland: Penguin (N.Z.), 1982.

_____ *Look Back Harder*. Ed. and Introduction by Peter Simpson. Auckland: Auckland University Press, 1987.

Davenport, Guy. *The Geography of the Imagination*. San Francisco: North Point Press, 1981.

Davey, Frank. *Reading Canadian Reading*. Winnipeg: Turnstone Press, 1988.

Davie, Donald. "Ezra Pound's Hugh Selwyn Mauberley." *The Modern Age*. Ed. Boris Ford. Harmondsworth: Penguin, 1963. 315-329.

Dewdney, Christopher. *Alter Sublime*. Toronto: Coach House Press, 1980.

Dixon, Peter. *Rhetoric*. London: Methuen and Co Ltd, 1971.

Dostoyevsky, Fyodor. *The Brothers Karamazov*. 2 vols.Translated with an Introduction by David Magarshack. Harmondsworth: Penguin, 1958.

Dowling, William C. *The Epistolary Moment: The Poetics of the Eighteenth Century Verse Epistle*. Princeton, NJ: Princeton University Press, 1991.

Duggan, Laurie. *Memorials*. North Adelaide: Little Esther Books, 1996.

Duncan, Robert. *Bending the Bow*. New York: New Directions, 1968.

Dunham, Rob. "A Sentence Like A Snake: A dialogue with E.D. Blodgett.". *CV/II*, 7:2 (April 1983). 27-32.

DuPlessis, Rachel Blau. *The Pink Guitar: Writing as Feminist Practice*. New York and London: Routledge, 1990.

Duwell, Martin. "A Wordy Bunch of Worthies." *Scripsi* 7:3 (1992): 145-150.

Easthope, Antony and John O. Thompson, eds. *Contemporary Poetry Meets Modern Theory*. Toronto and London: University of Toronto Press, 1991.

Easthope, Antony. *Poetry as Discourse*. London and New York: Methuen, 1983.

Eliot, T.S. "Ulysses, Order, and Myth." *Selected Prose of T.S. Eliot.*. Ed. Frank Kermode. London: Faber and Faber, 1975;*The Dial*, LXXV:5 (November 1923): 480-483.

Evans, Ivor H. *Brewer's Dictionary of Phrase and Fable*. London: Cassell, 1975.

Evans, Patrick. *The Penguin History of New Zealand Literature*. Auckland: Penguin (N.Z.), 1990.

Forbes, John. "Meet the New Boss (Same as the Old Boss)." *Scripsi* 7:3 (1992): 129-135.

Frye, Northrop. "Conclusion to a *Literary History of Canada*." *The Bush Garden*. Toronto: House of Anansi Press, 1971. 213-251.

Glickman, Susan. "From 'Philoctetes on the Island' to 'Tin Roof': the Emerging Myth of Michael Ondaatje." In Solecki (1985): 70-81.

Gray, Robert, and Geoffrey Lehmann, eds. *Australian Poetry in the Twentieth Century*. Port Melbourne: Heinemann, 1991.

Gunn, Thom. "Small Persistent Difficulties: Robert Creeley." In *Shelf Life: Essays, Memoirs, and an Interview*. Ann Arbor: University of Michigan Press, 1993. 87-95.

Hamilton, Edith. *Mythology*. New York: New American Library, 1967.

Harris, Max and Joanna Murray-Smith. *The Poems of Ern Malley*. Sydney: Allen and Unwin, 1988.

Harris, Robert. *JANE, Interlinear and Other Poems*. Sydney: Paper Bark Press, 1992.

Harrison, Jim. *Outlyer and Ghazals*. New York: Simon and Schuster, 1971.

Hawken, Dinah. *Water, Leaves, Stones*. Wellington, N. Z.: Victoria University Press, 1995.

Hejinian, Lyn. "From 'The Rejection of Closure'." In Hoover (1994): 653-658.

Hjartarson, Paul. "Introduction." *Da Capo*. Edmonton: NeWest Press, 1990. xi-xxii.

Homer. *The Iliad*. Trans. Robert Fitzgerald. New York: Doubleday, 1974.

Hoover, Paul ed. *Postmodern American Poetry*. New York: Norton, 1994.

Hornsby, Roger A., and T.V.F. Brogan. "Verse Epistle." *The New Princeton Encyclopedia of Poetry and Poetics*. Eds. Alex Preminger and T.V.F. Brogan, et. al.. Princeton, NJ: Princeton University Press, 1993. 1351-1352.

Howe, Susan. *Pythagorean Silence*. New York: Montemora, 1982.

_____ *Defenestration of Prague*. New York: Kultur Foundation, 1983.

_____ *My Emily Dickinson*. Berkeley: North Atlantic Books, 1985.

_____ *Articulation of Sound Forms in Time*. Windsor Vermont: Awede, 1987(a).

_____ "Where Should the Commander Be." *Writing*, 19 (November 1987[b]): 3-20.

_____ *A Bibliography of the King's Book or, Eikon Basilike*. Providence: Paradigm Press, 1989.

_____ *The Europe of Trusts*. Los Angeles: Sun and Moon Press, 1990(a).

_____ *Singularities*. Hanover and London: Wesleyan University Press, 1990(b).

_____ *The Birth-mark: unsettling the wilderness in American literary history*. Hanover and London: Wesleyan University Press, 1993(a).

_____ *The Nonconformist's Memorial*. New York: New Directions, 1993(b).

_____ *Frame Structures: Early Poems 1974 - 1979*. New York: New Directions, 1996.

Hunter, Lynette. "Form and Energy in the Poetry of Michael Ondaatje." *Journal of Canadian Poetry*, 1:1 (Winter 1978). 49-70.

Islam, Kurshidul, and Ralph Russell. *Three Mughal Poets: Mir, Sauda, Mir Hasan*. Cambridge, Mass: Harvard University Press, 1968.

Johnson, W. R. *The Idea of Lyric*. Berkeley: University of California Press, 1982.

Jones, D.G. *Butterfly on Rock: A Study of Themes and Images in Canadian Literature*. Toronto: University of Toronto Press, 1970.

_____ *A Throw of Particles*. Toronto: General, 1983.

Kamboureli, Smaro. *On the Edge of Genre: The Contemporary Canadian Long Poem*. Toronto: University of Toronto Press, 1991.

Kearns, Lionel. "If There's Anything I Hate It's Poetry." *Canadian Literature*, 36 (Spring 1968): 67-70.

Keats, John. *John Keats*. Ed. Elizabeth Cook. Oxford/New York: Oxford University Press, 1990.

Kenner, Hugh. *Gnomon: Essays on Contemporary Literature*. New York: McDowell Obolensky, 1958.

Kiyooka, Roy. *Nevertheless These Eyes*. Toronto: Coach House Press, 1967.

_____ *transcanadaletters*. Vancouver: Talonbooks, 1975.

_____ *Pacific Windows: Collected Poems of Roy K. Kiyooka*. Ed. Roy Miki. Vancouver: Talonbooks, 1997.

Kolodny, Annette. "Some Notes on Defining a Feminist Literary Criticism." In Brown and Olson (1978). 37-58.

Kroetsch, Robert. *Essays. Open Letter*. 5:4 (Spring 1983).

_____ *The Lovely Treachery of Words* . Toronto: Oxford University Press, 1988.

_____ *Completed Field Notes*. Toronto: McClelland and Stewart, 1989.

Lane, M. Travis. "Dream as History: a review of *the man with seven toes*." In Solecki, (1985): 150-155.

Lattimore, Richard. "'Introduction' to Sophocles 'Philoctetes'." *Greek Tragedies*, Vol. 3. Ed. David Grene and Richard Lattimore. Chicago: University of Chicago Press, 1960. 44-45.

Lawson, Alan. "Postcolonial Theory and the 'Settler' Subject." In Brydon (1995): 20-36.

Lecker, Robert. "Better Quick than Dead: Anne Wilkinson's Poetry." *Studies in Canadian Literature*, 3:1 (Winter 1978): 35-46.

Leggott, Michele. 1994. *DIA*. Auckland, N. Z.: Auckland University Press, 1994.

Levy, Reuben. *An Introduction to Persian Literature*. New York: Columbia University Press, 1969.

Lochhead, Douglas. *High Marsh Road*. Toronto: Anson-Cartwright Editions, 1980.

_____ *Tiger in the Skull: New and Selected Poems, 1959-1985*. Fredericton, NB: Fiddlehead, 1986.

Mandel, Ann. "Michael Ondaatje." *Canadian Writers Since 1960: Second Series (Dictionary of Literary Biography: Volume 60)*. Ed. W.H. New. Detroit: Gale Research Company, 1987. 273-281.

Mandel, Eli. *Stony Plain*. Erin, Ont.: Press Porcépic, 1973.

_____ *Out of Place*. Erin, Ont.: Press Porcépic, 1977.

_____ *Life Sentence*. Victoria: Press Porcépic, 1981.

_____ *The Family Romance*. Winnipeg: Turnstone Press, 1986.

Manhire, Bill. *Good Looks*. Auckland: Auckland University Press/Oxford University Press, 1982.

_____ *Zoetropes: Poems 1972-1982*. North Sydney: Allen and Unwin/Wellington: Port Nicholson Press, 1984.

_____ *The Brain of Katherine Mansfield*. Auckland: Auckland University Press, 1988.

_____ *The New Land A Picture Book*. Auckland: Heinemann Reed, 1990.

_____ *Milky Way Bar*. Wellington: Victoria University Press, 1991.

Mansell, Chris. *Day Easy Sunlight Fine*. In *Hot Collation*. Ringwood: Penguin, 1995. 95-163.

Marlatt, Daphne. "musing with mothertongue." *Readings from the Labyrinth*. Edmonton: NeWest Press, 1998.

Marshall, Tom. "Layering: the Shorter Poems of Michael Ondaatje." In Solecki (1985): 82-92.

Mason, R.K. *Collected Poems*. Christchurch: The Pegasus Press, 1963.

McCaffery, Steve. *Intimate Distortions*. Erin, Ont.: The Porcupine's Quill, 1979.

_____ *North of Intention*. New York: Roof Books/Toronto: Nightwood Editons, 1986.

McLuhan, Marshall, and Wilfred Watson. *From Cliché to Archetype*. New York: The Viking Press, 1970.

Middleton, Peter. "On Ice: Julia Kristeva, Susan Howe and avant garde poetics." In Easthope and Thompson (1991): 81-95.

Miner, Earl. *Japanese Poetic Diaries*. Berkeley: University of California Press, 1976.

Mujeeb, M. *Ghalib*. New Delhi: Sahitya Akademi, 1969.

Munton, Ann. "The Long Poem as Poetic Diary." *Open Letter* 6:2-3 (Summer-Fall 1985): 93-106.

Murray, Les. "Peter Porter *On First looking into Chapman's Hesiod*." In *Australian Poems in Perspective*. Ed. P.K. Elkins. St. Lucia: University of Queensland Press, 1978.

Nairn, Tom. "Demonising Nationalism." *The London Review of Books*, 15:4 (25 February 1993): 3-6.

Newlove, John. *Moving In Alone*. Lantzville, B.C.: Oolichan Books, 1977.

Nichol, bp, and Frank Davey. "The Book as a Unit of Composition." *Open Letter* 6: 1 (1985): 39-46.

Nichol, bp. *The Martyrology, Books 1 and 2*. Toronto: Coach House Press, 1972.

_____ *The Martyrology, Books 3 and 4*. Toronto: Coach House Press, 1976.

_____ *The Martyrology, Book 5*. Toronto: Coach House Press, 1982.

_____ *The Martyrology, Book 6*. Toronto: Coach House Press, 1987.

Olson, Charles. *Human Universe and other Essays*. Ed. Donald Allen. New York: Grove Press, 1967.

_____ *The Maximus Poems*. Ed. George F. Butterick. Berkeley and London: University of California Press, 1983.

Ondaatje, Michael. *The Dainty Monsters*. Toronto: Coach House Press, 1967.

_____ *the man with seven toes*. Toronto: Coach House Press, 1969.

_____ *Leonard Cohen*. Toronto: McClelland and Stewart, 1970.

_____ "Interview (by mail) with Michael Ondaatje." *Manna* 1 (March 1972): 19-22.

_____ *Rat Jelly*. Toronto: Coach House Press, 1973.

_____ "O'Hagan's Rough-Edged Chronicle." *Canadian Literature* 61 (Summer 1974): 24-31.

_____*There's a Trick with a Knife I'm Learning to Do*. Toronto: McClelland and Stewart, 1979(a).

_____, ed. *The Long Poem Anthology*. Toronto: Coach House Press, 1979(b).

_____ "An Interview with Michael Ondaatje (1975)." With Sam Solecki. In Solecki (1985): 13-27.

_____ *The Cinnamon Peeler: Selected Poems*. Toronto: McClelland and Stewart, 1992.

Perloff, Marjorie. *The Poetics of Indeterminacy: Rimbaud to Cage*. Princeton, NJ: Princeton University Press, 1981.

_____ *The Dance of the Intellect: Studies in the Poetry of the Pound Tradition*. New York: Cambridge University Press, 1985.

_____ *Poetic License: Essays on Modernist and Postmodernist Lyric*. Evanston: Northwestern University Press, 1990.

_____ *Radical Artifice: Writing Poetry in the Age of Media*. Chicago: University of Chicago Press, 1991.

Poe, Edgar Allan. *Literary Criticism of Edgar Allan Poe*. Ed. Robert L. Hough. Lincoln: University of Nebraska Press, 1965.

Porter, Peter. "Country Poetry and Town Poetry: A Debate with Les Murray." *Australian Literary Studies* 9:1 (1979): 39-48.

Pound, Ezra. *Guide to Kulchur*. New York: New Directions, 1952.

_____ *The Literary Essays of Ezra Pound*. Ed. T.S. Eliot. London: Faber, 1960.

_____ *The Cantos of Ezra Pound*. New York: New Directions, 1970.

_____ *Personae: The Shorter Poems*. Eds. Lea Baechler and A. Walton Litz. New York: New Directions, 1990.

Quartermain, Peter. *Disjunctive Poetics: From Gertrude Stein and Louis Zukofsky to Susan Howe*. Cambridge and New York: Cambridge University Press, 1992.

R.A.K. Mason. *Collected Poems*. Christchurch: The Pegasus Press, 1963.

Raphael, Frederic and Kenneth McLeish, trans. *The Poems of Catullus*. London: Jonathan Cape, 1978.

Redford, Bruce. *The Converse of the Pen: Acts of Intimacy in the Eighteenth-Century Familiar Letter*. Chicago: University of Chicago Press, 1986.

Reinfeld, Linda. *Language Poetry: Writing as Rescue*. Baton Rouge and London: Louisiana University Press, 1992.

Rich, Adrienne. *Leaflets: Poems 1965-1968*. New York: W.W. Norton and Company, Inc., 1969.

_____ *The Will to Change: Poems 1968-1970*. New York: Norton, 1971.

Ricou, Laurie. "Phyllis Webb, Daphne Marlatt and simultitude." In Newman and Kamboureli (1986): 205-215.

Roethke, Theodore. *The Collected Verse of Theodore Roethke: Words for the Wind*. Bloomington: Indiana University Press, 1961.

Rogers, W. E. *The Three Genres and the Interpretation of Lyric*. Princeton, N.J.: Princeton University Press, 1983.

Sanger, Peter. *Sea Run: Notes on John Thompson's STILT JACK*. Antigonish, NS: Xavier Press, 1986.

Scobie, Stephen. *Leonard Cohen*. Vancouver: Douglas and McIntyre, 1978.

_____ *bpNichol: What History Teaches*. Vancouver: Talonbooks, 1984.

_____ "His Legend a Jungle Sleep: Michael Ondaatje and Henri Rousseau." In Solecki (1985): 42-60.

_____ *Signature Event Cantext*. Edmonton: NeWest Press, 1989.

Scott, F.R. *The Collected Poems of F.R. Scott*. Toronto: McClelland and Stewart, 1981.

Sharp, Iain. "Review of Bill Manhire's *Zoetropes*." *Landfall 154* (1985): 237-240.

Sisson, C. H., trans. *Catullus*. London: MacGibbon and Kee, 1966.

Smith, A.J.M. "A Reading of Anne Wilkinson." *Canadian Literature*, 10 (Autumn 1961): 32-39.

Smith, Barbara Herrnstein. *On the Margins of Discourse: The Relation of Literature to Language*. Chicago: University of Chicago Press, 1978.

Solecki, Sam, ed. *Spider Blues: Essays on Michael Ondaatje*. Montreal: Véhicule Press, 1985(a).

_____ "Nets and Chaos: The Poetry of Michael Ondaatje." In Solecki (1985[b]): 93-110.

_____ "Point Blank: Narrative in *the man with seven toes*." In Solecki (1985[c]): 135-149.

Stead, C.K. *Whether the Will is Free*. Auckland and Hamilton: Paul's Book Arcade, 1964.

_____ "Preliminary: From Wystan to Carlos—Modern and Modernism in Recent New Zealand Poetry." *In the Glass Case: Essays on New Zealand Literature*. Auckland: Auckland University Press/Oxford University Press, 1981.

_____ *Geographies*. Auckland: University of Auckland Press/Oxford University Press, 1982.

_____ *Paris*. Auckland: Auckland University Press/Oxford University Press, 1984.

Storrocks, Roger. "The Invention of New Zealand." *AND*, 1 (August 1983): 9-30.

_____ "No Theory Permitted on These Premises." *AND*, 2 (February 1984[a]): 119-137.

_____ "To Postulate a Ready and an Understanding Reader." *AND*, 3 (October 1984[b]): 120-130.

_____ "'Natural" as only you can be': Some readings of contemporary New Zealand poetry." *AND*, 4 (October 1985): 101-123.

Sullivan, Rosemary. "At A Tension" (review of Sharon Thesen's *The Pangs of Sunday*). *Books in Canada*, IXX:5 (June/July 1990): 32-33.

Swift, Jonathan. *Journal to Stella*. 2 vols. Ed. Harold Williams. Oxford: Oxford University Press, 1948.

_____ *Stella's Birth-Days: Poems by Jonathan Swift*. Ed. Sybil Le Brocquy. Dublin: Dolmen Press, 1967.

The Compact Edition of the Oxford English Dictionary. New York: Oxford University Press. OED, 1971.

Thesen, Sharon. *Artemis Hates Romance*. Toronto: Coach House Press, 1980.

_____ *Holding the Pose*. Toronto: Coach House Press, 1983.

_____ *Confabulations: Poems for Malcolm Lowry*. Lantzville: Oolichan Press, 1984.

_____ *The Beginning of the Long Dash*. Toronto: Coach House Press, 1987.

_____ *The Pangs of Sunday*. Toronto: McClelland and Stewart, 1990.

_____ *Aurora*. Toronto: Coach House Press, 1995.

Thompson, John. *Stilt Jack*. Toronto: House of Anansi Press, 1978.

Tranter, John, and Philip Mead, eds.*The Penguin Book of Modern Australian Poetry*. Ringwood: Penguin, 1991.

Tranter, John. *At the Florida*. St. Lucia: University of Queensland Press, 1993.

Tulip, James. "Poetry Since 1965." In *The Penguin New Literary History of Australia*. Ed. Laurie Hergenhan, et. al. Ringwood, Victoria: Penguin, 1988. 475-492.

Wah, Fred. "Subjective as Objective: The Lyric Poetry of Sharon Thesen." *Essays on Canadian Writing*, 32 (Summer 1986): 114-121.

Webb, Phyllis. *Wilson's Bowl*. Toronto: Coach House Press, 1980.

_____ *Sunday Water: Thirteen Anti Ghazals*. Lantzville, B.C.: Island Writing Series, 1982.

_____ *The Vision Tree: Selected Poems*. Ed. Sharon Thesen. Vancouver: Talonbooks, 1982.

_____ *Water and Light*. Toronto: Coach House Press, 1984.

_____ "Ghazal-Maker." *Canadian Literature*, 112 (Spring 1987): 156-157.

Wedde, Ian, and Harvey McQueen, eds. *The Penguin Book of New Zealand Verse*. Auckland: Penguin (N.Z.), 1985.

Wedde, Ian. "Introduction." In Wedde and McQueen (1985): 23-52.

White, Patrick. *A Fringe of Leaves*. New York: Viking Press, 1977.

Wilcox, Leonard. "Postmodernism or Anti-Modernism?" *Landfall 155* (1985): 344-364.

Wilkinson, Anne. *The Collected Poems of Anne Wilkinson and a Prose Memoir*. Ed. and Intro. by A.J.M. Smith. Toronto: Macmillan Canada, 1968.

Williams, Mark, ed. *The Caxton Press Anthology New Zealand Poetry 1972-1986*. Christchurch: The Caxton Press, 1987.

Index

43

Poetry titles available from NeWest Press

Fragmenting Body etc

Douglas Barbour

Innovative long poems by a well-known poet and critic, including an elegiac sequence for bpNichol and the title poem exploring aspects of what we mean by the body in the world.

1-896300-17-0 • $14.95 CDN • 9.95 US

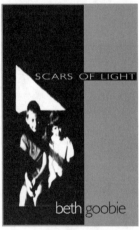

Scars of Light

Beth Goobie

A collection of narrative poems tracing the surface memory of an abused child, and unearthing the terror found in ordinary places such as parks and playgrounds and piano lessons in the front room.

0-920897-73-8 • $13.95 CDN • 9.95 US

The Wireless Room

Shane Rhodes

A stunning first collection of poems ranging from studies in western pastoral history though highflying evocations of sub-atomic particles to deeply personal poems about and for parents.

1-896300-15-4 • $14.95 CDN • 9.95 US